"When I first read Hegel, Marx, and the Frankfurt School as an undergraduate, I struggled to make sense of them. I did slightly better a few years later as a graduate student. Carl Trueman has written the introduction that I wish I had to help guide me in my understanding. *To Change All Worlds: Critical Theory from Marx to Marcuse* isn't a red-meat, bomb-throwing broadside, but a careful and nuanced presentation of a variety of controversial views. While a Christian must ultimately reject critical theory, that doesn't mean there aren't helpful insights from which we can benefit. Trueman shows us the way."

—**Ryan T. Anderson**, president, Ethics and Public Policy Center

"Carl Trueman ranks among the most important Christian thinkers of our time, a superb scholar and engaging writer with the clarity of a C. S. Lewis and a gift for explaining the issues shaping modern life. *To Change All Worlds* is no exception. It's a brilliant exploration of critical theory and its impact on the central question we now face as a society: Who and what is a human being? It's an absolutely essential reading."

—**Charles J. Chaput**, O.F.M. Cap., archbishop emeritus of Philadelphia

"In his characteristically lucid and accessible style, Carl Trueman explains the often abstruse revolutionary ideas of critical theory by introducing us to its early thinkers and foundational texts. Avoiding polemical broadsides and expressing nuanced appreciation for some of critical theory's insights, *To Change All Worlds* nevertheless demonstrates that its spirit of negation can deconstruct our categories and tear down our institutions but can propose nothing of positive value to erect in their place."

—**Aaron Kheriaty**, scholar, Ethics and Public Policy Center

"There is perhaps no issue more debated and less understood today than critical theory. In *To Change All Worlds,* Carl Trueman offers a learned, accessible, and judicious history of critical theory and its challenges to traditional assumptions about truth and human nature."

—**Thomas S. Kidd**, research professor of Church history,
Midwestern Baptist Theological Seminary

"If Carl Trueman didn't exist, we would have to invent him. In this important volume, he presents a masterwork on critical theory. The strategic importance of this book lies in the fact that it is no superficial analysis. This is a work of front-line scholarship that reads like a novel and unfolds like a detective story. Once again, Carl Trueman offers a book that will shape the mind of this generation, and he does so by taking the reader back through several decades and exposing the framework of critical theory—and then by taking on the theorists themselves. You can't afford not to read this book."

—**R. Albert Mohler, Jr.**, president,
The Southern Baptist Theological Seminary

"A brilliant book, beautifully written. Trueman is a literary sensei. Readers familiar with historic critical theory and the Frankfurt School will enjoy Trueman's dissection of key themes and concerns. Those new to critical theory will have a master-class guide in Trueman and his uncanny ability to make complex, almost obscurant ideas accessible and captivating. *To Change All Worlds* highlights the sagacity of some of the social analysis of critical theory and the discerning questions it raises, while exposing its bankrupt presuppositions and spurious solutions. If you want to better understand the foundation of modern day critical social theories and downstream woke ideology, buy this book."

—**Pat Sawyer**, lecturer, UNC-Greensboro

"Long before words like 'intersectionality,' 'heteronormativity,' and 'ableism' entered our lexicon, Karl Marx and the critical theorists of the Frankfurt School laid the foundation for the ideology that undergirds these concepts. *To Change the World* is Trueman at his best, translating the abstruse often-opaque texts and ideas of the early critical theorists into accessible, easily-grasped prose through illustration, analogy, and example. His book is a must-read for those seeking to understand the historical origins of the 21st century progressive zeitgeist."

—**Neil Shenvi**, author and apologist

"'Ideas have consequences' is a well-worn phrase. No more is its truthfulness self-evident than with the trickle-down effects of ideas like critical theory, a constellation of arcane ideas developed by intellectuals, but which has also succeeded in thoroughly revolutionizing American intellectual and cultural life. Carl Trueman's *To Change All Worlds* is an invaluable source for every Christian who is asking why America's thought systems and thought patterns seem to have shifted in light of critical theory's influence. Trueman writes with elegance, accessibility, and the convictions necessary to evaluate critical theory from the perspective of historic Christian orthodoxy."

—**Andrew T. Walker**, associate professor of Christian ethics and
public theology, The Southern Baptist Theological Seminary

TO
CHANGE
ALL
WORLDS

TO CHANGE ALL WORLDS

CRITICAL THEORY FROM MARX TO MARCUSE

CARL R. TRUEMAN

B&H
ACADEMIC®
BRENTWOOD, TENNESSEE

For Todd.

With deep thanks for your friendship over these many years.

CONTENTS

ACKNOWLEDGMENTS

The most pleasant task of writing a book is thanking those who helped make it possible. I am grateful to Madison Trammel and his team both for suggesting that I write a basic introduction to the origins of critical theory and for seeing the project through to publication. Thanks are also due to Paul Kengor and Robert Rider of the Institute for Faith and Freedom at Grove City College for the provision of research assistants throughout the research and writing phase. Those assistants—Joy Stockbauer, Emma Peel, Jacob Adams, and Michael Halley—proved invaluable. My teaching assistant, Isaac Willour, was also helpful in chasing down some useful resources when not grading quizzes for me. Thanks too to my colleagues in the BARS department at Grove City College, to the dean, Dr. Paul Kemeny, to the provost, Dr. Peter Frank, and to the president, the Hon. Paul McNulty, for fostering such a delightful working environment. Last, thanks to my wife, Catriona, who has throughout our marriage supported all my projects and allowed me the most vital of resources: time to read and to write.

I dedicate the book to my good friend, Todd Pruitt.

.

CHAPTER 1

The Importance of Critical Theory

Introduction

"Critical theory" has in recent years become a major bone of contention in American culture. The term has taken on a life of its own, such that it functions as kind of shibboleth for both conservatives and progressives. Are you for it or against it? That is the blunt either-or test of loyal membership on both sides of the political divide, typically played out at levels of sophistication dictated by the character limits for a Tweet. In particular, critical race theory has become a focal point for Americans eager to litigate the country's racial divides and the long shadow of slavery and segregation. Rather like those other buzzwords or phrases—cultural Marxism, white privilege, heteronormativity—the vocabulary has taken on a life of its own, and is often wielded with utter conviction in the battles that take place online among those on both sides who have mastered the moralizing rhetoric without ever having reflected upon the theoretical background from which it emerged.

1

That is where this book will, I hope, prove useful. I am by trade and training an intellectual historian. That means that my primary interest is in how ideas and schools of thought come into being, what their origins are, what claims they make about the world in which we live, and what their significance—cultural, intellectual, historical, ideological—might be. I am not concerned first and foremost with the truth or coherence of the ideas and movements I study so much as with the various aspects of their historical and cultural significance. And so this study is an attempt to expound the critical theoretical ideas of a few chosen thinkers associated with the early development of critical theory in order to help us engage with more clarity on some of the most pressing issues of our own age.

And what are those issues? An immediate response might well point to the use of critical theory in schools, colleges, public policy making, and the media. That certainly covers some of them, but I want to suggest that there is a much deeper issue in our modern world that makes some knowledge of critical theory important in ways that go beyond what we might call these broadly political concerns. It is the issue of anthropology, the understanding of what it means to be human.

The year in which this book was completed—2023—was the eightieth anniversary of C. S. Lewis delivering the lectures that later became the small but important volume, *The Abolition of Man*.[1] In 1943, Lewis astutely identified a deep anthropological crisis facing the West. To put it more bluntly, the West was losing its ability to define what it means to be a human person. And if that was true in 1943, how much more so is it today, when a basic anthropological question such as "What is a woman?" is proving too complicated for some of the finest public minds to answer with any conviction or clarity?

This is where critical theory becomes important. Once we step back from pressing political concerns, it is clear that the critical theorists, from an early figure such as Theodor Adorno to later figures such as Gail Rubin, are

---

[1] C. S. Lewis, *The Abolition of Man* (New York: HarperOne, 2015).

all wrestling with the question of what, if anything, it means to be human? Critical theory is, of course, an umbrella term for a variety of different and even incompatible approaches. The Marxism of an Adorno is not the queer theory of a Rubin. But all share this in common: a basic preoccupation with anthropological questions.

This is not to defuse the contemporary political significance of critical theories. All critical theories—at least, all truly critical theories—are revolutionary. But it is to set them in the context of our times and to see them as one set of responses to that age-old question which has in the flux and volatility of modernity taken on peculiar urgency: What is man? Is he defined by making and producing or by consuming? Are biological relationships important or not? What does the good life look like? How has technology changed our understanding of human nature? Has it liberated us or enslaved us? Is sexual desire part of our core identity? Does the universe have a moral shape? Is there such a thing as "human nature"? Are we free agents or merely functions of broader cultural forces? And, of course, the pointed question so succinctly expressed by Pilate: What is truth? Christians wrestle with these questions, intensely so in our chaotic contemporary world. And critical theorists do so as well. If nothing else, we share with them a set of serious questions about the human condition that demand serious answers.

If the challenge facing Christians—and all members of Western society today—comes down to basic questions such as these, questions that all touch on the deeper issue of how we define human nature, then it behooves us to be aware of the manner in which the discussion is being pursued. This then is the principle which guides the exposition of aspects of critical theory which follow. This book is neither a polemic nor is it an attempt to show how aspects of critical theory might be appropriated within a Christian context. Local bookstores carry titles that do these things.[2]

---

[2] On the polemical side (with varying degrees of sophistication and success), see Voddie Baucham, *Fault Lines: The Social Justice Movement and Evangelicalism's Looming Catastrophe* (New York: Salem, 2021); Helen Pluckrose and James Lindsay,

Polemicists sometimes fail first to expound what they criticize, and so the exposition itself is profoundly skewed by the polemical intention. Such persuade no one but those already convinced of the evil at hand; and I am an historian, not a theologian or philosopher, so I make no strong claim to being able to synthesize Christianity and critical theory. You may be puzzled by what appears at times to be my enthusiasm for critical theory. I am not enthusiastic about it at all, but I see my task as explaining it on its own terms and so have kept criticism in the main expository sections to a minimum. Just as if I were writing a book on *Moby Dick* or Shakespearean tragedy, I address the texts of critical theory as examples of individuals attempting to grapple with the deep questions of the human condition from which we can learn, even as we may disagree with the underlying philosophies being expressed. A number of the chapters do end with a reflective postscript, but these are intended as suggestive, rather than prescriptive, and thus offer food for further thought rather than a Christian critical theory.[3]

Nor is this book a profound contribution to the secondary scholarship on critical theory. It is no more than an introduction to the topic. Almost every one of the thinkers and issues I discuss is subject to a range of nuanced—and sometimes not so nuanced—interpretations. My purpose is to explain

---

Cynical Theories: How Activist Scholarship Made Everything about Race, Gender, and Identity—and Why This Harms Everybody (Durham, NC: Pitchstone, 2020); Michael Walsh, *The Devil's Pleasure Palace: The Cult of Critical Theory and the Subversion of the West* (New York: Encounter Books, 2017). While not specifically focused on critical theory, Roger Scruton's *Fools, Frauds and Firebrands* (New York: Bloomsbury Continuum, 2015) also contains useful polemical discussion of relevant thinkers.

[3] Those interested in further, deeper reflection on critical theory from a constructive Christian perspective should consult Christopher Watkin, *Biblical Critical Theory: How the Bible's Unfolding Story Makes Sense of Modern Life and Culture* (Grand Rapids: Zondervan, 2022); also (from a more critical perspective) Neil Shenvi and Pat Sawyer, *Critical Dilemma: The Rise of Critical Theories and Social Justice Ideology—Implications for the Church and Society* (Grand Rapids: Harvest House, 2023).

the basic elements of early critical theory—in historical context—so that, if interested, you will be both educated and encouraged to read more on the subject. And as I point out numerous times in the text, early critical theory really does set the basic foundations for its later iterations, and so time spent grappling with its historical origins does illuminate the present.

The Underlying Issue

It is perhaps useful at this point to set forth in brief compass the central problem that Christians should have with critical theory. This is not (obviously) to say that interacting with critical theory is not useful. This whole book is an attempt to help with such interaction. But the main problem with critical theory, at least of the stream discussed in this volume, is its anthropology, its understanding of human nature. Standing in the tradition of Hegelian Marxism, there is a deep suspicion of essentialism, that is, the belief that things have stable "essences" or, we might say, that things have fixed qualities that determine who or what they are and are thus how they are to act. In other words, when it comes to human beings, the very idea of human nature as something stable across time and cultures and that carries with it significant moral implications for how we live, is basically rejected. The early critical theorists would thus see accounts of "human nature" as attempts to grant some kind of absolute authority to the contingent moral vision of a particular time or society. And that, of course, collides with any claim that human beings are, for example, made in the image of God and therefore made with particular ends in light of which they should order their lives. This is a theme that will lie in the background of much of the narrative and analysis of this book. It also explains one of the great problems that critical theory exhibits: an inability to articulate a clear vision of what the future of human society should look like. In short, it makes the theory far more critical than constructive, and more comfortable with dismantling what is than in describing what should be in anything other than the most generic and vague terms.

A Personal Project

My own interest in critical theory dates to the 1980s when I was first introduced to aspects of Marxist theory with reference to ancient, and then Reformation, history. At the time, the ideas fascinated me but they seemed to be fading in significance, replaced by the new forms of critical theory emerging under the influence of French thought, specifically that of Michel Foucault. In fact, Foucault eschewed the grand schemes that underlay the Hegelian Marxism of earlier critical theorists.[4] And so for some decades critical theory, as I understood it, seemed to be something of historical interest and part of a bygone, late modernist age. And then 2020 happened, Black Lives Matter hit the prime-time headlines, critical race theory (CRT) gripped the popular imagination, and every virtue-signaling Twitter warrior felt the need to opine (in 280 characters or less) in support or opposition to critical theory. Ordinary churches had to reckon with what had been a fairly obscure legal philosophy. And denominations such as the Southern Baptists suddenly had to wrestle with whether CRT was compatible with biblical Christianity.

In February of 2021 I published an essay, "Evangelicals and Race Theory" in *First Things*.[5] In it, I reflected on the appropriation of critical theory, specifically CRT, by elements within the evangelical Protestant world. In the course of this essay, I connected the contemporary debates taking place in America to the earlier work of a group of European thinkers who were connected to what is known as the Frankfurt School—the name given to those involved with the Institute for Social Research at the Goethe University in Frankfurt.

---

[4] Foucault made it clear in his 1970 inaugural lecture at the Collège de France that escaping from Hegel and his intellectual legacy was an imperative of his project: see his "The Order of Discourse" in Robert Young, ed., *Untying the Text: A Post-Structuralist Reader* (Boston: Routledge and Kegan Paul, 1981), 48–78, esp. 74.

[5] Carl R. Trueman, "Evangelicals and Race Theory," First Things (February 2021), https://www.firstthings.com/article/2021/02/evangelicals-and-race%20-theory.

The response to my article in general was polarizing. Many loved it, many hated it. And from the latter a number of criticisms emerged as consistent themes. First, some said that the examples on which I had focused were from scholars such as Ibram X. Kendi, who were not really exponents of CRT. That claim has since been refuted by the Catholic philosopher Edward Feser, who has demonstrated the influence of CRT on scholars such as Kendi.[6] The second criticism—the one that both amused and annoyed me—was that, in setting CRT against the background of the Frankfurt School, I had myself indulged in a form of racism, turning a movement for black liberation into a derivative of white male philosophy. More than anything else, that line of criticism lies in the background of my personal interest in writing this book.

Why the Frankfurt School?

Given that this book addresses the thought of men who were all dead before 1980 and long before CRT became a topic of mainstream cultural conversations, some justification for my decision to focus on Max Horkheimer and his colleagues seems necessary. To start with the "whiteness" criticism: it is true that most of the early Frankfurt School came from families that were economically and socially privileged. And they were most definitely European. But most of them were also Jewish, a far more significant category for understanding the cultural and political dynamics of the early twentieth century. That is a vitally important point, given that their project began in Germany in the late 1920s and early 1930s and was thus conceived against the background of the rise to prominence and then power of the brutal ideological anti-Semitism of the Nazi Party under its leader, Adolf Hitler.[7]

---

[6] Edward Feser, *All One in Christ: A Catholic Critique of Racism and Critical Race Theory* (San Francisco: Ignatius, 2022).

[7] See Stuart Jeffries, *Grand Hotel Abyss: The Lives of the Frankfurt School* (London: Verso, 2016). This is an excellent and accessible history of the Frankfurt

Indeed, as we shall see, wrestling with why Nazism and Fascism were proving so attractive to the working classes of Europe was the central concern of
their theoretical work during this time. Key figures also had to flee Germany
for their lives, including Theodor Adorno, Max Horkheimer, and Herbert
Marcuse. Walter Benjamin, a close friend of the School, blended Jewish
eschatological mysticism, criticism, and Marxism. Benjamin committed sui-
cide in 1940 on the border between France and Spain when refused entry to
the latter. He was escaping the Nazi regime. To be clear, I am no advocate of
their approach to critical theory; but it would still seem reasonable to conclude that these men knew more of marginalization, persecution, and physical oppression than most, if not all, of the CRT advocates who enjoy tenured
positions at American institutions of higher education or who blithely Tweet
about racial oppression on their new Apple iPhones from the comfort of
a Starbucks. "Whiteness" is frankly a useless and irrelevant category when
parsing the ethnic conflicts the early members of the Frankfurt School faced
as young academics. It really has a rather specifically American reference and
tends to reduce the various ethnic struggles of the world to the categories
that have so shaped American history and social conflicts. The struggles of
Jews—and thus of Jewish members of the Frankfurt School in the 1920s,
'30s, and '40s—simply do not conform to the narratives of racial oppression
that dominate American politics.

But there are also positive connections between the Frankfurt School
and later critical theorists. Well-known race activist and sympathizer with
CRT, Angela Y. Davis, was a student of Marcuse. Edward Said, doyen of
postcolonial studies, was deeply read in figures such as Georg Lukács and
Adorno. And Franz Fanon may not have studied in Frankfurt but was also
influenced by the Western Marxism of which the Frankfurt School was
a part. And one does not need to look for such direct links to see how
today's CRT rests upon the same broad philosophical assumptions that were

School which draws attention to the importance of Jewishness for understanding
its work.

articulated by the earlier Frankfurt theorists: for example, an awareness of the social construction of culture, of the manipulative nature of ideologies that "naturalize" social systems, hierarchies and categories, and the importance of power to understanding how reason (and knowledge) are understood and produced. To these categories, we can add a number of significant polemical targets shared in common: capitalism, colonialism and imperialism, the monogamous nuclear family, patriarchy, and traditional religion.

It is my belief that in each of these areas, the fundamental logic of critical theory can be found in the work of the early Frankfurt School. The basic rules of the game are established there. This is not to claim that later theorists have not made important contributions. In fact, while some later theorists—for example, Judith Butler—do stand in the same philosophical line of reflection rooted ultimately in the work of Georg Hegel, others have taken inspiration from a very different source, the post-structuralism of Michel Foucault, with its fundamental rejection of all totalizing systems. Hegel, Marx, and Freud—all lodestars for the early Frankfurt School—are the preeminent boogeymen of such critique, offering as they did systematic accounts of the world and how it is to be understood.[8] Nevertheless, the similarities between the two streams are such that a study of Horkheimer and company is enlightening with regard to the concerns and significance of all branches of critical theory. After all, both the Frankfurt School and Foucault's philosophical system were concerned with the historical conditions and social structures that governed what counted as rational thought and knowledge. The former spoke of false consciousness and ideology and the latter, of epistemes and discourses of power; but the point each made was substantially the same: that which appears true and natural in a given

---

[8] For an account of Marx and Freud and their significance for understanding modern notions of selfhood, see my *The Rise and Triumph of the Modern Self: Cultural Amnesia, Expressive Individualism and the Road to Sexual Revolution* (Wheaton: Crossway, 2020). Butler is interesting in this context: strongly influenced by Hegel, her gender theory also draws extensively on Foucault.

society is not "true" or "natural" in any intrinsic, given, or transcendent way. Rather these are things that are produced by historical circumstances and serve the interests of power. In answer to that basic question, What is man?, both streams thus offered answers that shared significant affinities with each other, seeing contemporary understandings of human nature as contingent and functions of dominant ideologies.

In addition, the early Frankfurt School have something else to commend them: their philosophical depth and sophistication. Those who claim that attempts to set CRT against the background of the Frankfurt School are rooted in "whiteness" are historically wrong. The claim also impoverishes reflection on critical theory as an historical philosophical phenomenon. As with all movements, later iterations tend to assume as given that with which earlier generations wrestled firsthand. This can lead to a truncated understanding of the real significance of a tradition of thought and to a simplification of deep critique into cheap clichés of the kind that populate X. To study the early founders of a movement, however, is to study the foundations of its thought and thus potentially to gain a much deeper understanding of what the movement represents.

The early members of the Frankfurt School were entrenched in the Western philosophical tradition. They were familiar with the work of the German idealists, of Immanuel Kant, Johann Fichte, Friedrich Schelling, and Hegel. They understood Marxism against this background and had a grasp of the various problems and questions the tradition raised. There is again a real irony to advocates of postcolonialism or CRT not being aware of this. The notions of historical change, for example, or of political revolution to which they are both beholden are products of this Western thinking. Intellectual expressions of anti-Westernism in the West are deeply indebted to Western patterns of thought and political tastes. Yes, Hegel was by today's standards a racist and Western chauvinist, but that very critique of Hegel rests upon Hegelian foundations.

Hegel was the dominant influence in the development of critical philosophy in the nineteenth century as we will see in the discussion of

Marx in chapter 2. His emphasis upon the historical contingency of thought gave a solid philosophical grounding to the distinction between nature and culture and to the fact that societies change over time. One might describe him as offering a philosophical account of historical consciousness. That has, of course, become a commonplace in modern discourse. We are today familiar with the idea that things change over time, that one cannot simply compare the fourth, the eighteenth, and the nineteenth centuries without taking account of the wider historical contextual differences between them. And critical race theorists are heirs to these insights of which Hegel was perhaps the most influential exponent. That many of them have not read Hegel does not mean that they are not indebted (albeit indirectly) to him and his heirs in the critical Marxist tradition of the Frankfurt School. Indeed, critical race theorists need to grasp this in order to fully understand the genealogy of their own thinking.

While much of what follows will be a dispassionate account of the origins and development of early critical theory, I will add here a personal note: it is my opinion that the early critical theorists were not simply more self-conscious (and often more sophisticated) in defining themselves with reference to the broader philosophical tradition; they were also addressing a far more substantial question than many of their heirs and successors today. Marx once cited Hegel as saying that all great historical events occur twice, to which he added the sardonic comment that he failed to realize the first time as tragedy, the second as farce. There is a sense in which I believe the same can be said about critical theory. Its origins lie in attempting to explain the rise of Nazism, the Holocaust, and the self-inflicted horror which Europe endured in the twentieth century. The big questions continued in the years after the civil rights movement of the fifties and sixties, when CRT was used to make arguments about the long-standing effects of slavery and Jim Crow in the broader cultural mindset of the United States. Today, however, critical theorists deploy their skills in defending drag queen story hour, the use of preferred pronouns, and pressing for a more inclusive Oscar ceremony. One might be forgiven for thinking that a school of thought that began as a serious attempt to think through issues of life and death, of what it meant to be human and to be free, and which produced dense articles and thick tomes that drew deeply on profound philosophy has degenerated into an idiom that rather neatly expresses the therapeutic concerns of Western capitalism—often via X—and is frequently put to the service of self-indulgence and manufactured victimhood. That is an argument for another day—but it serves to justify my choice of the early Frankfurt School as my object of study. However wrongheaded it was, it was not a trivial project concerned with ephemera. It was a serious attempt to understand one of the most serious and destructive moments humanity has ever faced.

Why Is the Frankfurt School Relevant Today?

As you may have inferred thus far, the Frankfurt School remains relevant because it offers foundational insights into the concerns of critical theory as it has developed over the decades, even those inspired by others strands of philosophical criticism of culture, such as that offered by Foucault. But it is also true that the early Frankfurt School addressed questions and issues that remain of pressing importance today.

We live in a world where politics is polarized. We live in a world where powerful personalities on the right and the left have emerged as messianic figures. We live in a world where it is increasingly clear that arguments purporting to be based on science and reason can be used to curtail personal freedom. The entertainment industry is more and more obviously engaged in shaping cultural values and expectations. Consumption of goods has become the purpose of life. And behind all of these lurks that question of what it means to be human, if indeed it means anything at all. On all these questions and more, the early Frankfurt School has something to say, and in a typically deeper way than their contemporary successors. The relevance of these questions is thus not in doubt. The pressing issue—and one to which we shall return in the conclusion—is the extent to which critical theory can be a useful source for answers.

First, however, we need to understand the background and then the content of the Frankfurt School's approach. That requires us to go back into the early nineteenth century and discuss the role of two particular thinkers: the German philosopher G. W. F. Hegel, and his apostate disciple, the political thinker and activist Karl Marx. Without some grasp of the contribution of these men, we can have no real understanding of that contribution of the Frankfurt School. Once we have outlined their thought, we shall move on to two key Marxists of the twentieth century: Karl Korsch and Georg Lukács, who helped to bring Hegel back into Marxist discussion. Then we turn to the Frankfurt School, to see how they distinguished critical theory from traditional theory, wrestled with the problem of instrumental reason, developed a theory of sexual revolution, and subjected modern media to scrutiny in terms of its political impact. Again and again throughout this exposition, we shall see that the question lies just below the surface.

Even though the Frankfurt School has insightfully framed questions about the human condition and has legitimate concerns about objectifying persons, it does not offer compelling answers to the anthropological problems that it raises. It is clear on what humanity is not—the alienated individuals that capitalism has produced. But what humanity *is* is not so clear. Indeed, at the end what emerges is something akin to Mephistopheles in Goethe's great drama, *Faust*. Here is how the demon describes himself to Faust:

> I am the spirit that always negates, and rightly so, since everything that comes into existence is only fit to go out of existence and it would be better if nothing ever got started.[9]

---

[9] Johann Wolfgang von Goethe, *Selected Works* (New York: Everyman, 2000), 780.

Sadly this is the impression that critical theory leaves in our minds. It is clear on what is wrong with society—pretty much everything—but it lacks the ability to articulate in clear terms what should replace it. It ultimately offers no vision of what it means to be human, whether because (as with the Hegelian Marxists) human nature has yet to be realized or, with the more postmodern critical theorists, it is ultimately a meaningless question. Therein lies its tragedy.

CHAPTER 2

Hegel, Marx, and the Origins of Critical Theory

Introduction

Mention critical theory to someone today, and the chances are that the subsequent conversation will focus on matters such as race or sexuality or gender. The reason for this is simple: the current iterations of critical theory reflect precisely those issues which dominate the political and social discourse of our day. While this is understandable, it can also mean that the discussion proceeds with little or no understanding of the origins and development of what we might call the critical theoretical spirit. Some might argue that this is of little importance: the world of today is not the world of 1930s Germany, where the first generation of self-conscious critical theorists were honing their ideas; still less is it the world of the debates among the successors of the German philosopher G. W. F. Hegel in the 1840s that produced Karl Marx. Yet it is my conviction—and the underlying argument of this book—that the concerns of contemporary critical theorists rest upon or have affinities with the arguments and positions of those earlier generations, such that today's debates can be better understood against this deeper historical background. Issues of power, of consciousness, of exploitation, and of manipulation (among others) are shared in common by critical theorists across the generations, whether they look back to the Hegelian tradition of Marx and company or to the post-structuralist work of Michel Foucault. And thus a knowledge of the origins of critical theory is very useful, perhaps even vital, for an accurate understanding both of the inner logic, public significance, and political ambitions of the critical theorists of today.

Of course, in many conservative circles, the mere mention of Karl Marx or Marxism is likely to produce an immediate negative reaction. Indeed, the term "cultural Marxism" has become one of the preferred social media terms for critical theory, used with abandon by those who are fully confident that they oppose it but may have very little real understanding of what it claims. Like all such terms used as political pejoratives—"white privilege" being perhaps its counterpart for the left—its purpose is not to promote conversation but rather to close it down. And yet it does point to one very important fact: the origins of modern critical theory do lie in the thought of Karl Marx, and so discussion of Marx is important for understanding the foundations of the broad critical theoretical tradition. Yet, as today's critical theorists emerge from a prior line of thinking, so did Marx. After all, nobody emerges from a cultural vacuum, and therefore our narrative must begin not with Marx himself but with the philosopher upon whose thought Marx both drew positively and also reacted somewhat against: G. W. F. Hegel.

The Importance of Hegel

To grasp the significance of Hegel for later critical theory, it is important to understand something of his philosophy as it touched on the matter of history.[1] Now, Hegel came of age in a world where philosophical discussion was dominated by the thought of Immanuel Kant. His own work therefore formed perhaps the most important part of the ongoing discussion of Kant that took place in German philosophy in the decades after Kant's death. Kant's project, most famously developed in his three *Critiques—of Pure Reason* (1781/87), *of Practical Reason* (1788), and *of Judgment* (1790)—was an attempt to set forth the conditions by which human knowledge was possible. The thrust of his argument was that human beings know things not as they are in themselves but in accordance with the way in which the human mind is structured to know them. Thus, when I look at the lamp on my desk, it occupies space and continues through time. Kant argued that these aspects of its existence—space and time—are actually categories that exist in my mind and which make sense of what I perceive. They are not to be understood as qualities of the lamp itself. Knowledge is thus a kind of synthesis between that which can be known and the way in which I as a human being know things.

Kant's thought set the trajectory for subsequent German philosophy in its emphasis upon the mind as key but also provoked revisions and critiques within the very tradition of thinking for which he was the most important source: German idealism. Idealism was marked by its preoccupation with the ways in which individuals thought. We might perhaps say that idealists focused philosophy on the intellectual sphere of the knowing subject, that is, the individual who was doing the "knowing."

In terms of the history of critical theory, Hegel's major contribution to German idealism was his insight that the way human beings think does

---

[1] The best introduction to Hegel is Peter Singer, *Hegel: A Very Short Introduction* (Oxford: Oxford University Press, 2001). A very readable scholarly treatment is Robert C. Solomon, *In the Spirit of Hegel* (Oxford: Oxford University Press, 1983). For a summary discussion of Hegel's influence on the early Frankfurt School, see James Gordon Finlayson, "Hegel and the Frankfurt School," in Dean Moyar, ed., *The Oxford Companion to Hegel* (Oxford: Oxford University Press, 2017), 718–42.

change over time. Kant's philosophy gave a good account of how the structure of the mind shaped knowledge of the world. The role of the individual subject in the act of knowing was central. Just as the person looking at the world through rose-tinted glasses sees everything as having a rosy tint, Kant saw the categories with which the mind of the knower operated as decisive for knowledge. No one knows the world as it is in itself. They know only the world as the human mind organizes the data it perceives in accordance with the mind's own structure. Yet one thing that Kant did not significantly address was the issue of how historical process might affect the nature of thought. For him, the categories by which the mind knew things remained static over time and thus the question of whether an ancient Athenian and an eighteenth-century Prussian knew things differently was of little or no interest.

Hegel, by contrast, was deeply interested in the historical dimension of human thought. He observed that the ways in which men and women thought and related to each other did change between places and epochs. And in this insight lies one of the keys to later critical theory. In a sense, critical theorists who build upon Hegel, such as Theodor Adorno, are asking a similar question to Kant: Under what conditions is knowledge possible? But they move the question from the essential structure of the human mind to the contingent structure of the society in which the individual lives and in which "knowing" occurs. What constitutes knowledge for them is therefore deeply connected to social and cultural conditions and thus the critique of reason, to borrow Kant's phrase, is of necessity a critique of society.

Hegel is key to this development. He relativized human thought by arguing that the human perception of the world was also profoundly shaped by the subject's location in history and society. The ancient Athenian, the medieval European knight, and the nineteenth-century Prussian merchant all thought in different ways even if the basic Kantian epistemological categories of time, space, etc., remained as constants of the human mind. This is most accessibly expressed in his *Lectures on the Philosophy of History*.[2] Here he traces how the concept of universal freedom emerged in history. In the East—in China and India, for example—there was despotism. Only one person— the ruler, the emperor—was free. Then, in Greece and in ancient Rome a consciousness emerged that freedom belonged to more but still only a subset, a few, of humankind. Finally, in the Germanic lands and thanks to the impact of Christianity, the idea that all human beings are free came to be understood. In each epoch, the way of thinking actually shaped the lives of men and women; only as thought changed was humanity ultimately liberated.

Two things are of great importance here for later critical theory. First, there is the significance of historical process as separating what we might call culture from nature. History was a story of becoming, not being. It was dynamic, not static. Hegel saw the way people think at any given point in time as a result of the historical process and not as representing the way things necessarily had to be. In China, there was not a practice of universal freedom, but the lack of that practice was the result of the country's position in cultural history, not some law of nature. The concept of freedom was therefore itself a product of historical process and to be understood as such.

Freedom cannot exist in the abstract. To use the traditional notions of freedom with which we in the West generally operate, we can be free from something or free for something. Thus, I can be free in the sense that I am not incarcerated and therefore not radically restricted in my movements. And I can be free to vote, if I am a citizen living in the United States, in the sense that I have that right granted to me under the Constitution. But to say that I am free and to say no more than that is meaningless. Freedom is a relative term whose meaning is determined by the context in which I live. Context thus has a deep impact on who I am because it shapes the very categories by which I think about myself and the world in which I live.

---

[2] G. W. F. Hegel, *Lectures on the Philosophy of History*, trans. Ruben Alvarado (Aalten, Netherlands: Wordbridge, 2011).

One important implication of Hegel's thought here should be clear: human thought, beliefs and behavior are relativized by the historical process. At any moment in time, the thinking and the behavior of any given society is contingent, not a necessary function of some transcendent human nature. Human beings can believe in God or deny his existence. They can think freedom is important or overrated. They can ride horses or drive cars. The Englishman's preference for tea is not an intrinsic function of a transcendent human nature but rather the result of the society in which he lives, just as the same can be said for the American woman's preference for coffee. Neither preference represents a truer vision of authentic humanity, but each refers rather to particular human beings in particular societies.

This insight presses against a common human intuition, one that assumes that the way in which we think and act is somehow natural and normative for all humanity and that differences from our norms are therefore to be seen as deviations from what it means to be truly human. In fact, human thought and behavior are historically and culturally conditioned. Again, this will be important for critical theorists who will not only see their task as critiquing the tendency of societies to see themselves as natural, as the way things have to be, but will also press behind this to expose what they see as the manipulative power games that underlie the way cultures understand themselves.

Of course, if all Hegel had done was point to the fact that history is important and that patterns of behavior and thinking changed over time, he would have still made a useful contribution to the history of thought. However, he made a second important contribution that sets the stage for Marx and thereby for critical theory: *he did not just see history as a process of continuous becoming rather than a static reality; he also saw this becoming as rooted in conflict or, perhaps to use a less loaded term, dialectic.*

The most famous passage in which Hegel expresses this idea is that of the story of the lord and the bondservant, in his work *The Phenomenology of the Spirit*, a vast and complicated book in which he attempted to explain the nature and origin of self-consciousness.[3] The lord-bondservant passage was key to his argument. It also became extremely influential in twentieth-century continental philosophy because it was the subject of a series of lectures by the Russian émigré thinker Alexander Kojève in the 1930s. Present at these lectures was a veritable who's who of people who went on to shape French philosophy in the subsequent decades: Jean-Paul Sartre, Maurice Merleau-Ponty, and Jacques Lacan, among others.[4]

The lord-bondservant passage is a thought experiment. The background to it is Hegel's belief that for a being to be self-conscious, it needs to be recognized by another self-conscious being. The term *recognized* here does not have its common-sense meaning whereby someone might recognize the person passing them on the street as a neighbor or coworker. Rather it has the sense of being seen as somebody of particular value. For example, the British subject who is knighted by the king is thereby recognized as somebody of significant value to British society. Conversely, the person who is looked down upon by another is being recognized as somebody that person considers to be of less value than himself. This, of course, has an impact on how the person thinks of himself: to be honored by the king leads to a feeling of importance and satisfaction; to be treated by somebody as a dog leads to feelings of resentment, weakness, and inadequacy.

Hegel demonstrates this understanding of self-consciousness through the lord-bondservant dialectic. Two individuals meet on a plain. Each has a desire for the other to recognize him as superior and so a fight ensues. Of course, the obvious demonstration of ultimate superiority, is for one to kill the other, thereby exerting total control and power over his opponent. But that would be self-defeating: once the loser is dead, then there is nobody left to recognize the victor. For the victor to know himself as victor, he needs

---

[3] G. W. F. Hegel, *The Phenomenology of Spirit*, trans. Michael Inwood (Oxford: Oxford University Press, 2018), 76–82.

[4] See Alexander Kojève, *Introduction to the Reading of Hegel: Lectures on the Phenomenology of Spirit*, ed. Allan Bloom (New York: Cornell, 1980).

the defeated one to stay alive so that he can acknowledge him as such. Thus, the victor merely subordinates the loser to himself and turns him into a bondservant, thereby making himself the lord. This situation, however, is not fully satisfactory or stable. First, recognition from a bondservant is not that satisfying. We can see this when we think of how having one's contribution to society recognized by the king or the President would be thrilling: it is the exalted status of the king or President that makes the recognition impressive and satisfying. But to be recognized as significant by somebody we regard as our inferior is scarcely as satisfying because of the lowly status of the one recognizing us.

Second, there is an ironic twist in the story: as time goes on, the lord becomes rather lazy, since he is given recognition by the bondservant as the latter serves him, cooks his meals, arranges his schedule, tends his garden, and performs other tasks at his command; but in doing these things, in recognizing the lord in this way, the bondservant has gained a whole set of skills that make him in a sense more powerful and competent as a human being than the lord. And so at some point the positions become reversed: the lord ends up dependent upon the bondservant.

The thought experiment might seem trivial but it contains deep truths about how we live. We all typically think of ourselves, and indeed behave, in ways that are profoundly shaped by the manner in which others treat—recognize—us. Whether it is a husband and a wife, a parent and a child, a teacher and a student, an employer and an employee, human self-understanding and human actions are the result of negotiated relationships involving hierarchies, expectations, desire, and power. I am who I am because of the relationships I have to others and the way that they treat me. When someone shows me respect, I feel good about myself. When they treat me with disdain, I feel bad. And ongoing relationships also involve change. The bride and groom on their wedding day are not the same people that they are on their twenty-fifth anniversary. As they live together, they change because of their personal interactions. There is a dynamic to the relationship by which their self-consciousness is reshaped over time as they share their lives together, have children, and face life's ups and downs. The way they think about each other, the things they consider important, and the ways they behave will all likely change over time.

We can also press this a little further. At the heart of Hegel's thought is the notion of freedom and how freedom emerges in the process of history. Think of the lord and the bondservant: Yes, the bondservant recognizes the lord as lord, but he scarcely does so freely or willingly. He is compelled to do so because the lord is more powerful and demands this of him. The relationship that exists is thus one involving significant tension: the bondservant dislikes giving coerced recognition because it severely curtails his freedom; but the lord knows that coerced recognition is not as good as that which is freely given. Think, for example, of a married couple: each partner wants the other to use the phrase, "I love you," freely and spontaneously; if they suspect that the phrase is spoken unwillingly or out of fear, then that reflects not a happy, satisfying marital relationship but one that we might call dysfunctional or defective. The relationship between the lord and the bondservant is like this latter one, marked by imbalance of power and by ongoing struggle.

For anyone familiar with later critical theory, the connection with Hegel here should be obvious. Self-consciousness is shaped by the social environment in which we find ourselves. What it means to be a person is defined by the network of relationships and roles within which we are set. The critical question thus becomes the extent to which those relationships, institutions, communal practices, and expectations force us into roles and identities that hinder us from flourishing.

There is also the importance of freedom in recognition for being truly human, something that the lord-bondservant passage highlights and indeed indicates as emerging from personal interaction and struggle. Social hierarchies constitute relationships of power, and therefore the identities those hierarchies create and enforce are themselves functions of power and idioms by which power and hierarchy can be expressed. Such issues lie at the heart of much later critical theory, and the concern for power and its manipulative connection to social structures and identity is a constant across the critical theoretical landscape, both Hegelian-Marxist and post-structuralist. Think of radical feminism with its desire to break free of the behavior that men expect from women—for example that they dress in certain ways, play particular roles in the home and in society at large, etc. It is a debate about recognition—the terms by which men recognize women and the recognition that men demand from women. And for the critical theorist, these terms of recognition cannot be separated from the socially constructed relations of power that shape them. The same applies to race: the stereotype of how members of particular racial groups are expected to act again finds its analog in Hegel's notion of recognition.

This historicist concern for human self-consciousness in Hegel is thus foundational both to the development of Marxism in general and to critical theory in particular. In its emphasis on the contingency of human life in terms of its thought, its institutions, and its behavior, it opens the way for a critique of the same. And in the lord-bondservant passage, we see how power relations provide much of the dynamic for this. In retrospect, it is no surprise that Hegel's thought will be put in the service of a political project that is revolutionary at its very core: that of unmasking attempts to "naturalize," and thus absolutize, social relations that maintain exploitation and manipulation of one group by another.

Karl Marx

Karl Marx is of vital importance to the development of critical theory.[5] First, his vision of philosophy as a means for revolutionary change is one

---

[5] A good introduction to Marx is Peter Singer, *Marx: A Very Short Introduction* (Oxford: Oxford University Press, 2018). The literature on Marx is inevitably vast and also diverse in its interpretations of his thought. For a good collection of essays that present the "state of the art," see Matt Vidal, Tony Smith, Tomás Rotta, and Paul Prew, *The Oxford Handbook of Karl Marx* (Oxford: Oxford University Press, 2019).

that lies at the heart of the Frankfurt School. Second, his critical appropriation of Hegel involved the development of key ideas such as alienation and ideology that will be deployed by later critical theorists. Third, his rejection of the idea of human nature as possessing an essence which could be abstracted from history shaped the anti-essentialism that is central to critical theoretical approaches. And finally, his own critique of Hegel foreshadows in significant ways the kind of work that was to become standard fare for later generations of critical theorists.[6]

The philosophical background to Marx is German idealism. This is a stream of philosophy that developed in the late eighteenth and early nineteenth centuries in the wake of the work of Immanuel Kant. Kant was concerned with how knowledge of anything was possible and his answer, as noted in chapter 1, was that human beings do not know things as they are in themselves but as the human mind perceives them in accordance with its own organizing principles of categories. Idealism as a broad tradition flowing from Kant was thus preoccupied with the relation of human beings as perceiving subject to the things perceived. Put more simply, it focused upon the human mind in its relation to the world that it perceives.

Of more immediate significance for Marx is the contribution of G. W. F. Hegel to German idealism. For Hegel, history was a dynamic process consisting of an ongoing dialectical process that consisted of three

---

[6] For a summary of Marx's connection to Hegel see Shuangli Zhang, *Marx and Hegel* in Moyar, 647–69. More detailed discussion can be found in Sidney Hook, *From Hegel to Marx: Studies in the Intellectual Development of Karl Marx* (Ann Arbor: University of Michigan Press, 1966); David McLellan, *The Young Hegelians and Karl Marx* (London: MacMillan, 1969); also Michael Heinrich, *The Life of Marx and the Development of His Work: volume I: 1818–41 Karl Marx and the Birth of Modern Society*, trans. Alexander Locascio (New York: Monthly Review Press, 2019). This is the first volume of a project trilogy. Volume 2 will include discussion of the critical period of the 1840s where Marx's radical appropriation of, and reaction to, Hegel is to be found.

steps: one or more ideas or concepts are considered to be fixed and unal-
terably true; as we reflect on those concepts, a contradiction emerges
in them; and this moves to a higher category that embraces both the
idea and its negation. This sounds rather obscure, and certainly Hegel's
prose does not make the idea easy to grasp, but an example brings out
his point. Imagine a community where freedom is understood as every
individual being able to do exactly what they wanted whenever they want
to. A problem quickly emerges: the result is total anarchy which, among
other things, prevents many people (the weak, for example) from doing
whatever they want. Thus a reaction sets in and a despot takes over. But
then it becomes apparent that freedom is effectively annihilated. And so
a third form of thinking about how human beings should organize their
community emerges in the form of a representative democracy. Here
there is an idea—freedom; its negation—despotism; and its resolution—
representative democracy. It is this kind of dynamic that will influence
Marx, although he will ground the movement not in ideas but in material things, specifically how human beings are connected to the means of
production: who owns the raw material; who owns the factory where that
is made into product; who turns the raw material into that product; and
who owns that product.

Marx's relationship to this philosophical background is important, for
he both builds upon it and transforms it in a powerful, political way. Central
to Marx's contribution is his pressing of philosophy toward the achievement of political revolution. Visitors to Highgate Cemetery in London will
see this epitomized in two quotations from his works that are engraved on
the marble monument that marks his grave. One is the famous statement,
"Workers of all lands unite," drawn from the *Communist Manifesto*; the second is taken from a manuscript written in 1845 but only published after
Marx's death, his *Theses on Feuerbach*. This was a brief set of notes Marx
wrote on the philosophy of Ludwig Feuerbach, a disciple of Hegel and an
influence on Marx's own thinking. The quotation is of the eleventh thesis,
which reads in the original as follows:

> The philosophers have only *interpreted* the world in various ways;
> the point, however, is to change it.[7]

In this single sentence Marx drew a line under the previous philosophical tradition. In his mind philosophy had come to an end and it was time to set off in a new direction. He then used this as the basis for setting forth a principle that would become a hallmark both of Marxist thought in general and critical theory in particular.

What did Marx mean by declaring philosophy to be at an end? Clearly, he did not mean that there was no further need to think about and reflect on this world and its meaning, for he himself was to spend the rest of his life doing precisely that. Rather, he meant that the tradition of philosophy which flowed from Plato to Hegel had finished. While this tradition comprised a myriad of different philosophies, they all had in common a basic separation of the rational concepts they articulated from the social background in which they occurred. Kant's critiques, for example, never asked the question about what kind of a world it was that fostered or found value in such critiques. Philosophy therefore needed to contextualize itself in order to have a critical handle on its own significance.

Marxist philosopher Andrew Feenberg elucidates this point with reference to Plato's *Republic*. In Plato's ideal state, the lower orders are unfit to rule because they are too preoccupied with private affairs. The ruling elite, by contrast, are qualified to rule because they have no private attachments—they are not even allowed to know their own children. Through a Marxist lens, Plato wrestles with and assumes the permanence, indeed the naturalness, of a basic conflict of public and private interest and thus seeks a rational solution with the nature of government. Yet a moment's reflection reveals that the nature of the solution can only be deemed "rational" if the

---

[7] Karl Marx and Frederick Engels, *Collected Works*, vol. 5, *Marx and Engels 1845–1847* (New York: International Publishers, 1976), 11. Hereafter *CW*.

conflict between private and public interest is absolute. Plato assumes the perennial stability and importance of the public-private distinction. If, however, that very distinction is seen to rest on a historically contingent and (in the strictest sense) unnecessary social convention (the ownership of private property by individuals) then the rationality of the argument itself becomes contingent.[8]

Marx's point in the eleventh thesis, therefore, is that the task of philosophers (or perhaps we might now call them "theorists" in order to make clear the historical break) is a critical one of pointing beyond the way people think about the world to the underlying social conditions which make such thinking appear rational, necessary and coherent. As with later critical theorists, Marx is asking a critical question: what social conditions lead to the definitions of what counts as truth and knowledge at any given point in time? So far, so Hegelian. But then Marx adds a transformative, active dimension to the philosophical program: once the theorist exposes the material conditions that lie behind how a society thinks, the possibility of resisting the status quo—and resisting the way the status quo makes us all think—becomes real. In short, the theorist's task is to make social change possible by making it conceivable. And that is done by tearing down the illusory absolutism of the established "natural" ways of thinking and acting. As noted, it is a perennial tendency of us all to assume that the way we and our society think and operate is natural and normative. By disabusing us of this, Marx believes he can liberate us for social change. Philosophy of this type is thus not simply descriptive, analytic, or explanatory. It is in a deep sense revolutionary because it has as its purpose the transformation of society. This is a note that the critical theorists of the Frankfurt School will take as their lodestar.

---

[8] Andrew Feenberg, *The Philosophy of Praxis: Marx, Lukács and the Frankfurt School* (London: Verso, 2014), 18–20.

Ideology

Closely connected to this new vision of philosophy or theory is Marx's notion of *ideology*. The term is commonly used today to refer to a particular set of beliefs that somebody might hold with a high degree of conviction. This is most obviously reflected in the adjective *ideological* which is generally applied as a pejorative by critics to their opponents' actions or claims that they believe are driven not so much by fact or objective assessment of evidence as by prior commitments to a particular cause, typically one that might be described as political.

The term originates with French aristocratic thinker Antoine Destutt de Tracy who coined it in the late eighteenth century to refer to the study of a body of coherent and rational beliefs, a form of what we now call the sociology of knowledge.[9] In Marxism, however, the term takes on a distinctly different meaning with deep political significance. Now, Marx's use of "ideology" is not entirely consistent across the body of his work but there are nonetheless a number of basic elements that characterize the term that are of importance for the subsequent development of critical theory.[10]

Marx's most famous early use of the word occurs in *The German Ideology* (*TGI*), a set of manuscripts written with his friend and collaborator Friedrich Engels in 1846. While the work remained incomplete and unpublished in Marx's lifetime, and so presents interesting interpretive challenges to scholars of Marx, it is of great importance in understanding both his later theory of history and the rise and concerns of critical theory. Here he not only set out in brief compass his theory of historical development by class struggle but also reflected upon the nature and importance of language and ideas with

---

[9] For an older but still useful introduction to the sociology of knowledge, see Peter L. Berger and Thomas Luckman, *The Social Construction of Reality: A Treatise in the Sociology of Knowledge* (New York: Anchor, 1967).

[10] On the various nuances of Marx's use of the term, see Michael Rosen, *On Voluntary Servitude: False Consciousness and the Theory of Ideology* (Cambridge: Polity, 1996), 168–222.

regard to the historical process and to the broader material conditions of human existence.

The text begins with the observation that it is production—the intentional making of things—that marks human beings off from other animals. A moment's reflection reveals the substantial truth of this: beavers, for example, build dams but they do it instinctively and as a means of survival. Only human beings build bridges, and not typically because they need to for survival or are hardwired to do so. Rather, humans do such a thing because they choose to. Furthermore, they might also build the bridge using special materials or a particular design not simply for reasons of utility but for reasons of aesthetics and taste. Human production is characterized by freedom and intention. That is one of the things that makes the species unique.[11]

Now, it is hardly an insight to observe that human beings make things, whether tools, or carpets, or buildings. In Marx, however, this becomes key to understanding what it means to be human at any given point in time. Our relationships to the things we make—to the raw materials, to the process of making, to the ways in which the products are exchanged—are what define us as human beings. Thus, the basket weaver in the fourteenth century and the factory worker in the nineteenth century experience their "human nature" in different ways. This is Hegel, refracted through a materialist lens.

What Marx does in *TGI* is extend this notion of production to ideas. Human beings do not only make material things. He also claims that they manufacture ideas and concepts. After all, if it is material production that

---

[11] *CW* 5, 31. There is a vigorous debate within Marxism concerning the extent to which Marx believed in "human nature" as a stable, universal category. This was influentially denied by the French Marxist, Louis Althusser but has been ably defended by Norman Geras: see his *Marx and Human Nature: Refutation of a Legend* (London: Verso, 2016). Also useful is the extended introduction to Marx's *Economic and Philosophical Manuscripts of 1844* by onetime member of the Frankfurt School, Erich Fromm: *Marx's Concept of Man* (London: Continuum, 2004), 1–69.

makes us who we are, then the ways in which we think about these acts of production and the purposes to which we apply them are central to how we think about ourselves. The world of ideas rests upon the world of materially productive work.[12]

A simple example illustrates this. The principle that one should obey those in authority, whether in the workplace or the broader political sphere, is something that many people intuitively regard as a good thing. We might acknowledge that on occasion a boss or a ruler can be corrupt or incompetent, and we might in such cases allow for carefully qualified resistance to their authority. Even in those cases we follow careful guidelines: complaints procedures at our places of work or voting for another candidate at the next election. But the principle of obedience is seen as good. The question is, why do we see it as such? Marx would argue that we see it in this way because it serves the economic interests of those in authority. The principle is not grounded in the will of God or in the idea that it reflects some objective moral structure that is intrinsic to the universe. It is grounded in the need of the bosses and the political leaders to have some means of cultivating or even enforcing a particular pattern of behavior among workers and citizens that suits their economic purposes. The ruling class may offer arguments based on God or on the natural morality that inheres in the universe, but that is *ideology*: it is a set of ideas that hides what is really going on in the material circumstances of the world by a process of what Marx calls "mystification."

For Marx, the problem with the idealism of a philosopher like Hegel is that he fails to take account of this and thereby fails to see the significance and priority of material conditions in the formulation of ideas.[13] Hegel is fascinated by the emergence of the concept of freedom, for example, but

---

[12] *CW* 5, 36.

[13] "It has not occurred to any of these philosophers [the Young Hegelians] to inquire into the connection of German philosophy with German reality, the connection of their criticism with their own material surroundings." *TGI* in *CW* 5, 30.

he sees this as a process involving ideas, not as something grounded in real material and economic relations. There is a sense, of course, that Hegel's approach makes intuitive sense since ideas seem to have tremendous power. Ideas are often what seem to motivate us, whether it be love for a person, belief in the justice of a cause, or the notion that a particular pattern of behavior will make our lives better. But for Marx our intuitions are not a pellucid guide to reality. Rather, they are themselves produced by the material circumstances in which we find ourselves. Indeed, in a dramatic inversion of Hegel, Marx declares:

> It is not consciousness that determines life, but life that determines consciousness.[14]

By giving priority to ideas, Marx sees Hegel and his followers as having engaged in a mystification of reality. They have located power and the dynamic force of history in ideas and thus obscured the fact that it is material circumstances, specifically economic processes connected to production, that are the real engine of society and the foundation of thought. Marx too is interested in how an idea such as that of individual freedom emerged; but he wants to know what material conditions and what economic relations gave birth to it and are served by it.

This move by Marx is of profound political significance because, in unmasking the material foundations of ideas, he also raises the question of how those ideas function and whose interests they serve. If they are mystifications of social and economic relations, then they must be serving a political purpose: that of naturalizing the status quo in a manner that precludes fundamental criticism of the status quo. If the philosopher's task is to change the world, then the philosopher must engage in fundamental critique of the world along lines which expose these mystifications.

---

[14] *CW* 5, 37.

It is important to note here a common misreading of Marx's claim, one that actually achieved canonical status in the Marxist-Leninist tradition, particularly as held by the Third International. This considered ideology to be a neutral concept, a mere expression of economic interests with no active significance. What this means is that ideology—the system of ideas that represent a society's values and priorities—is a reflection of underlying social realities and thus stands in a simple relationship of cause and effect to society's economic structure. This receives some support in *TGI* from Marx drawing an analogy with a *camera obscura*, a device which simply reflects the world around on a screen, but upside down.[15] As with photographs, the resultant image is determined straightforwardly by what is actually presented to the camera, be it a landscape or a village green. Ideology functions as an image of what is real.

Yet a careful reading of Marx indicates that ideology is not simply an epiphenomenon that expresses underlying economic (and thus political) interests. Rather it is itself both a function and a component part of the economic system. In other words, ideology serves a purpose in shaping reality as people experience it and in providing them tools whereby they can engage it. Ideology actually serves to constitute reality.

We can illustrate this with the example of American slavery. Clearly, slavery plays an important role in the pre-Civil War economy. Various ideological formulations connect to this: assumptions of racial hierarchies, of the "natural" fact of slavery, even perhaps notions that slavery is good for the slaves. These reflect the economic structure, but they also reinforce and perpetuate it. Thus, attempts to outlaw slavery might be met with arguments about the slaves' inability to fend for themselves. The ideology is therefore not merely reflective of the status quo. It is constitutive of it as well. It

---

[15] "If in all ideology men and their relations appear upside-down as in a *camera obscura*, this phenomenon arises just as much from their historical life process as the inversion of objects on the retina does from their physical life process." *CW* 5, 36.

reinforces it and maintains it. It provides tools for defending and protecting it.[16] In short, it has an active, not merely a passive function. Ideological constructions are the idiom and the instruments by which the struggle between competing classes is engaged. This is the point Marx is making.

Here lie in seed form some of the impulses of later critical theory. The argument, akin to that of Hegel, is that the way people think is a fundamental part of who they are. And thus as the way they think changes, so they too change. Now, if those ways of thinking can themselves be challenged and overthrown, then the societies committed to them can also be changed in revolutionary ways. Therefore, the critique of ideology—the exposure, for example, of its inner contradictions or its failure to account for all of reality—is in and of itself transformative and revolutionary. The Marxist revolution must be pursued in part at the level of the criticism of ideas, even though it is material conditions that are the truly important foundation of society.

We can grasp this point using a simple example. The factory worker who has known nothing but the drudge of production line work from the moment he left school intuitively assumes that this is just the way the world is. He thinks of himself as a worker, not a boss. He shows up to work on time and does the task he is assigned to do all day long, day after day. At the end of each week, he receives his paycheck. His assumption is that his status is fixed by the order of nature: there are factory owners and there are factory workers, and he belongs to the latter class. But if he can be encouraged to imagine the world differently, to see ownership of the factory not as something natural to the bosses but, say, as an act of theft by the boss; if he can be brought to see that the money the bosses use to buy factories,

---

[16] "All the struggles within the state, the struggle between democracy, aristocracy, and monarchy, the struggle for the franchise, etc., etc., are merely the illusory forms—altogether the general interest is the illusory form of common interests—in which the real struggles of the different classes are fought out among one another." *CW* 5, 46–47.

pay wages, and hold positions of authority in society, is really intrinsically worthless and that it is labor—the worker's own labor, *his* own labor—that is the important thing, the foundation upon which everything else is built, then immediately his own self-understanding will change as will his attitude to the boss and to his social position. He will realize that, far from being immutably weak and impotent, the working class can be an explosive force for political change. He will have seen through the ideology of capitalism and thus be in a position to challenge and overthrow the capitalist system because he now knows where real power lies: in the work of his own hands, not the arcane operations of the financial sector.

Ideology and Religion

Perhaps the most dramatic example that Marx gives of ideology is that of religion. In this area he draws on the concept of *alienation* that is found in Hegel but developed in a specific way by Hegel's younger disciple, Ludwig Feuerbach. Feuerbach is important for Marx because he shifts the philosophical discussion away from the idealism of Hegel toward a more strict materialism. Thus, when it comes to religion, Feuerbach sees the question of God as not being a matter of theology—Does a god exist? What kind of a god is he? Rather, he gives an account of the phenomenon of religion as arising from humanity's material circumstances. We might cast the question this way: Why do people believe in God, even though there are no metaphysical grounds for so doing? The answer for Feuerbach is that religion is a sign of human alienation. Alienation, like ideology, will become an important concept in the formation of critical theory. We will discuss this in more detail in the next chapter, but it is worth noting here that one of the symptoms of alienation in Marx is the persistence of religious belief.

Feuerbach considers the concept of God to be a psychological projection of all the things that human beings see as good in themselves onto a cosmic being who embodies all of these in unchanging perfection. For this reason, Feuerbach declares that theology is really anthropology. What he means is that the concept of God is simply the divinized essence of humanity: God's attributes are really human attributes, projected in an idealized form. They seem different because real human beings never embody the idealized form of human nature as represented by the idea of God. And this has an inhibiting effect: human beings have come to respect and to worship this projection and in so doing cement the difference between themselves and "God" in a way that means they no longer aspire to qualities they now consider divine. In so doing, they are alienated from their own nature. Religion, in other words, prevents them from realizing their potential and from being truly human.[17] Religion also has for Feuerbach a sinister, manipulative dimension that has clear affinities with Marx's position:

> Wherever morality is based on theology, wherever the right is made dependent on divine authority, the most immoral, unjust, infamous things can be justified and established. I can found morality on theology only when I myself have already defined the Divine Being by means of morality. . . . To place anything in God, or to derive anything from God, is nothing more than to withdraw it from the test of reason, to institute it as indubitable, unassailable, sacred, without rendering an account *why*. Hence self-delusion, if not wicked, insidious design is at the root of all efforts to establish morality, right, on theology.[18]

---

[17] "Religion, at least the Christian, is the relation of man to himself, or more correctly to his own nature (i.e., his subjective nature); but a relation of it, viewed as a nature apart from his own. The divine being is nothing else than the human being, or, rather, the human nature purified, freed from the limits of the individual man, made objective—i.e., contemplated and revered as another, a distinct being. All the attributes of the divine nature are, therefore, attributes of the human nature." Ludwig Feuerbach, *The Essence of Christianity*, trans. George Eliot (New York: Harper and Row, 1957), 14.

[18] Feuerbach, 274.

These similarities indicate that Marx is deeply indebted to Feuerbach on religion. The element of suspicion is key to understanding both. Like other post-Enlightenment modern thinkers—Nietzsche and Freud being two further examples—Marx is not particularly interested in whether religion is true. He assumes it is not. Rather, he (again like Nietzsche and Freud) is interested in why it persists. And this is where Feuerbach is useful to him, supplemented by his own critical philosophy. For Marx, as for Feuerbach, religion is symptomatic of alienation, of the fundamental dehumanization of man.

The *Contribution to the Critique of Hegel's Philosophy of Law* contains Marx's most famous description of religion as "the opium of the people." But this comment needs to be set within the broader context of the passage within which it occurs. Marx starts with the Feuerbachian point that man makes religion and that religion is "the self-consciousness and self-esteem of man who has either not yet found himself or has already lost himself again."[19] Marx then proceeds to argue that the struggle against religion is central to the political struggle because it is in effect the struggle against the alienating illusions that religion represents, "the world of which religion is the spiritual aroma." This then set the stage for Marx's famous description of religion:

> Religious distress is at the same time the expression of real distress and also the protest against real distress. Religion is the sigh of the oppressed creature, the heart of a heartless world, just as it is the spirit of spiritless conditions. It is the opium of the people.[20]

The point Marx makes here is that the existence of religion indicates that all is not well with the world. It is an expression of suffering and a protest against the same. Thus, he interprets the religious commitment of, say, poor peasants or impoverished industrial workers as indicating two things: that

---

[19] *CW* 3, 175.
[20] *CW* 3, 175.

they are not happy and comfortable in their current condition and that they aspire to something better. They know that hunger and want are not good and so they look to find something that will provide a rationale for their circumstances and some hope for the future—maybe a sovereign God who works all things for good, and a heavenly rest when they finally leave this vale of tears. The problem for Marx is that this prevents individuals from facing the reality of their conditions and then doing something about them. This places the criticism of religion at the heart of the revolutionary project Marx is developing:

> To abolish religion as the illusory happiness of the people is to demand their real happiness. The demand to give up illusions about the existing state of affairs is the demand to give up a state of affairs which needs illusions. The criticism of religion is therefore in embryo the criticism of the vale of tears, the halo of which is religion. Criticism has torn up the imaginary flowers from the chain not so that man shall wear the unadorned, bleak chain but so that he will shake off the chain and pluck the living flower. The criticism of religion disillusions man to make him think and act and shape his reality like a man who has been disillusioned and has come to reason, so that he will revolve around himself and therefore round his true sun. Religion is only the illusory sun which revolves round man as long as he does not revolve around himself.[21]

If the purpose is to change the world, not merely to describe it, as Marx's famous eleventh thesis on Feuerbach claims, then here we see something of what that means: the critique of religion is not simply for the purpose of demystifying or disenchanting the world. Rather, it is part of changing the world, of tearing down the illusions by which men and women shield themselves from having to face reality. For Marx, religion is indeed an opium—an analgesic and a hallucinogenic that defuses the felt need to change the

---

[21] CW 3, 176.

world. It facilitates man's abdication of his own responsibilities to himself and alienates him from what he truly should be. Revolution thus demands that religion be criticized—not merely debunked as false but also exposed as manipulative, as serving broader class interests, and thus as oppressive. It is ideology. When believed by the poor, it is false consciousness. It represents the basic alienation that lies at the heart of an unjust society. And critiquing it as such is to be part of the basic revolutionary move toward social justice.

In connecting religion to suffering caused by the economic inequities of the capitalist system, Marx also points to the fact that the alienation which it represents is intimately connected to how human beings relate to the products that they make. In his *Economic and Philosophical Manuscripts of 1844*, another set of notes that were not published until long after his death, Marx applied the concept of alienation to labor. This theme will become very important in the development of Marxism in the early twentieth century, as we shall see in chapter 3. Suffice it to note at this point that alienation, and its manifestation in religion, was a key theme in the early, Hegelian Marx, a point to be rediscovered by his successors, most notably Georg Lukács and then the Frankfurt School.

The Foundations Laid

With the writings of the early Marx, drawing upon the legacy of Hegel, we see several emerging ideas that are going to be important for critical theory. At the most general level, there is a consciousness of history as a process that manifests itself, among other things, in the ways in which individuals and societies think, the values they embody, and the manner in which they organize themselves. This in turn means that such things are contingent: they do not have to be the way that they are; rather, the status quo at any given moment in time is itself the net result of an historical process.

This opens up the possibility for the kind of new philosophy for which Marx advocates. According to Marx, the old philosophy, stretching from ancient Greece to Hegel, described the world. Even with Hegel it fell short of setting itself against the background of the social and material conditions in which it existed. That is where the new philosophy—the critical philosophy or, perhaps better *theory*—of Marx and his heirs will set a new course. It will integrate philosophical and sociological concerns. But it will not stop there: it will do so with the purpose of changing, not merely describing, the world. That is the burden of the eleventh thesis on Feuerbach and, quite literally, Marx's epitaph on his tomb in Highgate Cemetery.

To do this, the early Marx lays the groundwork for some important concepts. Ideology, false consciousness, and alienation all play their part. And yet even as Marx sets forth these basic ideas, a significant and important question emerges, one that attempts to answer that which gives birth in the twentieth century to the critical theory of the Frankfurt School. That question, of course, is how does it happen that false consciousness comes to dominate the minds of the working class? In other words, how does the ideology of the bourgeois capitalist become the intuitive view of the world held by the proletariat? It is one thing to point out that it does so, that somehow the workers believe that their best interests are served by preserving a system that enables, reinforces, and perpetuates their exploitation. It is another thing to explain what causes this.

To put this in a pointed way: it is not enough to say that ideology serves interests—that is, that people believe that which works to their own advantage or benefit. The whole point of *false consciousness* is that the ideas which it embodies do not serve the interest of those who hold them. The poor are not benefited by religious belief that helps them to rationalize the unjust status quo. The proletarian factory worker on subsistence wages is not helped by thinking that private property is legitimate and therefore his own poverty is just or unavoidable or mere collateral damage. So why do such classes of people meekly adopt such thinking?

One standard answer, and one that proved very influential in some forms of Marxism in the late nineteenth and early twentieth centuries, deploys what is called the base-superstructure model.[22] This idea is that economic relations—the real reality—are foundational and that the ideology of false consciousness is in effect a superstructure that simply rests on top of this base. In short, the way people think merely reflects the needs and concerns of the dominant class. It is thus an effect and rather passive in the process. This is a position consistent with the camera obscura analogy for ideology we noted earlier. This has implications for Marxist thinking, in that it makes economics, not ideology, the primary focus of revolutionary activity. It also potentially points to a kind of materialist determinism: the process of history involves capitalism ultimately collapsing under its own contradictions, and this will lead automatically to the triumph of the proletariat and the advent of communist society. In short, according to Marxist logic, as capitalism crushes the workers, the workers will inevitably become conscious of their suffering, of its cause, and of their historical destiny as the class that carries the end goal of history. But what happens if the historical and economic processes do not deliver the promised revolution? What resources does Marxism have to draw upon at that point? Marxists had to face that question in the early twentieth century and thereby set the stage for the rise of a new form of Marxism, one that revisited the early Marx in an attempt to build differently upon his legacy. It is to this trajectory that we now turn.

---

[22] For a very helpful summary of the meaning and significance of these concepts, see the entry under "base and superstructure" in Ian Fraser and Lawrence Wilde, *The Marx Dictionary* (New York: Bloomsbury, 2013); also Jorge Larrain, "Base and Superstructure" in Tom Bottomore, Laurence Harris, V. G. Kiernan, and Ralph Miliband, *A Dictionary of Marxist Thought*, 2nd ed. (Oxford: Blackwell, 1991), 45–48.

CHAPTER 3

The Crucible of the Critical Imagination: Karl Korsch and Georg Lukács

Introduction

While the Marx of the 1840s had clearly been indebted to the philosophy of Hegel in his development of his thinking, his later work—particularly the monumental *Capital*—tilted away from the kind of categories he used in the 1840s—particularly that of alienation—and toward more clearly economic concerns. While scholars debate the extent to which a "later" Marx breaks with an "early Marx," there is no disagreement about whether the nineteenth-century international socialist movement that he helped to inspire and which he influenced was strongly economic in its approach, as reflected in its dominant organized expression, the Second International. So what happened to trigger the renewed interest in Hegel and the early Marx that became a hallmark of the critical theorists of the Frankfurt School? To understand this, we need to look at the fate of the Second International and the response this caused in the thinking of a new and young generation of Marxist intellectuals.

Karl Kautsky and the Failure of Orthodox Marxism

After the death of Marx, the organizational and intellectual leadership of international socialism was eventually assumed by the Second International, a somewhat amorphous confederation of socialist groups from around the world that existed from 1889 to 1916. The Second International provides important background to the rise of critical theory because of the way in which it gave prominence to a strictly economic articulation of Marxism that was ultimately regarded as a failure both in terms of its political organization and its explanatory power regarding the actual movement of history.

The key figure in this context was the Czech Marxist Karl Kautsky. Kautsky was one of the authors of the so-called Erfurt Program, a document adopted by the German Social Democratic Party in 1891. More significant for the history of Marxist theory is the official commentary that Kautsky wrote on this, entitled simply *The Class Struggle*.[1]

In *The Class Struggle*, Kautsky advocates an economic and evolutionary approach to communism. His argument is that capitalism is doomed to perish under the unsustainable weight of its own economic contradictions. It will over time extract more and more out of less and less, plunging the working class into deep economic pain that will eventually cause a reaction. Capitalism will effectively cause its own self-destruction and, as it does so, the working class will expand, drawing in others who find themselves being crushed by the growing demands of an increasingly discredited system. And at that point, the wheels of history will deliver the communist revolution. The work's basic point is summarized in its stirring last paragraph:

---

[1] For an English translation of the text, see Karl Kautsky, "The Class Struggle (Erfurt Program)," *Marxists Internet Archive*, accessed January 21, 2023, https://www.marxists.org/archive/kautsky/1892/erfurt/index.htm.

The more unbearable the existing system of production, the more evidently it is discredited, and the more unable the ruling parties show themselves to remedy our disgraceful social ills, the more illogical and unprincipled these parties become and the more they resolve themselves into cliques of self-seeking politicians, the greater will be the numbers of those who stream from the non-proletarian classes into the Socialist Party and, hand in hand with the irresistibly advancing proletariat, follow its banner to victory and triumph.[2]

This approach was later decried by many as "vulgar Marxism," positing as it did an essentially straightforward cause-and-effect connection between economic history and socialist revolution.

Kautsky's influence on the Second International served to cultivate a certain passivity toward revolution. Revolution was not something one could truly work to bring about; rather, it was something for which one had to wait, given that it was the result of productive forces that effectively negated the significance of individual actions and effort. Indeed, it is arguable that this led to the eventual disintegration of the Second International. It would seem reasonable to ask why one needed socialist organizations at all if the process of capitalism's collapse was the result of its own intrinsic contradictions, rather than of active revolution.[3]

Kautsky's approach did have this to commend it: it was clear and coherent, offering a simple cause-and-effect analysis of the processes

---

[2] Karl Kautsky, "The Class Struggle: Socialism and the Property-Holding Classes," *Marxists Internet Archive*, accessed January 21, 2023, https://www.marxists.org/archive/kautsky/1892/erfurt/ch05.htm.

[3] Kautsky expresses his passive approach to revolution neatly in the following quotation: "The task of Social Democracy consists, not in bringing about the inevitable catastrophe but in delaying it as long as possible, that is to say, in avoiding with care anything that could resemble a provocation or the appearance of a provocation." Quoted in David McLellan, *Marxism after Marx*, 4th ed. (London: Palgrave Macmillan, 2007), 32–33.

of history where economics was foundational and everything else mere epiphenomena. The only problem was that real history did not work out in quite that way. The idea that communism required the prior existence of an advanced capitalist society was severely challenged in 1917. Revolution succeeded in agrarian Russia but in the following year failed in industrialized Germany. And the crude, economic Marxism of Kautsky and the Second International had no way to give an account of why this should be. Indeed, when Lenin and the Bolsheviks seized power in Russia in 1917, it was no surprise that Kautsky did not approve. The Bolsheviks were working too fast and not at the pace that historical process demanded. And yet, if this was the case, could Kautsky's Marxism really offer anything other than passively waiting until history delivered on its proletarian promise?

Kautsky's Marxism also in practice denied significance to ideas. Economic relations were not only the most basic elements of society, they were also the only ones of real significance. In this account of Marxism, ideas became mere reflections of these underlying economic realities, effects that flowed from deeper causes of which individuals were unaware. There was therefore little or no need for ideological critique of society because the question of consciousness, whether of a class or of an individual, was not in itself an important one. If revolutionary consciousness was a necessary prerequisite for revolution, economics—not arguments—would bring it to life.

By 1920, therefore, the problem for Marxist theory was becoming obvious. While the Bolsheviks had enjoyed revolutionary success in Russia, this was not because classical economic Marxism had proved itself to be true. Rather, the success had come about in contradiction to the expectations of such, given that Russia was not industrialized and thus had neither a significant bourgeoisie nor industrial proletariat. Germany, by way of contrast, was highly industrialized, had well-developed middle and working classes, had no strong tradition of democratic institutions to provide the sense of social enfranchisement which might defuse class tensions, and had just lost a war of unparalleled carnage in a most catastrophic fashion. Yet despite all of these propitious circumstances, its communist revolution had failed. This presented Marxism with two problems: one of which was immediately obvious, the other of which would emerge during the 1920s. First, why did the revolution fail in a country where it should have stood the best chance of succeeding? And, second, why in the subsequent years did significant numbers of the German working class move toward the reactionary parties of nationalism rather than toward the internationalist cause of the communists? These are two variations on the basic question noted at the end of chapter 2: Why do people so easily submit themselves to voluntary servitude by internalizing ways of thinking that go against their best interests? It is the problem of what early critical theorists dubbed false consciousness.

Faced with this challenge, two Marxist thinkers in particular looked back to the Hegelian roots of Marx's thinking in order to challenge the orthodox Marxism of Kautsky and company by returning the issue of consciousness to a key position: Karl Korsch and Georg Lukács. Both happened to publish their key works on this topic in 1923, in the wake of the Russian success and the German failure.

Karl Korsch: Marxism and Philosophy

Karl Korsch (1886–1961) was a German Marxist, although he fled Germany in 1933 on the night of the Reichstag fire (the incident that allowed Hitler to consolidate his power) and, after sojourns in Denmark and England, settled in the United States in 1936, where he remained as an academic until his death. Early involvement in left-wing politics and the conviction that the German revolution failed because of lack of ideological preparation shaped his distinctive contribution to the development of Marxist theory.[4]

---

[4] On Korsch's life and thought, see Patrick Goode, *Karl Korsch: A Study in Western Marxism* (London: Macmillan, 1979); Douglas Kellner, ed., *Karl Korsch:*

Korsch's 1923 essay, *Marxism and Philosophy*, represented a ground-breaking contribution to Marxist thinking. It was a call for Marxism to return to its Hegelian roots in an effort to make it more effective as a revolutionary force. Pitched specifically against the kind of economic determinism which the thinking of Kautsky and the Second International represented, it offered an alternative pathway to revolution and, in doing so, pointed to a number of concerns that have affinity with the later developments represented by critical theory. Indeed, three are of particular interest: Korsch's understanding of the function of philosophy in the politics of culture; his concept of society as a totality; and the notion of truth which underlies his thinking.

Korsch's understanding of the importance of philosophy for a revolutionary political program builds on a point made by Hegel, that philosophy is the spirit of an age expressed in thought. The implication of this political program is that one can learn about an era by looking at the dominant philosophical patterns to which it gives expression. We see this in our own day, where oppression and victimhood are often characterized less in the strictly economic or material terms of an earlier era and more in individual psychological and therapeutic categories. What our societies value most or how our societies see the world—in our case psychological health and the means of achieving such respectively—are articulated by the dominant approaches to law, education, and social organization.

Taking this principle of Hegel, Korsch observes that the heyday of Hegelian thought in German intellectual life came to an end by the close of the 1840s, followed by a period of philosophical stagnation before a revival of Kantianism in the 1860s. Korsch comments that the typical historian of ideas, merely focused on the strictly intellectual elements of the story, cannot really understand why this takes place, either in terms of the rise of

---

Revolutionary Theory (Austin: University of Texas, 1977); Karl Korsch, *Marxism and Philosophy*, trans. Fred Halliday (London: New Left Books, 1970).

Hegelianism after Kant or its rapid decline midcentury. This is because the typical historian of ideas misses a central point: there is an important relationship between the changes taking place in society and the philosophies that have plausibility at any given time. In other words, the philosophies that thrive in a given culture are philosophies that connect positively to broader phenomena taking place within that culture.

For Korsch, Hegel is a revolutionary thinker: his philosophy of historical change was the philosophy of the bourgeoisie, offering a philosophical rationale for overthrowing the old feudal regime and the establishment of the middle class as the dominant social and political force. It was also what Korsch calls an "objective component of the total social process of a real revolution."[5] Thought, or philosophy, was vital to social revolution. The critical theorist, Herbert Marcuse, makes substantially the same observation about Hegel in his 1941 study of the philosopher, *Reason and Revolution*: German idealism is itself part of the dramatic social revolution that takes place in German society in the early nineteenth century.[6]

Korsch can thus explain the rise and fall of Hegelianism in terms of the rise to dominance of the middle class, the bourgeoisie. In the late eighteenth and early nineteenth centuries, the middle class was rising and displacing the old landed gentry as the dominant social group. France is the most explosive example of this, with its bloody revolution. But, citing Marx to the effect that the French do in the realm of practice what the Germans do in the realm of theory, he sees the German revolution as being an intellectual one. In short, the revolutionary transformation of society as a result of the rise of the bourgeoisie found philosophical expression in a system of thought that prioritized change (and change driven by conflict) at its core, rather than one which operated with static categories. But once the revolutionary transformation had been achieved and society stabilized, the

---

[5] Kellner, *Karl Korsch: Revolutionary Theory*, 34.
[6] Herbert Marcuse, *Reason and Revolution* (n.p.: Wolfhaus, 2020), 3–12.

Hegelian philosophy of change ceased to represent the spirit of the age and was eventually replaced by a repristinated Kantianism with its stability and its transcendentals.[7]

Underlying this is a key assumption that will have analogs in critical theory. The bourgeois mistake is to assume that philosophy—the explanation of society—is an external analysis of society and not actually a part of society itself. For Korsch, it is not just a description of the way things are. It actually does something, whether that be challenging the status quo or justifying the same. It is not neutral, objective, or external to social practices. To imagine that it is merely descriptive or explanatory, is a classic example of false consciousness.[8] It grants an independent status to philosophical theory as something that stands above society itself. It thereby hides the fact that philosophy serves class interests. Korsch by contrast wants to bind theory and practice together: for him, the philosophical analysis of society is part of society, a social act. Thus, when that analysis is of the Hegelian variety, something that relativizes the present and thus has revolutionary potential, it is itself part of that revolution. Now, Marxism, with its radical materialism, has risen as the revolutionary successor to the old Hegelian idealism. It represents an active challenge to the now dominant bourgeoisie who once looked to Hegel as their revolutionary theoretician but abandoned him once they had the status quo that suited their social ambitions. Marxist materialism is thus the successor to Hegelian idealism and, like the latter in its heyday, is a revolutionary act. In short, to think like a Marxist is also to act like a Marxist and vice versa. The criticism of society is at its core revolutionary activity. In the words of Douglas Kellner:

> *Marxism and Philosophy* was intended to provide a restoration of the philosophical dimension of Marxism and the importance of

---

[7] Korsch, *Marxism and Philosophy*, 40.
[8] Korsch, 73.

ideological struggle for revolutionary practice, much as Lenin has restored the political dimension of Marxism and the importance of revolutionary political struggle.[9]

In short, Korsch believes that Marxists need to understand the importance of the criticism of ideology as a means of raising revolutionary consciousness.

The point might seem somewhat arcane but becomes easier to grasp once two further concepts are clarified. The first is the fact that Korsch sees society as a *totality*.[10] This means that society has to be understood as a whole, with all of its aspects interrelated. Now, Korsch understands society as having three levels: the economic structure (and the social relations it determines) is the most basic and most important; the state and the laws that uphold the state are the next level, giving the economic relations the status of being natural; and then there is ideology, the various ideas, intuitions, narratives and traditions that make up a society's self-consciousness. Ideology is nonsense in that it is a mirage of unity that hides the reality of social contradictions and class struggle, but that does not mean it is not important. Indeed, Korsch regards it as necessary, for it is what makes communal activity possible. Only when there is a shared sense of the whole can society function.

In adopting this tripartite division, Korsch explicitly agrees with what he dubs "vulgar Marxism" (i.e., the strict economic Marxism of the Second International) in making economic factors basic, but, unlike them, he refuses to grant independent and decisive significance to the merely economic. All three areas—economy, law, and ideology—are part of the totality and need to be understood as functioning in relation to each other and therefore as ripe for criticism.[11]

This is an important insight that can be illustrated using some obvious examples: it may be that the worker is exploited by the factory owner, but

---

[9] Kellner, *Karl Korsch: Revolutionary Theory*, 37.

[10] Korsch, *Marxism and Philosophy*, 52.

[11] Korsch, 73–78.

the worker is typically not exploited by direct force. He is not frog-marched from his home to the factory gates each morning and then forced at gunpoint to work ten hours on the production line. Rather, he goes willingly. Likewise, the men who fought in the trenches and the women who worked in the munitions factories in the First World War did so willingly, thereby serving an imperialist cause. Such a cause was not in the interest of their liberation but rather of their continued oppression, but they did so because they wanted to serve their country. The state and its laws, and the ideology of the time, all shaped their consciousness and thus led them to behave willingly in certain ways. We might put this in a more colloquial way that yet brings out Korsch's point: the "system" controls their thinking and their behavior.

We can elaborate Korsch's point yet further with the example of a law against vagrancy. If begging or sleeping in cardboard boxes under a bridge are illegal, then they are illegal for all, the rich, the poor, and all points in between. It seems to treat everyone as an equal. Yet in practice what does the law do? A Marxist in the critical tradition of Korsch would no doubt argue that it restricts the freedom of the poor, that it presents the inevitable victims of an unjust capitalist system as morally culpable for their own victimhood, and protects the property of the rich. In short, it serves the interest of capitalism by hiding or excusing its problems and offering a means of naturalizing its evils. It serves the economic system and reinforces its ideology but is not reducible to being a simple effect of either one. Its relationship to them is part of the totality.

For Korsch, an important part of revolutionary Marxism lies here, in the practical interpretation of human consciousness and how it is formed by the interrelated economic, legal/institutional, and ideological spheres.[12] And this is what legitimates ideological critique. Indeed, it is what makes ideological critique a vital part of the Marxist revolutionary project: the

---

[12] Leszek Kolakowski, *Main Currents of Marxism* (Oxford: Oxford University Press, 1981), 3:310.

destruction of false consciousness is necessary for the development of true consciousness. As Marx claimed with respect to religion, tearing away false hope (or false despair) is necessary to promoting real hope and the action that is based upon such. Of course, Korsch is not an idealist and does not believe that the mere criticism of ideas in itself will bring about revolutionary change. But the fact that society is a totality means that the revolutionary project must address all three levels: economy, state and law, and ideology. And in the realm of ideology, this means raising awareness of how the three elements interconnect. There is, to use the Hegelian/Marxist terminology, a dialectical relationship here, one where each of the three stands in interactive and critical relationship to the others. Economic factors are foundational but they do not stand to law and to ideology in a straightforward cause-to-effect relationship. The situation is more complicated than that and exposing this complex interrelationship is the task of the Marxist critic.

Ideological critique is thus an important component of the revolution. It serves to expose the system of cultural values and practices as nonsense, as deceptive, and as rationalizing the kind of behavior that serves the bourgeois cause and thus the oppression of the proletariat. It thus plays its part both in raising the consciousness of the oppressed and in opposing the oppression to which they are subject. To use the idiom of later critical theorists, ideological critique serves to expose the latent power relations that culture serves to disguise by presenting itself as natural. For Korsch, these power relations are determined by economic factors; whereas for modern critical theorists, power is more diffuse, intersecting with race, gender, sexuality, ethnicity, age, etc. But the basic issue—that ideology is an instrument of power and oppression—remains a constant theme from Korsch to the present day.

This then points us to an important assumption in Korsch's thinking: his notion of truth. Typically, most people operate with a common-sense notion of truth understood in terms of a correspondence between a statement and a reality. "The cat is on the mat" is true if there is indeed a cat on the mat, and false if the cat is in fact outside on the lawn. That is analogous to the kind of philosophy that Marx criticizes in his eleventh thesis on Feuerbach and which Korsch criticizes in his rejection of the idea of philosophy standing apart from, or above, society as a disinterested description or analysis of the same. Such philosophy is not revolutionary because it does nothing to challenge the status quo. It is a form of what Korsch dismisses as "naïve realism," a problem he sees in vulgar Marxism and which, as he somewhat sarcastically notes, was actually rendered implausible by the critical philosophy of Kant, something the "vulgar socialists" seem to have missed.[13]

In fact, in holding to a naïve realism as the way in which we know things, such philosophy is not actually "true" in the deepest sense, however much it might appear to correspond to the way the world is. Naïve realism offers a simplistic view of the world and does no more than justify the status quo as natural and necessary. As such, naïve realism does not represent the concept of truth with which Korsch is operating.

For him, what makes a philosophy, idea, or theory true is not its simple correspondence to reality. Reality, after all, cannot be accessed in a straightforward, nonideological manner. Rather truth values are determined by whether a particular idea or claim furthers the revolutionary cause. Korsch finds precedent for this in Marx's second thesis on Feuerbach:

> The question, whether objective truth can be attributed to human thinking is not a question of theory but a practical question. Man must prove the truth, i.e., the reality and power, the this-worldliness of his thinking in practice. The dispute over the reality or non-reality of thinking which isolates itself from practice is a purely scholastic one.[14]

What Marx means is that truth needs to be reconceptualized not as an idea but as a practice. Do ideas work to achieve the revolutionary change in

---

[13] Korsch, *Marxism and Philosophy*, 76.
[14] *CW* 5, 6. The passage is quoted by Korsch, *Marxism and Philosophy*, 82.

society for which Marxism aims? If yes, they are true. If no, they are false. This is the notion of truth with which Korsch is operating.

As a result, the normal criterion of truth—correspondence to reality—is irrelevant. The important thing is whether the idea destabilizes the status quo and tilts the world toward the realization of revolution. Again, there is an affinity here between Korsch's Marxism and the modern critical notion of constructing alternative narratives to expose injustice and challenge those who hold power. Such a strategy often infuriates conservatives but it lies at the heart of the critical theory project. If all truth claims are ideological, then it is their practical ideological value that determines their truth value. Responses that demand evidence for claims miss the point of such theoretical critique: the very demand for evidence—indeed, the definition of what does and does not count for evidence—arises out of the ideological structures of the society or culture within which the demand is made and evidence defined. They can thus be dismissed by a critical theorist as simply being part of the dominant ideology, an attempt to present the interests of the powerful as if they were the disinterested truths of nature.

There is a problem here—a problem we will encounter on numerous occasions with critical theory. It is the question of how one might know that a particular idea destabilizes society in a way that advances the revolutionary project. There are, after all, ways of thinking that destabilize the status quo that do not tilt toward Marxist revolution. Korsch is writing in 1923, on the very eve of the rise of Fascism and Nazism—forces that are going to revolutionize a number of European countries but hardly in a progressive Marxist direction. In order to know that an idea advances the progressive cause, one surely needs some cogent and relatively elaborate vision of what a Marxist society might look like in order to judge such. And that would seem to push philosophy into the realm of an objectivity that Korsch's focus on ideology and historical process precludes. It is, in short, the problem of articulating a utopian vision from the standpoint of someone who denies that anyone can stand outside of the historical process and offer an objective view of the truth. As we will see with, for example, Herbert Marcuse, it is much easier to criticize the status quo in order to tear it down than it is to offer a clear account of what is to replace it.[15]

To return to Korsch and the truth of revolutionary action, he is asserting that ideas and their expression are in themselves actions. This is, of course, true. When I say something, I do something. Thus, if I say to someone, "You are a fool!," I might appear to be describing him, but what I am really doing is putting him in his place, asserting my superiority over him, and making him look weak to any onlookers. Korsch sees cultural and social criticism along the same lines. It is not descriptive; it is a transformative, revolutionary act. Thus, cultural criticism, while not the whole of revolutionary action, is nonetheless an important, if not vital, part of it. The very activity itself is for the purpose of transforming the consciousness of the proletariat.

Toward the end of *Marxism and Philosophy*, Korsch offers a summary of his approach which captures nicely the essence of his thinking about the need for a critical theory of culture:

> All these forms [economic and legal theories, art, religion, and philosophy] must be subjected to the revolutionary criticism of scientific socialism, which embraces the whole of social reality. They

---

[15] In an oft-quoted passage in *The German Ideology*, Marx offers his own brief account of what life in the communist utopia will be like. Seeing one of the key problems of capitalist society as the division of labor—the apportioning of different tasks to different people in industrial society (and thus the division of people from each other and from the fruits of their labor)—he sees communist society as overcoming that: "In communist society, where nobody has one exclusive sphere of activity but each can become accomplished in any branch he wishes, society regulates the general production and thus makes it possible for me to do one thing today and another tomorrow, to hunt in the morning, fish in the afternoon, rear cattle in the evening, criticize after dinner, just as I have a mind, without ever becoming hunter, fisherman, shepherd or critic." *CW* 5, 47. Even if we understand Marx as offering a somewhat poetic account of how we think of ourselves rather than about the advent of radically transferable skills and vocations, it seems that such a passage is nothing more than a pipe dream, inconceivable at the level of theory, let alone in practice.

must be criticized in theory and overthrown in practice, together with the economic, legal, and political structures of society and at the same time as them. Just as political action is not rendered unnecessary by the economic action of a revolutionary class, so intellectual action is not rendered unnecessary by either political or economic action. On the contrary it must be carried through to the end in theory and practice, as revolutionary scientific criticism and agitational work before the seizure of state power by the working class, and as scientific organization and ideological dictatorship after the seizure of state power.[16]

In short, the bourgeois world's existence as a totality requires a comprehensive revolutionary response, of which cultural criticism—a means of raising the consciousness of the proletariat—is to be a vital part.

Georg Lukács

As Marxism struggled to come to terms with the success of the Russian Revolution and the failure of its German counterpart, Korsch was not the only thinker to seek inspiration and help in the Hegelian roots of Marxist thought. Nor, indeed, was he to prove the most important. That title really belongs to a Hungarian thinker named Georg Lukács who had started his writing career as a literary critic and then became politically and philosophically radicalized. Thus, in 1923, he published one of the most important texts of Marxist philosophy ever penned: the collection of essays entitled *History and Class Consciousness*.

Lukács is a controversial character, both politically and intellectually. Politically, his service to the Hungarian communist government of Bela Kun (1919), and then to the Stalinists of the 1950s and the post-1956 Hungarian Communist Party, led the late English conservative philosopher

---

[16] Korsch, *Marxism and Philosophy*, 84.

Sir Roger Scruton to refer to him simply as evil. Intellectually, his various changes of direction within the broader Marxist tradition—typically coinciding with the exigencies of political survival or advancement—make it hard to establish what his real, stable philosophy was—if indeed he had one. Yet he is also arguably the most important Marxist philosopher of the twentieth century and an important influence upon critical theory.[17] Edward Said, a foundational thinker in postcolonial studies, for example, frequently cited Lukács as an influence.[18]

For our purposes, his 1923 work, *History and Class Consciousness*, makes key contributions in areas that are of significance for the development of critical theory: the nature of Marxism, reification, and alienation. And, as with Korsch, he does this by returning to a more Hegelian form of Marxism in response to the crude Marxism of the Second International, with a particular interest in the notion of consciousness as a key concern of revolutionary thought.

The Definition of Orthodox Marxism

Writing in the aftermath of both the end of the Second International and the wake of the Russian Revolution, Lukács faces the question of what exactly orthodox Marxism is. There are a number of contenders for the title—the approaches of Karl Kautsky, Rosa Luxemburg, and V. I. Lenin being just three. What Lukács does is adopt a definition which completely sidesteps any formal dogmatic content in terms of, say, objective laws of economics

---

[17] There is a large amount of scholarship on Lukács. The most helpful introduction is George Lichtheim, *George Lukács* (New York: Viking, 1970). The best study in English is G. H. R. Parkinson, *Georg Lukács* (London: Routledge, Kegan, Paul, 1977). For Lukács's influence on the Frankfurt School, see Andrew Feenberg, *The Philosophy of Praxis: Marx, Lukács and the Frankfurt School* (London: Verso, 2014).

[18] See Timothy Brennan, *Places of Mind: A Life of Edward Said* (New York: Farrar, Straus, and Giroux, 2021), 76.

or history, in favor of a more subtle approach. In the opening chapter of *History and Class Consciousness*, he states that, even if every individual thesis of Marx was proved wrong, it would not require any Marxist to abandon Marxism. This is because of his reorientation of what constitutes orthodoxy:

> Orthodox Marxism . . . does not imply the uncritical acceptance of the results of Marx's investigations. It is not the "belief" in this or that thesis, nor the exegesis of a "sacred" book. On the contrary, orthodoxy refers exclusively to method.[19]

This move is akin to Korsch's approach to truth: truth does not lie in objective, transcendent laws but rather in the method that pushes history forward. This method, for Lukács as for Korsch, is dialectical.

To grasp the nature and significance of this dialectical method for Lukács, it is helpful to clarify what he is not claiming, or at least what he is not merely claiming. Marxism is famous for seeing history as a process, and specifically as a process driven by economic factors. But if that was all there was to Marxism, such would not represent a claim to a particularly distinctive approach. That economics influences the flow of history is something many non-Marxist historians would accept without question. Further, that history is a process that involves change would not be a particularly controversial assertion. But process and change can be understood in different ways.

Take, for example, a simple matter of cause and effect. When a hammer strikes a nail, the nail sinks into the wood panel. There has been change. But it is important to notice that neither the hammer nor the nail are actually changed in themselves in this process. They remain the same. The same applies to a bowling ball striking the pins. The pins go flying in all direction but are not intrinsically changed and neither is the ball.

By contrast, Lukács's dialectical method not only posits history as a process but also sees the various parties in that process as being changed by

---

[19] Georg Lukács, *History and Class Consciousness: Studies in Marxist Dialectics*, trans. Rodney Livingstone (Cambridge: MIT, 1971), 1.

the process. Economic and class conflict does not simply involve the clash of static interest groups. It involves the transformation of those groups as well. For Lukács, this is the key insight of Marxism and draws from Hegel's ideas of history and of recognition. As we noted in chapter 2, the relationship between the lord and the bondservant is not a static one: as the bondservant serves his lord, he gains skills that slowly but surely transform the relationship and his consciousness of the relationship. The change in him and the change in his relationship to the lord are inseparable. His consciousness has no status that exists in separation from the concrete reality of his existence in relation to his lord.

Following Marx's own taxonomy of history, Lukács sees humanity as developing though several stages. In feudalism, the world seemed natural. Nothing much changed from generation to generation. Space and time held tremendous natural authority and human beings thus thought of themselves as natural creatures with a given identity. We can easily grasp what Lukács is pointing to: in medieval Europe, for example, most people were born, grew up, worked, played, married, reproduced, and eventually died in the same place, a place that barely changed from the day of their birth to that of their death.[20]

Capitalism transformed all this. Industrial technology and the expansion of the marketplace served to attenuate the power of nature and reorganize human relations. It transformed human relationships in geographical and legal terms. The flux of this world made human beings aware that they were social creatures. And it created two antagonistic classes, the bourgeoisie and the proletariat. And the bourgeoisie as the dominant class expressed its existence in social and cultural forms that made its world, the world of capitalism, seem rational and thus the best one, ruled by instrumental, scientific reasoning and principles that reflected not class interest but the natural, objective way of organizing society.[21]

---

[20] Lukács, 19.
[21] Lukács, 19–20.

For Lukács, however, as for Korsch, there is no true objectivity. The fact that the world as currently constituted claims that such exists is a trick, a manipulative move that hides what is really going on. Capitalism poses as a scientific, rational phenomenon. Yes, there are periodic crises—economic crashes—but these are always presented as failures of the system, the result of imperfect understanding or as deviations. Lukács argues that, on the contrary, they actually belong to the very system itself: capitalism involves inherent contradictions that cause periodic crises; the crises are therefore capitalism doing what it has to do, along with all the suffering and social ferment such generates. That it presents itself under another guise is a central problem. And the task of the critic is to expose these. That does not involve stepping outside the system. Rather it involves exposing the inner contradictions of the system for what they are. It requires dialectical thinking that sees the whole of society not as the equivalent of a smooth, harmonious machine but as involving conflict and contradiction. It is a form of immanent critique that serves to foster a revolutionary consciousness.[22]

As with later critical theorists, Lukács sees science as playing a key ideological role here. As we will see in chapter 5, Max Horkheimer and Theodor Adorno see the role of scientific rationality as historically operating in a dialectical way, first overthrowing the old religious metaphysics that undergirded the ecclesiastical and religious authorities of the Middle Ages and then as becoming a dominant ideology that serves to subjugate and dehumanize individuals. Lukács anticipates this:

> When the ideal of scientific knowledge is applied to nature it simply furthers the progress of science. But when it is applied to society it turns out to be an ideological weapon of the bourgeoisie. For the latter it is a matter of life and death to understand its own system of production in terms of eternally valid categories: it must think of capitalism as being predestined to eternal survival by the

---

[22] Lukács, 10.

eternal laws of nature and reason. Conversely, contradictions that cannot be ignored must be shown to be purely surface phenomena, unrelated to this mode of production.[23]

Science as an idiom has a veneer of objectivity to it. It claims simply to describe and explain reality in terms of principles that are detached and disinterested. Lukács (as later critical theorists) rejects that. For him, science serves an ideological purpose, naturalizing that which is actually socially constructed and which serves the political interests of the powerful. This is a theme that permeates later critical theory, whether of the Marxist or non-Marxist kind.

Reification

Perhaps Lukács's most important contribution to Marxist thought—and a concept that has traveled well beyond the bounds of Marxism—is that of reification, an idea he expounds in the most famous chapter of *History and Class Consciousness*, "Reification and the Consciousness of the Proletariat." Put simply, reification is the ascription of objective reality and intrinsic power to things that are really social relations.[24]

This has its roots in Marx's understanding of the commodity fetish, something he discusses at length in *Capital*. The idea is a complicated one and Marx expends considerable time in expounding it, but its essential elements are relatively straightforward. He takes the basic idea of the fetish from the way in which the term is used by his contemporaries relative to

---

[23] Lukács, 10–11.

[24] The influence of Lukács's theory of reification on the Frankfurt School, especially Adorno, was immense. But Lukács's later submission to Stalinist orthodoxy and repudiation of much of his earlier work made him a decidedly ambiguous figure and one not explicitly cited as often as his evident influence would lead one to expect. See Titus Stahl, "Lukács and the Frankfurt School," in Peter E. Gordon, Espen Hammer, and Axel Honneth, *The Routledge Companion to the Frankfurt School* (London: Routledge, 2019), 237–50.

religious objects. In this context, a fetish is a material thing—say, a statue or a relic of a saint—to which mysterious power is ascribed. Marx sees a similar thing being done with commodities in capitalist society. There is a difference, however, between the religious fetish and the commodity fetish: the former's power is a fiction; for the latter it is real. But here is the key point: this real power is not a power that is intrinsic to the object; rather, it is a power that is given to it by the social relations within which it operates. Thus, in capitalist society, different producers produce different commodities but only come in to social contact with each other when those commodities are exchanged. This gives the commodity itself the appearance of intrinsic power, of being the means by which social interaction is made possible and takes place; what this hides is the fact that it is the means by which the commodity is produced—the labor of the one producing the commodity—which gives it its real value.

The example of money is a helpful way of elucidating this idea. Now, money is not strictly a commodity but the means by which commodities are exchanged in a capitalist system. Indeed, it is the universal measure of the value of all things in the capitalist world, from the products of the factories to the labor of the factory worker and therefore of the factory worker himself. Nevertheless, it is perhaps the best illustration of the kind of fetishism Marx is critiquing. Paper money is intrinsically worthless: the paper, the ink, and the process involved in printing it are the same for a one-dollar bill as for a fifty-dollar bill. Today, when we often do not even use material bills or coins but simply trade in pixels on a screen, the point is perhaps even more dramatic. Money in terms of its material reality is basically worthless. And yet we ascribe value to it as the basic means for judging the comparative worth of other, real things, whether food items, precious jewels, or even human beings. Why do we do so? Because we can exchange it for commodities. It has become the universal means by which we apportion value to everything else. The real value of those things is hidden from us: for Marxists, it is the labor put in to producing them. But we treat money as if it has the real power. In short, the social relationship that makes the production of commodities possible—exploitation of the workers by the factory owners—is invisible to us. This helps to create a culture where the means of exchange of commodities—money—takes center stage as that which is truly deemed "real." Money becomes the mysterious means by which all things are valued and compared, even people, given the centrality of wages to capitalist society. Most significantly, it also shapes our view of reality whereby we come to see exchange and exchange value as embodying the fundamental reality of human society. Commodities, and the exchange of those commodities, is what life is all about.

Lukács's notion of reification builds upon this idea. As previously noted, reification ascribes objective reality to things that are really a matter of social relations. In the words of Lukács:

> The essence of commodity-structure has often been pointed out. Its basis is that a relation between people takes on the character of a thing and thus acquires a "phantom objectivity," an autonomy that seems so strictly rational and all-embracing as to conceal every trace of its fundamental nature: the relation between people.[25]

Again, an example will help to clarify the phenomenon to which he is pointing. Take the term "the economy." Use of this is commonplace today. "The economy is growing," "Inflation is having an impact on the economy," and "The government will address the issues facing the economy in its budget" are all phrases with which we are familiar and which we might think we intuitively understand. But if we pause and ask ourselves what "the economy" is, the problem becomes apparent. There is no "economy" out there in the sense that there is a city called Washington, DC in the United States or a cathedral named St. Paul's in London. The economy cannot be photographed. It cannot be put into a test tube and analyzed for its chemical composition. It is a construct. In reality, what we call "the economy" is the

---

[25] Lukács, *History and Class Consciousness*, 83.

sum of the social relations of individual human beings engaged in what we refer to as economic activity.

One might respond by saying that yes, of course this is the case and that therefore the term "the economy" is helpful as shorthand. But a moment's reflection reveals that the term does more than simply describe the sum of social relations. It quietly asserts that the whole ("the economy") is greater than, and prior to, the parts (the individual activities to which it refers). We might put this in common parlance: once we start talking in terms of "the economy" then the term takes on a life of its own and becomes in society's consciousness a basic objective unit of reality that carries with it intrinsic and foundational authority. Thus, for example, the demands of "the economy" become paramount in policy and decision making; the needs of the individual disappear from consideration. Human beings are eclipsed in light of this greater putative reality.

Lukács sees capitalism as slowly but surely driving this "commodity structure" through all levels and aspects of society. Prior to the triumph of capitalism, methods of exchange involved personal relationships.[26] A couple of examples help to illuminate Lukács's point. We can imagine a village blacksmith in medieval times shoeing the horse of the local farmer in return for a side of pork or a hefty piece of beef. But with the advent of capitalism and the triumph of money as the principle of exchange, an increasingly impersonal element enters the picture. It takes some time to transform everything, so that even early capitalism retains a certain respect for human beings as human beings, but eventually it captures the cultural consciousness. Perhaps the contrast between Mr. Fezziwig and Ebenezer Scrooge in *A Christmas Carol* illustrates this. Fezziwig may be a capitalist, but he treats his employees with kindness and decency, throwing a Christmas ball for them each year; Scrooge by contrast hates Christmas and treats his clerk, Bob Cratchit, simply as a cost item in his budget. For Fezziwig, his staff

---

[26] Lukács, 86.

are people. For Scrooge, Cratchit is measured purely in cash value—not a human but a commodity, a thing.

This last example points to the interesting inversion that Lukács sees capitalism as causing: things become persons, and persons become things. Again, an example will help to clarify this point. Once the economy is seen to have an objective existence of its own, then the people who work within the economy have their identity from their relationship to "the economy" and not to each other. John becomes merely one among many workers who can be swapped out for any other worker at any point. He loses his intrinsic value as a person because his value is measured in terms of his labor power, power that he exchanges for money. In fact, as a worker, his value becomes defined purely by the wage he earns, not by the things he produces. Unlike the medieval craftsman, John works on a production line, and the things he makes have no connection to his individuality whatsoever. He is simply paid to pull a lever, turn a wheel, or flip a switch. He is a thing, a line item on a balance sheet, not an individual. The world has become a place where everything is rationally calculated in terms of its monetary value. The mechanism of exchange becomes the reality; everything else is subordinated to this. He is an object, a thing, not an individual person.

Lukács uses this to develop his own distinctive Marxist theory of revolution, where the proletariat becomes a commodity but then becomes aware that this is so and thereby conscious of its own agency and ability to make itself "real" by seizing the means of production. To use his somewhat opaque Hegelian terminology, the working class is both the subject and the object of history. Like the bondservant in Hegel's thought experiment, the proletariat comes to realize that its bondage is a confidence trick played by the bourgeoisie and is thus able to act to liberate itself.

The plausibility of Lukács's theory of revolution is only of tangential interest here. What is significant is the effect that he sees reification having upon the worker. It *alienates* him. And with his discussion of alienation, Lukács is the first major Marxist thinker to bring back into discussion an important idea found in Marx's *Manuscripts of 1844*, and this will prove a significant topic both in western Marxism and in the development of critical theory.[27]

Alienation

While alienation does not play an explicit role in the writings of the later Marx, it is a theme of his work in the early 1840s. Indeed, perhaps the most famous section of the *Manuscripts* is that dealing with alienated (estranged) labor. Here, Marx delineates the impact of industrialized labor upon the worker and sees it as alienating in four related ways, but to understand his argument we must first understand how Marx understands human nature. As we noted in chapter 2, for Marx, human beings are distinguished from other creatures in that we are free and make things as acts of free will and intention. This means that who we are and the things we make and how we make them are intimately related. But in a society built upon industrialized capitalism, this relationship is transformed, with productive labor taking on a new characteristic, that of alienation. Once the means and fruits of my labor do not belong to me, then there is a very real sense in which I no longer belong to me. I have ceased to be a free agent. Marx makes this point by arguing in the *Manuscripts* that alienation has four dimensions.

First, industrial labor alienates the worker from the products of his labor. The worker labors but what he produces does not belong to him. Instead, he is paid a wage. Thus, any personal value he feels from his work is not the result of the thing he produces but of the money he takes home. Second, it alienates the worker from his own productive activity: his productive activity does not belong to him but to another, the person who pays him and thereby purchases his labor. A fundamental aspect of his being is really the

---

[27] What is remarkable is that Marx's *Economic and Philosophic Manuscripts* were not published until 1932 in Moscow. Lukács thus only came into contact with them some years after writing *History and Class Consciousness*.

property of somebody else. Third, this then alienates him from himself and from his own body: his labor ceases to be the means by which he expresses himself and becomes merely the means by which he earns money that then enables him to meet his individual needs. In this way, he lacks the thing that makes him a human—his free, spontaneous productive activity—and so is alienated from his own humanity. And, finally, this alienates him from other human beings, for as man is alienated from himself so he sees the being and labor of others in the same light.[28] As Dan Swain has expressed it, "those who engage in wage labor are alienated both from those they work *for* and those they work *with*."[29] In short, the alienation of man from himself leaves him feeling powerless against the forces of capital—money, private property, the bourgeoisie—even though he should be the powerful one, given that it is he who actually produces things, not money nor banks nor factory owners.

In a passage of rhetorical power, Marx describes the means and effect of this alienation as follows:

> *Political economy conceals the estrangement inherent in the nature of labour by not considering the* **direct** *relationship between the* **worker** (labour) *and production.* It is true that labour produces wonderful things for the rich—but for the worker it produces privation. It produces palaces—but for the worker, hovels. It produces beauty—but for the worker, deformity. It replaces labour by machines, but it throws one section of the workers back to a barbarous type of labour, and it turns the other section into a machine. It produces intelligence—but for the worker, stupidity, cretinism.[30]

---

[28] See *CW* 3, 273–82.

[29] Dan Swain, "Alienation, or Why Capitalism Is Bad for Us," in Matt Vidal, Tony Smith, Tomás Rotta, and Paul Prew, *The Oxford Handbook of Karl Marx* (Oxford: Oxford University Press, 2019), 365.

[30] *CW* 3, 273. Ernest Mandel describes the effects of alienation as follows: "Work is no longer a means of self-expression for anybody who sells his labor time. Work is just a means to attain a goal. And that goal is to get money, some income to be able to buy the consumer goods necessary to satisfy your need. In

The worker does not enjoy the fruits of his labor and his life is actually degraded by the nature of his industrialized work. And what is important to note in this passage is the opening line: the nature of political economy hides this problem by its refusal to consider the direct relationship between the worker and the product. That which gives pleasure to the bourgeoisie is built upon the dehumanizing of the proletariat, but the middle classes never notice this.

This phenomenon can be illustrated with a modern example. Most of us in the West own smartphones. They are useful, even fun, gadgets to possess. They can even have a certain pleasing aesthetic. Indeed, Apple built its brand not only on its products' ease of function but perhaps even more so on their simple, clean, attractive appearance. Yet the smartphones we own are made with components produced by slave labor in China. The work those men and women do is dehumanizing and harsh. It denies them dignity. It is utterly alienating. They do not enjoy the fruits of their labor. But the advertising that sells these products does not connect them to the way in which they are produced, nor to the slaves who produce them. In other words, it conceals the alienation that they represent. For someone in the United States, the smartphone is a plaything; for the slave in China, it is the product of alienated labor.

The significance of all this for Lukács and then the development of critical theory is that reification is a function of alienation. We noted in chapter 2 that Feuerbach and Marx saw religion as involving a projection of idealized human attributes onto a putative divine being called "God" and that this was a form of alienation because those ideal attributes should be realized in human beings themselves. In Lukács's thought, the ascription of

---

this way a basic aspect of human nature, the capacity to perform creative work, becomes thwarted and distorted. Work becomes something which is not creative and productive for human beings, but something which is harmful and destructive." Ernest Mandel and George Novak, *The Marxist Theory of Alienation* (New York: Pathfinder, 1980), 27.

power to things, and the transformation of persons into things or subjects into objects, is also a matter of alienation, and it has the name *reification*.

Critique of reification involves the exposure of the roots of this alienation: the rise to dominance of commodity exchange as the way of thinking about all relationship. And making people conscious of the social relations that exist behind the capitalist mode of production is therefore central to revolutionary Marxism's critical task. To realize what it means to be truly human is to move beyond the alienation that capitalism involves; and to do that, the proletariat must become conscious of its alienation, of the forces that seek to make workers think of themselves as things, as having only cash value, and as being easily replaceable with any other worker. Put another way, a key part of the revolutionary project involves showing people their alienation by exposing the effect of reification and thus what it is that cuts them off from their humanity and prevents them from truly being the free creatures they should be.

Lukács sees bourgeois ideology as hiding this alienation in a specific way: its ability to isolate elements of society so that they are not seen as part of an organic whole. It isolates its various elements in such a way that nobody sees the whole picture, and so nobody is able to critique the whole picture. To return to the contemporary example of smartphones: the slave labor that makes the phone possible is conducted far, far away and hidden from the eyes not only of the customer but of the salesperson, the truck driver, and almost all of those involved in the chain that brings the components together to be assembled, distributed, and handed over to the one who finally purchases the product. To the one making the purchase, the phone is simply an attractive consumer good, not the product of a system which ultimately depends upon human exploitation.

For Marxists like Lukács, capitalism must do this because, of course, they do not think that the system ultimately makes sense. It is not a cogent, coherent whole but a system predicated upon self-contradictions. And since no one can see the whole picture, the bourgeoisie can (as noted by Korsch too) present the periodic crises of capitalism as aberrations rather than as essential parts of a self-contradictory system. And one of the ideological tools for this, according to Lukács, is that reason and rationality can be abstracted from the historical process and consequently presented as a neutral, disinterested tool for describing reality. The key to revolution then becomes the ability to see how the various isolated particulars of capitalist culture connect to each other and yet ultimately make no sense as a whole.

For Lukács this is an area where great works of art can help, for they often portray the contradictions within society before those contradictions become more generally apparent. It is indeed no coincidence that Lukács's earlier, pre-Marxist career was that of a literary critic.[31] Thus the genre of tragedy reveals tensions and fault lines that exist with a society that contradicts itself. We might think, for example, of the plot of Sophocles's *Antigone* where the eponymous heroine is caught between loyalty to family and loyalty to the king in a manner that proves unresolvable and ends in her death. Or, to use an example from modern society, in Franz Kafka's *The Trial*, Joseph K. is conscious of himself as an individual but has his individuality denied and crushed by a powerful and impersonal bureaucratic state. In this context, the work of the critic is to connect the artwork to the broader nature of society in order to show the contradictions that the latter embodies. In the same way, Lukács's famous essay, "Reification and the Consciousness of the Proletariat" can be read as a long and detailed history of German idealist philosophy, showing its connections to the rising forms of bourgeois society and its values in the nineteenth century.[32]

Korsch, Lukács, and Later Critical Theory

You may well be wondering at this point why we have spent so much time analyzing a specific development within Marxism in the early decades of the twentieth century. There are not too many Hegelian Marxists (beyond the

---

[31] Lukács, *History and Class Consciousness*, 175–76.
[32] Lukács, 83–222.

likes of Slavoj Žižek) dominating the news headlines. And the class-based concerns of Marxists like Korsch and Lukács seem rather straightforward and traditional compared to the more exotic and complicated taxonomies of intersectionality, queer theory, and gender studies. So how does this discussion help us to understand the kind of critical theories—racial, sexual, gender, queer, etc.—that grip the popular imagination today?

In fact, there are a number of elements of this Hegelian Marxism that anticipate the concerns not just of the early critical theorists but of their later successors. The first is that both men represent a shift on the left toward seeing what we might call psychological categories as key to the revolutionary struggle. Concern for consciousness and for the way in which societies encourage people to think about themselves and their relationship to others is central to both men and continues to be part of the general political culture of our own day. While for earlier generations the notion of oppression had a distinctly economic form—for example, one was oppressed if one was poor or unable to find a job—in today's political discourse one can be oppressed if one's identity or feelings are not acknowledged, as the fierce debates about pronouns and "deadnaming" with regard to transgender issues indicate. Of course, for Korsch and Lukács, the ultimate concerns were economic and the revolution for which they looked was one that had a fundamentally economic shape; but in bringing consciousness to the fore, they paved the way for conceptualizing the political struggle in more psychological terms and the struggle for liberation as far more than simply an economic one.

In this connection, their understanding of the interconnection of all cultural phenomena—economic, institutional, legal, and ideological— clearly points toward the kind of broad cultural critiques in which critical theorists engage. They see no place outside of the political structures of the culture from which to offer a view from nowhere. Everything interconnects and is therefore a legitimate object for critique. Further, though this term is decades away from becoming part of the critical theory playbook, their work certainly gestures toward the concept of intersectionality. Power is not simply a matter of an economic base determining a cultural superstructure. It is far more complicated than that, involving the interplay of cultural elements. Once the notion of economic class ceases to be the driving force of analysis, the way is open for the kind of more complex analysis of discourses of power in later critical theories of race, gender, and queerness. None of these are consciously anticipated by Korsch or Lukács, but they can be seen as consonant developments with their move to dethrone hardcore economic determinism and replace it with a more elaborate and sophisticated analysis of how ideologies are formed and operate.

But, as previously stated, perhaps the most significant contribution of Lukács is that of reification. Indeed, we might with little exaggeration say that this concept is the central preoccupation of critical theories in general. The treatment of people as things and of subjects as objects is key to the work of critical theorists of gender, sexuality, and race because each of these is pitted against the kind of essentialism that puts normative content into general terms that are then used to categorize people. In other words, they reject forms of reification that can then (in their view) be used to marginalize or demonize particular groups. Once, for example, what it means to be normatively human is identified with white male heterosexuality or American values or stiff-upper-lip Englishness, those who do not conform are in trouble. Indeed, they may themselves be placed into other reified but deviant categories that are really a reflection of the discourses of power that constitute a given society. Reification is a form of essentialism. And critical theory rejects essentialism in all of its forms as inherently oppressive.

Finally, both Korsch and Lukács see theory as a part of revolutionary practice. Its purpose is not to describe the world but to be a part of changing the world, in line with the aspirational claim of Marx's eleventh thesis on Feuerbach. And it is to the elaboration of that idea at the hands of the early Frankfurt School member, Max Horkheimer, that we now turn.

A Postscript on Reification

Lukács's concept of reification is arguably one of the most important for critical theory, perhaps even its central concern. When categories take on a life of their own and become a means of placing individual persons into boxes or assessing them simply in terms of labels, then something significant is happening. Indeed, so much of contemporary politics is preoccupied with precisely this issue: battles over speech codes, pronouns, what constitutes a slur, the notion of language as being in some sense violence—all of these things are really versions of what Lukács called reification. For him, reification was a function of the capitalist economy where exchange value (and thus money) was the universal principle for judging the worth of anyone or anything. Therefore, humans became just one more commodity in the marketplace. But reification does not require a commitment to a broadly Marxist understanding of economic relations; it plays upon a basic need for social interaction: the need for categories beyond that of a given individual in order to communicate and interact. We are social beings and necessarily understand ourselves through perceiving those things we share with others and those that distinguish us from them.

And therein lies the problem. As soon as we deploy general categories of discourse beyond that of the individual—whether it be the all-embracing "human being" or something based upon the reification of some less universal category such as race, ethnicity, sexuality, sex, or gender—we run the risk of dissolving persons into things. And this is where the sterility of much that passes for critical theory comes into play. What critical theory in its modern iterations does is seek to replace traditional categories of reification with alternatives. And so we now see the notions of "white," "heteronormative," and "cisgender," among others, supplanting the older reified categories that are now regarded as having served to maintain the established order of injustice and discrimination. These new categories—rather like the old—allow people to be dismissed out of hand and treated as objects, not free subjects. If I look at somebody and see them as merely an instantiation of "whiteness," I see them as a thing, not as a person.

Two effects flow from this. First, if the new categories gain traction then the established order is destabilized. That, as we shall see in chapter 4, is a key part of the difference between how the early critical theorists distinguished their work from what they dubbed "traditional theory." The critical theorist's calling is not merely to describe the world, as the philosophers had done, but to change it. Once the categories by which social interaction and stability were made possible and maintained have themselves been demolished or thrown into serious doubt, then the world that they represented becomes highly volatile. This is our world of today: institutions, law codes, and traditions built upon old categories of identity not only cease to be plausible but come to be seen as oppressive, unjust, and ripe for abolition.

But the second effect is this: that which replaces them creates its own hierarchies of power, its own ruling elites and its own marginalized and oppressed minorities. There are movements committed to critical theoretical approaches that eschew this: Marxists of the Lukács kind see the end of capitalism as bringing about the end of human alienation and therefore the collapse of the system via critique will not lead to new forms of oppression but to the end of history itself and to universal human liberation. In recent years, the vision presented by Black Lives Matter would seem to fall into this category. But less optimistic critical theorists—those whose understanding of the operations of power is detached from any aspirations to utopian politics—would surely concede that replacing one set of reified categories with another delivers no real and universal liberation. For example, does the "decolonizing" currently underway in school curricula and museums around the Western world really lead toward a more liberated, universal vision of the world? Or does it not rather replace the dominant categories of a previous era with those of the present? On a critical theoretical account, museums have always been organized in accordance with structures of cultural power. That applies to nineteenth-century British imperialists as it does to today's panjandrums of progressivism.

Only perhaps with the most radical queer theory—with the abolition of all categories—might such be achieved. But that scenario begs further questions: if all categories are abolished, is any kind of real society possible? Or, if all categories are destabilized, does power not remain in the hands of those who already possess it? After all, do we not already see hints of this latter situation if we ask the question of who really suffers when, for example, the traditional family is decried as oppressive? The wealthy progressives who live in the leafy suburbs and gated communities or the poor who live in the crime-ridden inner cities?

To put the matter of reification in Christian terms, it is a question of anthropology. What, if anything, grounds the categories by which we think about the human condition? Clearly a concept of "human nature" only takes us so far, given that we are free, intentional creatures and our lives are thus marked by particularities of the various cultures in which we live. We are each unique individuals with unique histories. Yet we also need to grasp that, when we look into the eyes of another human being, regardless of what particular category of identity might distinguish us from them, we look into the eyes of another human person, not a thing or an object. Critical theory can alert us to the reality of this problem but ultimately it cannot take us beyond the problem because of its radical suspicion of the power of our cultural frameworks to distort our vision. In this context, the Christian claim to see that the other is made in the image of God is simply a manifestation of a desire to reduce the other person to the categories of one's personal discourse and status quo as well as the power structures of the world that has constructed one's self and self-consciousness.

How can a Christian respond to this? I would suggest that it cannot be merely by way of argument. Reification is a real danger, as Lukács and those who came after him have warned. Rather, we have to address it in and through community, specifically the community of the church. With rituals such as the sacraments, liturgies that bind us together, the proclamation of the gospel which sets our lives within the categories established by God (creation, fall, redemption, and consummation), and the Spirit-filled life of the community that is constituted by and flows from such, we enact our humanity. Surely it is no coincidence that hospitality, the opening of one's home to others, is a key mark of New Testament Christianity. In such an act we relate to others as persons like ourselves, not as things. One can write endlessly about not treating the other person as an object. But if the problem is consciousness—how we intuitively think about ourselves and about others—the most powerful argument against such is not an argument; it is a way of life.

CHAPTER 4

The Frankfurt School: From Traditional Theory to Critical Theory

Introduction

Critical theory today is a term used to describe a variety of different disciplines: gender theory, postcolonial theory, critical race theory, etc.[1] While each of these disciplines has its own particular emphasis in terms of subject matter, they all share certain family resemblances. The emergence in the last forty years of the notion of intersectionality, with its sensitivity to the diffuse and complex ways in which power relations are manifested in society bears witness to this. It is also the case that there are different philosophical

---

[1] For a helpful summary of the central concerns and history of the various approaches included under the term "critical theory," see "Introduction: An Archaeology of the Western Subject," in Dino Franco Felluga, *Critical Theory: The Key Concepts* (London: Routledge, 2015), x–xxv; also Stephen Eric Bronner, *Critical Theory: A Very Short Introduction* (Oxford: Oxford University Press, 2017).

roots for some branches of critical theory. For example, those associated with Michel Foucault and French post-structuralism are more indebted to Nietzsche, with his acute sensitivity to the constructed nature of knowledge relative to power. Others, perhaps most notably Judith Butler, the guiding light of gender studies, are more deeply rooted in the Hegelian tradition. But neither stream is hermetically sealed off from the other. Critical theories share common themes and overlapping intellectual sources. Edward Said, the great postcolonial theorist, draws on both Foucault and Lukács; and Butler's Hegelianism does not prevent her from extensive use of Nietzsche and Foucault.

In fact, the basic concerns of later forms of critical theory—the socially constructed nature of reality, the manipulative nature of truth claims, the manner in which consciousness or (to use later terminology) discourses of power are formed, maintained, and operated, the purpose of theory as not so much to describe the status quo as to destabilize it, and the connection of intellectual work to political activism—can all be found in some form in the foundational work of the Frankfurt School from the 1940s through the 1960s. And as with later critical theory, the intellectual eclecticism—Hegel, Marx, Freud, Nietzsche—is also present from the early days. Indeed, there is a reason why, for many purists, "critical theory" and "Frankfurt School" are often treated as virtual synonyms: without the latter, there would likely be none of the later critical theories as we today know them. Thus, a knowledge of the Frankfurt School—its background and context, its major concerns, and its key players—is essential for understanding the later iterations of the tradition it inspired.

The Frankfurt School

The Frankfurt School is the name given to the members of the Institute for Social Research (ISR) at Goethe University in Frankfurt. The Institute was founded in 1923, emerging from a prior study group committed to Marxist discussion and analysis. Its most distinguished and influential director was Max Horkheimer, who took over the leadership of the ISR from Carl Grünberg. Under Horkheimer, the ISR became a focal point for some of the most acute dissident Marxist minds of the mid-twentieth century, including most notably Theodor Adorno, Herbert Marcuse, Erich Fromm, and Siegfried Kracauer. Walter Benjamin, the literary critic who combined Marxist thinking with messianic and mystical themes from Judaism, was also an important figure, though his relationship to the ISR was of a more informal, even if vitally influential, kind.[2]

Ethnicity was the common feature of this early generation of critical theorists: all were Jews from affluent, middle-class backgrounds, at a time when Nazism was rising to dominate German politics and culture. This is an important point, though often missed when critical theory is discussed as an abstract phenomenon (something, ironically, which stands in tension with the basic tenets of critical theory itself, with its concern for seeing all things within the total social and cultural context). To be a Jew in Germany in the twenties and thirties was increasingly to be an outsider to society and to be vulnerable to

---

[2] The best introductory history of the early Frankfurt School is that by contemporary cultural critic, Stuart Jeffries: *Grand Hotel Abyss: The Lives of the Frankfurt School* (London: Verso, 2016). Though written for a non-specialist audience, this book brings out the importance of the Jewish background of so many of the early critical theorists to their work. The standard history of the Frankfurt School is Rolf Wiggershaus, *The Frankfurt School: Its History, Theories and Political Significance*, trans. Michael Robertson (Cambridge: Polity, 1994). Still useful (especially for the figures covered in this book) is Martin Jay, *The Dialectical Imagination: A History of the Frankfurt School and the Institute of Social Research, 1923–1950* (Boston: Little, Brown and Company, 1973). Also worthwhile is David Held, *Introduction to Critical Theory: Horkheimer to Habermas* (Berkeley: University of California Press, 1980). An excellent collection of scholarly essays, covering many aspects of the Frankfurt School up to the present day is Peter E. Gordon, Espen Hammer, and Axel Honneth, *The Routledge Companion to the Frankfurt School* (London: Routledge, 2019). On Theodor Adorno, a good introduction is Andrew Bowie, *Theodor W. Adorno: A Very Short Introduction* (Oxford: Oxford University Press, 2002); also Gerhard Schweppenhäuser, *Theodor W. Adorno: An Introduction*, trans. James Rolleston (Durham: Duke University Press, 2009). On Marcuse, see Barry Katz, *Herbert Marcuse and the Art of Liberation* (London: Verso, 1982).

attacks and persecution. This factor gave the early Frankfurt School thinkers both an interesting vantage point on the culture in which they found themselves and added an existential urgency to their analyses. Whilst today's academics may well find that espousing some form of critical theory proves to be a rather useful career move, given the political tendencies of much of higher education today, this was not so for Horkheimer and his Jewish colleagues. Far from it. They occupied a politically vulnerable position and developed a philosophy that won them no friends in the German establishment of a society about to plunge into the dark night of National Socialism.

Indeed, the central issue for the early Frankfurt School was this rise of Nazism. The question with which they wrestled was this: Why was Nazism so popular? Its violent political philosophy emerged in a Germany that was arguably the most culturally sophisticated and technologically advanced country in the world. So why did it prove so vulnerable to such an authoritarian and barbaric movement? How had the land of Goethe become the fiefdom of Hitler? And given the Marxist commitments of the early members of the Frankfurt School, most urgent was the role of the working class in this. Why was the proletariat siding with the forces of oppression rather than liberation in the late 1920s and '30s? Germany had suffered a devastating defeat in a war marked by unprecedented levels of bloody carnage; it had been humiliated by the terms of the Versailles Treaty; it had seen galloping inflation and economic collapse; and it had no long-standing history of nationhood or of the national institutions that are part of such. Yet the working class was not moving as a unit toward supporting the revolutionary parties of the left. The Spartacist Revolution of 1918 had failed, having been ruthlessly suppressed, and the 1920s witnessed the increasing attraction of the nationalist parties of the right to the proletariat, the poor, and the dispossessed—the very people that classical Marxist theory assumed would move to the left as capitalism descended into crisis.

In this context, the move we noted in chapter 3 in Lukács and Korsch—the refocusing of attention upon consciousness rather than simply upon economics—was to prove attractive. Horkheimer and his colleagues desired to explain the anomalous behavior of the working class through a thoroughgoing analysis of how German culture worked. As a result, what emerged at the ISR was a multidisciplinary approach to the study of culture which drew not only upon Marx (read against the background of Hegel) but also Max Weber, Georg Simmel, Sigmund Freud, and the methods of empirical social research.

Yet the impulse (at least in theory) behind the work of the ISR was not simply to offer explanatory schemes for why things were the way they were. It was also an attempt to take seriously that burden of Marx's eleventh thesis on Feuerbach—to change the world, not merely to explain it. And this is where the critical nature of the ISR's work was so important, as laid out in an early essay by Max Horkheimer, "Traditional and Critical Theory." This is essential reading for anyone seeking to grasp the purpose of Frankfurt School critical theory.[3] In it, Horkheimer sets out the basic program: to develop an approach to cultural analysis that sees behind the claims of objectivity and necessity that the social status quo makes on its own behalf and exposes what forces are really at play.

Traditional Theory

In his essay, Horkheimer starts by offering an analysis of what he calls *traditional theory* as a means by which to underscore the innovative importance of the work of critical theorists such as himself. In essence, traditional theory is an analytical approach to reality that claims to provide an objective explanatory scheme for understanding reality. Quoting the philosopher Edmund Husserl, he states, "Theory in the fullest sense is 'a systematically linked set of propositions, taking the form of a systematically unified deduction.'"[4] In this sense, the

---

[3] Max Horkheimer, "Traditional and Critical Theory," in Max Horkheimer, *Critical Theory: Selected Essays*, trans. Matthew J. O'Connell (New York: Continuum, 2002), 188–243.

[4] Horkheimer, *Critical Theory*, 190.

basic model underlying the notion of theory is that of Enlightenment science, particularly mathematics. Indeed, Horkheimer knows that the tendency in such a model is toward making the method of the pure sciences normative for the whole of reality and seeing theory as something that can ideally be expressed using mathematical symbols.

In the next chapter, we will examine this theme as he and Theodor Adorno address it at length in their foundational text, *Dialectic of Enlightenment.* But it is something we have already noted in the discussion of Lukács who identifies science as "an ideological weapon of the bourgeoisie" because it applies static, transcendent categories and laws to all of life and thus gives the bourgeois status quo an apparently inviolable character.[5]

This is important. According to Horkheimer, traditional theory offers itself as an explanatory scheme for the particulars of reality which is in itself separable from that reality. This might appear to be a somewhat abstruse point, but an illustration helps to draw out its significance. Take the matter of work and wages. A traditional theoretical approach will attempt to establish the objective laws of economic activity—say, supply and demand— and then seek to understand labor relations and policy in terms of these laws. The laws thus have an unassailable prior authority to which the field of labor relations must then be subordinated. A theoretical framework put forth as merely descriptive of human behavior ends up becoming prescriptive for human behavior.

Several results flow from this approach. First, the human beings involved in the labor process cease to be human beings and become functions of what is essentially a mathematical equation. They are, to use a later cliché, merely cogs in the machine. As we saw in Lukács, people become things, and subjects become objects. Second, abstracted from the actual conditions of real life, the laws of supply and demand take on a life of their own. They cannot be subject to criticism any more than can the laws of gravity because they are assumed as basic truths by which the rest of reality is to be

---

[5] Lukács, *History and Class Consciousness*, 10–11.

interpreted. The cultural dominance of the model of scientific rationality ensures this.

This conclusion points to Horkheimer's main problem with traditional theory: its practitioners are completely unaware of the ideological framework that shapes their approach. Traditional theory presents itself simply as the truth, the naïve or disinterested description of the world and how it works. In fact, however, it represents the political interests of the power brokers of the society in which it has developed. This is in a sense the central point of critical theory: approaches that seem to be objective, commonsensical, or simply stating the obvious are in fact means by which the latent interests of the dominant group within society are asserted and protected. The systems of belief that support them have the appearance of unassailable and disinterested truth but are in fact highly manipulative.

Horkheimer summarizes this framework as follows:

> What scientists in various fields regard as the essence of theory thus corresponds, in fact, to the immediate tasks they set for themselves. The manipulation of physical nature and of specific economic and social mechanisms demand alike the amassing of a body of knowledge such as is supplied in an ordered set of hypotheses. The technological advances of the bourgeois period are inseparably linked to this function of the pursuit of science. . . . The conception of theory was absolutized, as though it were grounded in the inner nature of knowledge as such or justified in some other ahistorical way, and thus it became a reified, ideological category.[6]

Horkheimer's argument here is that "theory" has become a "thing," and it has thus been reified and taken on a life of its own. As such, it presents itself as a natural, neutral means of accessing and explaining reality. Specifically, this "theory" is rooted in the scientific method and discourse that emerges with the Enlightenment, with its concern to control and exploit nature,

---

[6] Horkheimer, "Traditional and Critical Theory," 194.

a concern that lies at the very heart of the capitalist enterprise where all things—even human beings—come to be seen as commodities that can be controlled and exchanged.

The Covid pandemic of the early 2020s provides an instructive example of that to which Horkheimer is here pointing. The phrases "science is real" and "follow the science" were the common rhetorical currency of myriad press conferences and government briefings around the world. Many news reports also began with the phrase, "The experts say . . .", typically meaning scientific experts. Now, setting aside the validity of any particular argument or policy that may have been justified by such language, what is interesting is how the language carried an intrinsic persuasive power and also assumed a reified notion of science. This is highly significant and touches on the structures of power within our culture.

First, the language of science carries power because our society has exalted science as representing an approach to reality and a body of knowledge that is disinterested, that just gives us the facts, so to speak. As with the laws of gravity, science is understood as having no political bias, no hidden agenda, no commitment either to socialism or capitalism. It does not matter if the President of the United States is Republican or Democrat; if he jumps from a window or from a plane in mid-flight, he will fall to the ground due to the gravitational pull of the earth. Thus, when a claim is justified by an appeal to science, our society, attuned as it is to the neutral, factual nature of science, will find such a claim to be inherently persuasive.

That leads to the second issue: the statement "follow the science" operates with a reified view of what science is. It implicitly claims that "science" is a thing, an existing body of knowledge about which there can be no real debate or discussion, just as the Statue of Liberty or the Sistine Chapel is a thing. But science is not so. Rather, science is a humanly constructed activity and not a "thing" to be discovered. This is not to claim that gravity itself is simply a social construct, a matter of the collective imagination of a particular society. Apples still fell from trees in societies where it was Aristotle, not Newton, who provided the content of scientific explanations.

But it is to say that the formulation of the laws of gravity and the role those laws play in society is not a given, not something that is simply "there."

Applying this to Covid, Horkheimer would thus raise two critical questions. First, what exactly is this "science" to which such authority is being ascribed? One would not have to reflect on this question for too long to realize that this "science" actually involves only a particular selection of scientific findings and that absolute consensus on the usefulness of masks, vaccines, and natural immunity does not exist (and that not simply among amateur pundits on X, but even among those society would otherwise regard as qualified to speak as scientists). So, Horkheimer would want to know, why do these scientists come to enjoy positive exposure on prime-time television while those others are marginalized? That raises the critical question of who makes authoritative decisions and how and why they have the power to do so.

But the issue is not simply one of power. There is also the fact that this use of science has a profoundly moral dimension to it that is not, strictly speaking, part of the scientific field of competence. Considered in itself, science is an explanatory discipline, not a morally prescriptive one. Take medicine, for example. A doctor can certainly tell you how to save a life. But if the doctor tells you why the life in question is worth saving, he must step outside of the scientific realm, strictly considered, and enter that of moral philosophy. Once science has been reified, however, it assumes a power—perhaps even an omnipotence—of its own such that its authority becomes comprehensive and irresistible. Thus, the scientist, the one who is in a sense the priest of this special type of knowledge, himself becomes powerful, omniscient, and able to opine on matters that a moment's reflection would reveal to be well beyond his actual sphere of competence.

What kind of society is it in which the scientific paradigm for knowledge becomes the predominant one and grants such comprehensive wisdom to scientists? In "Traditional and Critical Theory" Horkheimer uses the example of the delayed influence of Copernicus to illustrate this. Living from 1473–1543, Copernicus was very much a man of the late fifteenth and early sixteenth centuries. Yet his thinking only really became influential in the seventeenth century. From this, it is clear that it is not simply the intrinsic qualities of his thought that explained its ultimate success. Rather there was also the context of the society in which his thought was being received. Characteristics within the seventeenth century made his ideas more plausible and more acceptable than they had been in his lifetime.

Horkheimer's argument is that it was the general tendency of the seventeenth century toward a more mechanical, even mechanistic, view of the universe that served to make Copernicus's thinking a powerful, revolutionary force. In short, his ideas served to further a broader cultural transformation in which bourgeois thinking became dominant, based as it was upon calculation, predictability, and a growing sense that nature could be mastered by learning its immanent laws and turning them to human advantage. This provided the context for the triumph of Copernican science. It served to overthrow the old, medieval way of life and, once the bourgeoisie was established as the dominant class, reified the scientific method into something that claimed to stand outside of the flux of history. Thus, the bourgeoisie was able to maintain its dominance because it represented truth. It presented its social and cultural system as the way things should naturally be.[7]

Two points are worthy of note here. First, Horkheimer's debt to the Hegelian tradition is obvious. Hegel saw the dominant philosophy of a given age as revealing the heart or essence of the age. Here, Horkheimer sees the scientific method as revealing the priorities and concerns of the modern age, though with a Marxist twist: it is to be understood in terms of the broader framework of economic class interests. Hegel, to borrow a phrase from Marx, has been turned on his head and used to serve a materialist, rather than an idealist, approach to the world.

Second, we see a clear affinity between what Horkheimer is arguing and what we noted in chapter 3 concerning the earlier work of Karl Korsch. Korsch believed that Hegel's philosophy enjoyed its heyday in the early

---

[7] Horkheimer, 195–97.

nineteenth century because it was a philosophy of flux and change. Thus, it met with a positive reception among the rising bourgeois intellectuals for whom a means for change, and a means by which change could be justified, was profoundly attractive. Horkheimer here does the same with the scientific method: it rises to dominance because it serves a particular view of human beings and the world—the bourgeois view:

> The scholar and his science are incorporated into the apparatus of society; his achievements are a factor in the conservation and continuous renewal of the existing state of affairs, no matter what fine names he gives to what he does.[8]

In all of this we see a key element of critical theory: the exploration of the wider social and political context for understanding why ideas, even apparently nonpolitical, disinterested ideas, become powerful; and, further, the raising of the question of what such ideas actually do within society.

Yet if Horkheimer developed the discussion no further, he would not really have done anything more than offer a traditional theoretical critique of traditional theory. He himself acknowledges that "modern theoreticians of knowledge" (what we now call "sociologists of knowledge") accept that historical circumstances are important in analyzing intellectual developments.[9] In a similar way, Marx praised Feuerbach for replacing Hegelian idealism with the material reality of social existence as the means of understanding the world. But, as we noted in chapter 2, in the eleventh thesis on Feuerbach he suggested that the purpose of philosophy was not merely to describe the world but to change it. Thus, simply pointing to the sociological conditions that gave rise to the dominance, even the reification, of the scientific method did not in itself raise the analysis to the level of critical theory. It merely makes sociological theory normative. If the world is to be changed, theory needs to go further. It needs to be *critical*.

---

[8] Horkheimer, 196.
[9] Horkheimer, 195.

Critical Theory

Part of the answer to what makes theory *critical* rather than *traditional* lies in the overall framework within which the realm of ideas is understood to operate. Korsch and Lukács both speak of the need to understand society as a whole, as a set of interconnected beliefs, practices, and structures such that adjustments in one area always bring with them adjustments in others. As we noted in chapter 3, this avoids the cruder Marxism of the Second International that posited a one-way direction of causality, from the economic base to the ideological superstructure. While economics remains foundational, the relationship between this and a society's beliefs or ideology is rendered more complicated than a straight line from cause to effect.

Thus, when Horkheimer offers an analysis of the reasons for the dominance of the scientific method as the paradigm for traditional theory, the very act of highlighting that fact is in itself a potential act of critical theory. He regards such an analysis as exposing the ideological construction of something that previously seemed natural or commonsensical, and in so doing our consciousness (and therefore our relationship to the world) is transformed. But there is more to Horkheimer's critical theory than this. He also has a theory of how critical theory works.

Before outlining Horkheimer's theory of critical theory, there is an obvious problem that must be addressed. If he is correct (along with Korsch and Lukács) that there is no place to stand outside of the historical process and its ideological structures that would allow for an objective, disinterested account of reality, then there can be no critical theory that claims to be a disinterested view from nowhere. We saw this in the notion of truth that Korsch and Lukács expressed when they both denied the possibility of an expression of truth that corresponded simply to reality. Horkheimer is aware of this problem:

> The facts which our senses present to us are socially performed in two ways: through the historical character of the object perceived and through the historical character of the perceiving organ. Both

are not simply natural; they are shaped by human activity, and yet the individual perceives himself as receptive and passive in the activity of perception.[10]

Here Horkheimer makes a Hegelian point: the thing known and the one who knows are both part of an historical process; and the way in which the knowing subject knows the historical object is therefore part of the historical process. Knowledge or truth that stands outside of history—that which one might obtain from the view from nowhere—is therefore impossible.

We might illustrate this perspective with an example. Take, for example, the Statue of Liberty. The Statue of Liberty is architectural and political. It points to the ways such statues are produced and to the political points it is designed to make. Its significance is historical through and through. How I perceive it as an individual is also political, connecting to how I understand the symbolism upon which it draws and the significance of the location in which it is placed: the promise of liberty that it represents at a point in the Hudson River in New York that would be seen by immigrants immediately before they arrive on American soil. And even my notion of liberty, the category by which I interpret the statue, is itself a specific historical product of American history. But there might be another way to see the statue. I might have been related to someone who helped create the statue, perhaps someone who was badly injured in the process. The statue would then mean something different to me than to an immigrant gazing from the deck of a ship arriving in New York after a long transatlantic voyage.

In this, Horkheimer stands on a continuum with later theories of hermeneutics and with postmodern relativism whereby meaning is a subjective category rooted in the set of expectations that the knowing subject brings to bear on any given object. But Horkheimer is no relativist in the ultimate sense: his relativizing of all present knowledge does not mean that

---

[10] Horkheimer, 200.

he relativizes all future knowledge. There is a human reality for Horkheimer; it is simply one that has yet to be realized. How does Horkheimer know this? He knows it from the alienation that the current mode of existence involves:

> The collaboration of men in society is the mode of existence which reason urges upon them, and so they do apply their powers and thus confirm their own rationality. But at the same time their work and its results are alienated from them, and the whole process with all its waste of work-power and human life, and with its wars and all its senseless wretchedness, seems to be an unchangeable force of nature, a fate beyond man's control.[11]

Clearly rooted in a Marxist understanding of the relationship between production and alienation, this passage occurs in the midst of a discussion of German idealist philosophy. Horkheimer points out that Kant's notion of knowledge sees it as constructed by the human mind that engages the outside world in terms of certain categories that are part of the structure of the mind itself. Thus, the world as it is in itself cannot be known, but the world as received via the categories of human knowledge (e.g., space and time) can be known. There is thus a directly unknowable reality (the "thing-in-itself" to use Kant's terminology) behind human knowledge. Knowledge is reliable, stable, and universal because the thing-in-itself and the categories of the human mind are stable and universal. Seeing this tension between reality and a constructed perception of reality, Hegel historicizes this view and resolves it in a higher intellectual synthesis produced through the historical process itself. Horkheimer, as a Marxist, turns Hegel on his head: how we think about the world is shaped not by ideas but by the way in which material goods are produced and the relationship in which we stand to the means of production. What we think we know and how we think about the world and ourselves within it are functions of a historical process that is in essence

---

[11] Horkheimer, 204.

a deeply political one. The problem of alienated humanity is rooted in the problems of the capitalist economy.

In simpler terms, capitalism is a system that dehumanizes individuals by turning them into commodities. No longer are they individual persons with various creative powers. They are not subjects but objects. They are mere line items in a budget whose value is assessed by how much they cost the factory owner. That is not only how society treats them. Worse than that, it is how society teaches them to think of themselves. And traditional theory serves to justify that situation by placing "laws" over them—laws of efficiency, time and motion, and cost-benefit analysis, all of which lie at the heart of capitalist economic organization.

The problem is that the reality presented by the system and justified by the theory is itself dehumanizing and over time will be exposed as such. It is to this contradiction that critical theory addresses itself. Its purpose is thus not that of presenting an objective, disinterested reality for which to aim but rather of exposing the contradictions within the current system itself. And in so doing, it aims to raise the consciousness of members of society so that they can rebel against the system. Indeed, the articulation of critical theory is itself a part of revolutionary praxis. It is not a traditional theory because it does not attempt to describe reality; it is more a method that seeks to expose as political constructions those institutions, methods, habits of mind, and social relations which traditional theory justifies as "natural" and the way things have to be. It aims to destabilize the status quo. As Herbert Marcuse expresses it:

> Critical theory means to show only the specific social conditions at the root of philosophy's inability to pose the problem in a more comprehensive way and to indicate that any other solution is beyond that philosophy's boundaries.[12]

---

[12] Marcuse, "Philosophy and Critical Theory," in David Ingram and Julia Simon-Ingram, eds., *Critical Theory: The Essential Readings* (St. Paul: Paragon House, 1992), 5–19, 14.

The "problem" to which Marcuse is here alluding is that of knowledge: that Kantianism, for example, cannot pose the question of knowledge in a way that takes into account the specific social conditions in which it itself occurs. This indicates the limitations—the uncritical nature of its approach. In short, it rules out of bounds from the outset the most important questions—those that challenge the surrounding social system. Critical theory's task is to expose this limitation and indeed to expose it as intrinsic to the philosophical systems that traditional theories represent.

Alienation

A legitimate question to ask at this point is how critical theory can present itself as the correct way of understanding society without also claiming to be "true" in a way that its principal deferment of "truth" to the future denies. The answer is found in its concept of alienation. In this context, alienation is that which causes a fundamental discrepancy to exist between the claims of the dominant ideology and its actual practical results. Here is how Horkheimer expresses this:

> The collaboration of men in society is the mode of existence which reason urges upon them, and so they do apply their powers and thus confirm their own rationality. But at the same time their work and its results are alienated from them, and the whole process with all its waste of work-power and human life, and with its wars and all its senseless wretchedness, seems to be an unchangeable force of nature, a fate beyond man's control.[13]

What Horkheimer is claiming here is this: reason presses on human beings that certain ways of cooperating in society will lead to certain results. It will allow them to be truly human. As examples, we might use hard work, strong

---

[13] Horkheimer, "Traditional and Critical Theory," 204.

nuclear families, thrift, obedience of workers to the demands of bosses, etc. The promise of bourgeois society is that these institutions and values will enable you to flourish. Yet disasters still happen: wars occur; stock markets periodically crash; poverty remains real and is sometimes unavoidable even for those who do everything that "reason" demands of them. Typically, these crises and problems are presented as natural, as unfortunate but unavoidable side effects of the dominant system. Sometimes they might even be seen as evidence that the system is working properly (as in the language of "market correction" and "bubble" when there are significant collapses on the stock exchange). That kind of talk is, of course, what Marxists term *ideology*, a way of thinking about the world that hides the reality.

This points to the purpose of critical theory and to the radical extent of its ambitions, both of which separate it from traditional theory. Its purpose is to expose the contradictions in the ideological system, and it can do this by demonstrating that the system fails by the very criteria on which it bases its claims to truth. And its ambition is not simply to correct abuses within that system but to overthrow it as a whole. These two points are key to understanding critical theory and mark basic points of continuity between the work of the Frankfurt School in the 1930s and 1940s and the various contemporary claimants to the critical theory throne today, whether on race, ethnicity, gender, or sexuality.

The radical nature of the critical proposal is expressed with clarity by Horkheimer:

> The aim of this [critical theoretical] activity is not simply to eliminate one or other abuse, for it regards such abuses as necessarily connected with the way in which the social structure is organized. Although it itself emerges from the social structure, its purpose is not, either in its conscious intention or in its objective significance, the better functioning of any element in the structure. On the contrary, it is suspicious of the very categories of better, useful, appropriate, productive, and valuable, as these are understood in

the present order, and refuses to take them as nonscientific presuppositions about which one can do nothing.[14]

Critical theory therefore poses a comprehensive challenge to the way society is organized practically and justified conceptually. The very value scheme that a capitalist society uses to justify itself must be opposed and subject to thoroughgoing critique by setting the practical realities of such a society in opposition to the terminology used to naturalize or support those realities.

A Dialectical Approach

At the heart of the social problem to which critical theory addresses itself is the dialectical relationship between the individual and society as a whole. Society is produced by the activity of a large number of individuals coordinating their actions. But the result is that society, and its rules of engagement, become reified, take on a life of their own, and thus deny the significance of the very thing upon which they are in reality based: the intentional actions of free individuals. There is a contradiction between the individual and society, between belonging to a group and the individual's personal freedom. What critical theory does is expose this contradiction, not by focusing on the individual as opposed to the mass of society but rather by examining the relationship that exists between the two and seeing how they shape each other. We might put this another way: critical theory examines why it is that the terms of belonging and of being free, while presented by the culture as one and the same thing, actually stand at profound odds with each other.

We can illustrate this with two examples, the first using traditional Marxist categories, the second using modern technology. The factory worker believes that laboring forty hours a week on a production line enables him to be free because he has earned money that allows him to pay his bills and maybe have a little left for one or two luxuries—perhaps a drink at a bar

---

[14] Horkheimer, 207.

on Friday night or a vacation to the shore each summer. That is certainly the message that the capitalist system sends to him. But is he truly free? His work hours are set by the bosses. Maybe he only has to unwind at the bar on a Friday night because his work on the production line is such a monotonous drudge that he needs that moment of respite so as to be able to face the same drudge next week. And as for paying his bills—that is only an issue because of the existence of private property. In fact, the capitalist system has not made him free at all. It has made him a slave to his wages and to the system of private ownership that alienates him from the fruits of his own labor. The purpose of critical theory is to expose this reality.

Contemporary technology provides a second example. The promise of technology has always been that of personal liberation. When email became common in the 1990s, it was supposed to make correspondence more efficient. Now, rather than the cumbersome task of writing and mailing letters, one could simply sit at a keyboard and send out a swift message. A task that could take up a significant portion of the workday could be completed in the first half hour, leaving the rest of the employee's time free for other assignments. The reality, of course, is far different. The very ease and speed of email changed the nature of correspondence to the point where we now all receive far more communications that demand a reply—and often an instant reply—than ever before. Instead of liberating us from the burden of correspondence, emails (and now texts) have massively increased the amount of time devoted to seemingly never-ending messages that cry out for immediate response.

Two things are of note from this last example. The first, to which we shall return in more detail in the next chapter, is the phenomenon that fascinated early critical theorists: the way in which things that promise liberation transform over time into their opposite and become forms of oppression. This goes to the very heart of the dialectical process that critical theorists saw as central to understanding the history of society. The second is the way in which technology moves from being a tool over which human beings have control (or at least believe themselves to have control) to something which exerts total control over them. This is another example of reification. The human agent makes technology and uses it to transform the world but then technology takes on a life of its own and remakes the human agent in turn. As a result technology comes to set the terms for human engagement and to define the virtues—speed, efficiency, etc.—by which that engagement is to be evaluated and revised. In short, technology comes to determine what it means to be human. Of course, this second point is a function of the first.

This is not simply the case with email. Many of us find ourselves, to use the popular term, chained to our cell phones. We probably even choose our seats in the airport departure lounge on the basis of access to a power socket so that we can recharge the tiny devices that now organize our lives for us. And private space and time have disappeared. Employers can contact us anytime and anywhere, while many of us perform our once private lives on social media platforms. Are we masters of technology or slaves to it?

It is to this kind of issue that Horkheimer wishes to address critical theory. Traditional theory might well be able to explain the rise and impact of technology, but critical theory aspires to do something different: by raising consciousness of the disconnect between the claims of technology and the reality of a technologically-dependent life, critical theory aims to destabilize what appears to be a natural or irresistible state of affairs.

Horkheimer states it this way:

> Critical thinking is the function neither of the isolated individual nor of a sum-total of individuals. Its subject is rather a definite individual in his real relation to other individuals and groups, in his conflict with a particular class, and, finally, in the resultant web of relationships with the social totality and with nature.[15]

---

[15] Horkheimer, 210–11.

Horkheimer, of course, is a traditional Marxist in the sense that economic class (rather than race, gender, etc.) provides the fundamental category for analyzing society. Thus, he is particularly interested in the proletariat. This is important because critical theory, by placing social relations rather than abstractions at the heart of its philosophy, also points toward the category of experience as key. Critical theory seeks to explain the contradictions of human experience and, by so doing, to shape a revolutionary consciousness.

The proletariat is a good example of conflicted experience. On the one hand, technology gives the workers greater and greater productive power. Where once it took days to weave a piece of cloth, now this can be done by machines in a short period of time. Where once it was impossible to bring together raw materials from around the world, and thus impossible to make certain things, now that can be done with ease. And yet capitalism is subject to periodic economic crises. Globalization has drastically reduced the economic powers of individual nations, let alone individual workers. And economic competition and global interdependence has generated wars and conflict. All of this serves to foster a deeply conflicted proletarian experience of productive power and social impotence. And it serves the specific interests of those with power—those who control capital—not of society taken either as a whole or as a collection of individuals.[16]

It is here that Horkheimer breaks most clearly with the old-style economic Marxism of the Second International. Simply because the proletariat experiences life in such a contradictory and conflicted manner does not mean that the class as a whole will inevitably revolt against the economic system that is causing this. This is where the notion of false consciousness comes into play. For Horkheimer, the proletariat is no safe guide to understanding its own significance. In other words, the beliefs that working class individuals and groups may have about what is and is not good for them are not necessarily true.

---

[16] Horkheimer, 213.

False Consciousness

As we noted at the start of this chapter, in Horkheimer's day, the key issue for him and his Frankfurt colleagues was the support of large numbers of the proletariat for the nationalist movements of the German right, most notably the National Socialists. The fact that workers would see their best future hope lying in an authoritarian party that was funded in large part by the bourgeoisie and was committed to crushing communism and left-wing workers' movements was evidence that the economic process in itself would not bring about a proper proletarian class consciousness. Instead, it indicated the existence of a powerful form of false consciousness.[17]

As we noted in chapter 2, *false consciousness* is a term that refers to the fact that the exploited class likely does not understand itself as exploited, or at least does not understand the reasons for its exploitation. Thus, it will assume that its position can be improved by reforming the system. If the system claims to be just and holds forth a concept of justice but reality does not match up to these claims, then the system needs to be tweaked. One example might be the development of a welfare state. Capitalism presents itself as offering the possibility of prosperity for all if only individuals will work hard. Yet the boom-and-bust pattern of capitalist economies indicates that capitalism fails to deliver on this promise. A proletariat that is subject to false consciousness will assume that this boom-and-bust pattern represents a malfunction of the system and all that is therefore needed is a safety net to make sure that individuals are protected from destitution during the periods of economic depression. Thus, trade unions and political parties of what we might call the center left emerge, campaigning not for the overthrowal of the system but its reform. They assume the basic terms of the capitalist world.

This is where the truly radical—the truly critical—nature of critical theory becomes significant. Critical theory does not seek to critique the

---

[17] Horkheimer, 213–14.

contemporary system with a view to improving it. It seeks to critique the contemporary system with a view to overthrowing it entirely. And the radical nature of this cannot be overestimated. Even the terms of engagement—such concepts as freedom, justice, equality, happiness, etc.—must be thoroughly critiqued because all are currently defined in ways that serve the interests of the ongoing status quo.

Critical theory, therefore, is tasked with bringing to light the contradictions and the conflicts that lie below the surface of the world as experienced by those who live and work in it. It has to show that the very way of life that capitalism embodies serves to create the opposite of that which it promises, and it has to show that even the terms of discussion as set by capitalism have to be overthrown.

In an interview, Simone De Beauvoir—a key figure in the development of so-called Second Wave Feminism that, in a sense, was the true origin of modern feminism in its shifting of attention toward psychology, consciousness, and Marxist social criticism—made the following comment:

> Capitalism can certainly afford to allow women to join an army, allow women to join a police force. Capitalism is certainly intelligent enough to let more women join the government. Pseudosocialism can certainly allow a woman to become secretary-general of its party. Those are just reforms, like social security or paid vacations. Did the institutionalization of paid vacations change the inequality of capitalism? Did the right of women to work in factories at equal pay to the men change the male orientation of the Czech society? But to change the whole value system of either society, to destroy the concept of motherhood: that is revolutionary.[18]

---

[18] Simone De Beauvoir, "The Second Sex 25 Years Later," interview by John Gerassi, *Society* (Jan–Feb 1976), accessed April 4, 2023, https://www.marxists.org /reference/subject/ethics/de-beauvoir/1976/interview.htm.

Though not strictly a critical theorist, De Beauvoir here presents an argument consonant with the critical theory of Horkheimer. The capitalist system is perfectly capable of making concessions on the issue of women's rights and status in order to ensure its own stability and continuation. Even socialist parties that operate within patriarchal structures are able to accommodate reforms that appear to give women equal status to men without changing the underlying structure that keeps them subordinate. It is this structure, this system to which critical theory must address itself.

This need for radical reform is vital in understanding critical theory, both in its original Frankfurt form, and in its later iterations with regards to gender, colonialism, and race. It is not, for example, the case that critical theorists are pushing for justice or equality in terms understood by the current dominant society; it is that they are pushing for a complete overhaul of that dominant society, including those very concepts (such as justice or equality) as they are understood by the dominant society and as they are used to maintain the power structures of the status quo.

It is important to remember at this point that the critical theorist, and the critical theory to which he holds, is also part of the cultural whole of the age. Korsch and Lukács both called for a revision of the notion of truth, from something that was outside of the historical process, to something that was part of the historical process. The critical theorist's task, therefore, is not to bring the world as he sees it under the scrutiny of abstract or unhistorical principles of justice and equality. It is to make people aware of the historical contingency of these ideas, the ways in which they are being used by the dominant class, and the many ways in which they fail in practice to be what they claim in theory. Again, the purpose of critical theory is to destabilize the status quo by transforming the consciousness. Horkheimer sums it up in the following words:

> For all its insights into the individual steps in social change and for
> all the agreement of its elements with the most advanced traditional
> theories, the critical theory has no specific influence on its side,

except concern for the abolition of social injustice. The negative formulation, if we wish to express it abstractly, is the materialist content of the idealist concept of reason.[19]

In short, critical theory may draw upon other traditional theories—the work, for example of a sociologist like Max Weber—but its purpose is not to describe the world but, as Marx put it in his eleventh thesis on Feuerbach, to change it.

To make this point using a contemporary example, we might reflect upon the calls in the United States (and elsewhere) for the payment of reparations to the descendants of victims of the slave trade. How might a critical theorist think about such? Wherever one stands on this discussion, what is interesting is that the perceived problem of racial inequality is being solved in terms of the dominant capitalist system by the use of money. First, human suffering (and thus humanity itself) is being exchanged for money. That is the very problem that lies at the heart of capitalist society, as far as Marxist theory is concerned. Second, because the proposed solution operates within the terms of the system itself, the system remains in place and thus the cause of the problem is not actually addressed. If the racism that caused the issue is intrinsic to the system ("systemic," to use the contemporary term), then any solution generated by that system is no solution at all.

Critical theory of the purist kind could therefore assess reparations in one of two ways. They could be seen as just one more attempt to cover the cracks by apparently reforming the system while really leaving its basic structure in place. Or they could be interpreted as a means of destabilizing the system. A radical redistribution of wealth that contradicts the values of the system and generates class resentments might well push the system as a whole toward crisis and collapse through revealing the inner contradictions upon which it is built.

---

[19] Horkheimer, "Traditional and Critical Theory," 242.

An Example of Critical Theory in Action:
Marcuse on Repressive Tolerance

Horkheimer's vision for critical theory is exemplified in a famous 1965 essay by his colleague, Herbert Marcuse, "Repressive Tolerance."[20] This work was in its time very controversial, with advocates of liberal democracy seeing it as an attack on freedom of speech and members of the rising New Left as an argument against engagement with dissenting opinions.

It is useful as an illustration of critical theory for several reasons. Historically, its background clearly lies in Marcuse's experience of the rise of Nazism. The Nazi Party boasted about the fact that they would use democracy to destroy democracy, and that is exactly what they did. In doing so, they represented a perennial problem—and one that has only become more intense in our own age of social media: that of how far such things as the right to free speech can be extended before free speech itself is jeopardized by the results.

Methodologically, it offers a good example of the dialectical approach of the Frankfurt School of critical theory, in its claims that the rhetoric of freedom as used in capitalist liberal democracy is in fact a tool of oppression, and in its refusal to accept the terms of debate as set by the status quo. It also points clearly to the political goal of this form of critical theory.

Marcuse's basic argument is that the notion of tolerance, once a tool for shattering the traditional power of the old-style authoritarian state and church regimes, has itself become a means by which the new rulers are able to control their subjects. Essentially, tolerance now defuses transformative criticism of the status quo by setting out the rules of the game where criticisms can be made of the system but action to change the system can only be taken in ways that the system itself permits:

---

[20] Herbert Marcuse, "Repressive Tolerance" in *The Essential Marcuse: Selected Writings of Philosopher and Social Critic Herbert Marcuse*, ed. Andrew Feenberg and William Leiss (Boston: Beacon, 2007), 32–59.

Under a system of constitutionally guaranteed and (generally and without too many and too glaring exceptions) practiced civil rights and liberties, opposition and dissent are tolerated unless they issue in violence and/or in exhortation to and organization of violent subversion. The underlying assumption is that the established society is free, and that any improvement, even a change in the social structure and social values, would come about in the normal course of events, prepared, defined, and tested in free and equal discussion, on the open marketplace of ideas and goods.[21]

The point is clear: the working assumption of a liberal society is that the system by which the society operates is itself fundamentally sound. Any problems that appear—from wars to financial crises to racial oppression, etc.—are aberrations and will be solved by the system over time, if only basic liberal freedoms are respected. This then justifies the intolerance of anything that might move from a discussion within the system to an active challenge of the system.

For Marcuse, this means that those in power also stabilize the meaning of language and decide what words mean. Thus, a policy of rearmament can be presented as a path to peace.[22] Further, the claim that tolerance and freedom of speech allow for objectivity is also specious. Marcuse comments that when a newspaper publishes, for example, an article that is critical of the FBI next to one that is positive, the strict standard of objectivity is met: both sides of the case are presented. But set against the background of a culture where the default position is support of the FBI, it is always going to be the positive article that wins.[23]

---

[21] Marcuse, "Repressive Tolerance," 40.

[22] Marcuse, 42.

[23] Marcuse, 43. This also points toward the Frankfurt School's concern with the totality of culture and society and with the culture industry, a theme we will explore in chapter 7.

It is clear from this that contemporary manifestations of critical theory have much in common with the kind of thought espoused by Marcuse and the Frankfurt School. It may well be that the philosophical roots are somewhat different—Foucault, for example, rather than Hegel and Marx—but the concern for how culture shapes the way people think and how relationships of power shape the language and the concepts used is a clear point of continuity. Hence, the pressure that freedom of speech is under on college campuses and in wider Western society makes sense: once one assumes that culture is ideology, false consciousness or, to use the modern contemporary language, a discourse of power designed to empower some at the cost of excluding others, then the terms by which it asserts its virtues become the tools by which it actually exercises its vices.

Yet nothing we have noted so far in Marcuse's argument would not, strictly speaking, be available to some form of traditional theory. Acknowledging that those in power can use language in Orwellian ways, or noting that a society's broader framework of beliefs and values will shape how concepts such as "objectivity" play out in practice, is standard sociological fare. Where Marcuse's theory is truly critical lies in its practical political implications. Marcuse's analysis, by demonstrating the sinister linguistic game being played by the language of tolerance, presses toward the transformation of the terminology in a way that justifies an alternative, revolutionary political program. Language itself becomes a revolutionary tool.

Again, it is important to remember Marcuse's personal background here—a background he shared with most of the early members of the Frankfurt School: he was Jewish and had witnessed the rise of Hitler and the Nazi Party through the very democratic processes that were in theory designed to enhance freedom, not eliminate it. He had witnessed a dialectical move in history, where democracy had become its opposite with nightmarish consequences. And this had been accomplished using democratic language, mechanisms, institutions, and principles.

For Marcuse and his colleagues, culture is political and serves the purpose of cultivating false consciousness which lulls the oppressed into accepting, perhaps even welcoming, their oppression as a natural thing or as a price worth paying to live in a "free" society. Thus, the task of critical theory is to point out how this takes place and thus provide a justification and a framework for the transformation by proactive means. In short, not all speech should be protected, for some of it serves to justify oppression. Indeed, this also applies to the principle of free speech: this effectively neutralizes radical criticism by making it simply one form of valid speech among many that can be accommodated by the status quo.

Thus, the critique of the status quo must not stop at the level of theoretical analysis. It is not enough to say that democracy as it stands is a chimera. One might put it this way: to say democracy is a chimera or a fake and yet do so within the framework that the fake democracy permits is actually not to say anything at all. It is simply to recite a harmless liturgy that leaves things exactly as they were before. Critical theory is self-conscious criticism of the status quo that is part of revolutionary action. To quote Marcuse again:

> When tolerance mainly serves the protection and preservation of a repressive society, when it serves to neutralize opposition and render men immune against other and better forms of life, then tolerance has been perverted. And when this perversion starts in the mind of the individual, in his consciousness, his needs, when heteronomous interests occupy him before he can experience his servitude, then the efforts to counteract his dehumanization must begin at the place of entrance, there where the false consciousness takes form (or rather: is systematically formed)—it must begin with stopping the words and images which feed into this consciousness.[24]

There is a twofold revolutionary action that is required here: critique serves to destabilize the words and concepts upon which the status quo rests. That is the way in which critical theory is itself a form of action. And there is also

---

[24] Marcuse, "Repressive Tolerance," 51.

an action required by those who have the power to bring a state of affairs into existence: the obstruction, closing down, and elimination of those things that shape the false consciousness.

The question arises at this point of how one is to decide which words and ideas need to be suppressed. Marcuse's answer is to suppress those groups or ideas that promote "aggressive policies, armament, chauvinism, discrimination on the grounds of race and religion, or which oppose the extension of public services, social security, medical care, etc."[25] In short, his answer is anything that stands in the way of the development of a socialist society. Marcuse may be a critical theorist who rejects the idea of ahistorical truths, but his view of history is deeply marked by Hegel and Marx. History has a direction, the direction of freedom, and freedom conceptualized in a Marxist fashion. Thus, he has no difficulty in arguing for the suppression of bourgeois notions of freedom because he sees them as false and as designed to prevent true liberation.

Again, while there are many differences between the Hegelian/Marxist critical theory of Marcuse and some of the iterations of critical theory that are prominent today, such as those dealing with race and gender, there are also obvious affinities. This is one: the rejection of freedom of speech as understood in the Western liberal tradition, as a necessary social good.

Many in the West are confused by the recent rebellion against freedom of speech on college campuses. But the notion that freedom of speech is merely cover for allowing an unjust system to remain in place under a veneer of justice and fairness is not new with Black Lives Matter or campus speech codes on race, gender, and pronouns. Marcuse was voicing precisely the same concern in the 1960s.

A Postscript on Eating Meat and Leaving Bones

One point that is clear from the critical theory espoused by Horkheimer and colleagues is this: they believe that the concepts with which society

---

[25] Marcuse, 45.

operates—such things as justice, equality, fairness, legality, and the like—are all products of a particular form of society rather than transcendent categories of universal application. This is something that Christians attracted to critical theory need to take into account. One sometimes hears in discussion that one should "eat the meat and leave the bones" of critical theory. This is a cliché but one that sounds somewhat plausible. Is not all thinking somewhat eclectic? And if critical theory has some insights, can we not appropriate them for Christian purposes?

I will offer a broader reflection on the usefulness of critical theory in the conclusion, but there are a couple of observations on the specific "eat the meat and leave the bones" proposal that are worth mentioning here. First, we need to be very careful in advocating such eclecticism as, taken as a blunt principle, it has the obvious problem that it could be applied to anything, no matter how obviously wicked. One could, for example, "eat the meat and leave the bones" of Hitler's *Mein Kampf* or De Sade's *120 Days of Sodom*, but one would be unlikely to hear any Christian advocating such, and for good reason. And so when the concept is applied to critical theory, we need to take this into account and ask ourselves how exactly we might distinguish meat from bones. What we decide is meat and what are bones could well be a function of nothing more than broader cultural tastes, in the same way that, say, the sporting of a T-shirt with a hammer and sickle is acceptable while the wearing of one with a swastika is not. It is not that the former represents something more moral than the latter; it is merely that public taste for some odd reason finds the symbols of the old Soviet Union to be acceptable and Nazism not so. And just because critical theory appears to speak with a vocabulary that resonates with many of the concerns of our day—power, justice, marginalization—does not necessarily mean that it is using these terms in the same way as Christians do. We must therefore first address that critical question of the means by which the good is distinguished from the bad before we claim the meat/bones principle as being useful.

The second issue to be aware of is that, on Horkheimer's account of critical theory, the "meat" and the "bones" cannot be separated because the basis upon which one would discriminate between the two is grounded in the values of the current corrupt system. Critical theory itself denies the possibility of a place outside the system to be able to make such a distinction. If therefore we take one element of critical theory but separate it from the political ends to which it is connected, what remains (at least for those in Hegelian Marxist stream) is not really critical theory but rather the rhetoric of critical theory refracted through the lens of the concerns of society. The true critical theorist, one might say, is fully committed to critical theory not simply as offering a few insights but as comprehensively destabilizing the way society as a whole thinks and thus justifies itself. To truly take the meat off the bones is, strange to tell, likely to return critical theory back into the realms of traditional theory.

This is not to claim that critical theory is worthless, but it is to say that the way in which a Christian might choose to interact with it is not a simple or straightforward matter, still less a matter of trite clichés. It requires considerable care and carefully articulated distinctions. I believe such interaction is possible and can be fruitful but that "eat the meat and leave the bones" is simply not a very helpful way to explain how this should be done.

CHAPTER 5

The Problems of Enlightenment

Introduction

It is clear that the origins of critical theory lie both in the failure of a strictly economic Marxism to explain the path of European history in the early decades of the twentieth century and in the specific problem of the rise of Nazism and Fascism. Yet the questions it asks are not simply tied to the early twentieth century. The perennial attraction of violent politics, the Janus face of a technologically sophisticated world that can cure cancer yet produce weapons of mass destruction, and the inability of human beings to live together in harmony all continue to press in on us today. Why, we might ask, can we not find reasonable solutions to these things? And therein lies the problem: the questions of what is and is not reasonable, what counts as rational and irrational, are as important today as in the 1920s and 1930s when Europe witnessed the rise of extreme politics, right and left.

In this context, Nazism is particularly intriguing in a rather dark and gruesome way because it was the product of the most culturally sophisticated nation in Europe. That the land of Kant, Schiller, and Goethe became the seedbed of Hitler, the Gestapo, and the death camps is astonishing. Indeed, this raises far more questions than simply that of "Why did the working classes support the parties of the nationalist right rather than the Marxist left?" Perhaps a harder question is "Why did the glorious civilization to which the German Enlightenment pointed (and its intellectual and artistic culture in many ways embodied) give way to such violent, dehumanizing barbarism?" This question, of course, can be broken down into many more narrowly focused ones. For example, why did technology lead to war, to Auschwitz, and to murder on an industrial scale rather than to human liberation? Or, why did so many of the men at the Wannsee Conference at which the Final Solution was approved possess high academic qualifications from so many prestigious German universities?

In a sense, we could ask the same of earlier eras. The French Revolution aimed for liberty, equality, and fraternity but produced the Terror and then the despotic reign of Napoleon. Along the way, of course, it used Enlightenment technology to develop the guillotine, making the Terror possible. We might therefore summarize the problem that both Nazism and the French Revolution pose this way: How is it that things turn into their opposite, that high culture becomes barbarism, that liberating technology can become a means of destruction, and that language of freedom can be used to justify tyranny?

Such questions remain of perennial interest today. We are all aware of how politicians use language that appears to say one thing to justify the exact opposite. We also know that technology has not delivered on its promise to liberate us from the drudgery of work. As we noted in chapter 4, anyone who was in the workforce in the early 1990s will remember how the advent of email was supposed to make correspondence quick, easy, and something that could be dispatched early in the morning, leaving the rest of the day free for other tasks. That has not proved to be the case. That is not to suggest that the busyness of life as mediated through online communication represents the same moral challenge as the gas chambers at Auschwitz, but it is to highlight the fact that things often do seem to become the precise opposite of what they promised to be.

This is a simple way of understanding what the Frankfurt School meant by the term *dialectic*. We noted its role in Hegel and its influence on Marx and Marxism in earlier chapters. As we now move into substantial discussion of particular areas of interest in critical theory, it is important to remember that this is what Adorno, Horkheimer, and company are really interested in: What is it about the dynamic of the history of Western society that creates this situation where today's means of liberation become tomorrow's instruments of tyranny?

Before we can do this, however, it is important to note one thing that is sometimes missed when studying critical theory: the importance not only of the arguments proposed by the critical theorists but also of the form or style in which they make these arguments. We all know that written style often reflects the content or thought that is being expressed. The most obvious examples are from poetry and song, where the very form is part of the message. The Psalms, the blues, a love poem: in each case the words chosen, the order they are set, and the movement of ideas all connect tightly to the message being conveyed. It is the same with the critical theorists of the early Frankfurt School. The prose is often difficult and the arguments expressed in fragmentary ways. This is because they do not think the world is as it should be and thus the linguistic tools that this world provides here and now, while often giving the appearance of describing a stable world, are really hiding a deeper instability and incoherence. Thus, by presenting arguments in difficult prose and in often fragmentary or nonlinear forms, they force us to see that the world is not as stable and straightforward as bourgeois ideology would have them believe. The style itself is part of the polemic.

A Brief Excursus on Style

Given the argument of the last three chapters, we might characterize critical theorists as those who are concerned with the sociology of knowledge in a manner designed to lead to a transformation of society. While traditional sociologists of knowledge are concerned to explain the connection between social conditions and what counts as true, as good, and as beautiful, critical theorists are more ambitious: they see such explanations as changing the consciousness, or the viewpoint, of those who come to understand them in such a way that they will become conscious of how they can act as agents of revolution.

In this context, one frequent criticism of the Frankfurt School, and indeed of much critical theory in general, is that so much of it is obscure, packed with rebarbative jargon and long, meandering arguments that seem often to drift off into complete opacity.[1] How can consciousness be changed or how can critique have pungency if the form of that critique is couched in such abstruse and confusing prose? Indeed, there is a certain irony to the title of Adorno's broadside against Martin Heidegger (himself a master of obfuscation): *The Jargon of Authenticity*.[2] The Frankfurt School itself, and not least among them Adorno, generated more than their own fair share of jargon and prose that many ordinary readers might dismiss as impenetrable gibberish.

Yet to mock or dismiss critical theorists for inability to express themselves in clear prose and pellucid argument is to miss an important aspect of what they are doing: they are embodying in the form of their work their underlying understanding of the world in which they are operating. That might seem nearly as obscure as a piece of Adorno's prose, but it is not actually a difficult point.

---

[1] A notable exception to this criticism is critical race theory, a point noted by Helen Pluckrose and James Lindsay, *Cynical Theories: How Activist Scholarship Made Everything about Race, Gender, and Identity, and Why This Harms Everybody* (Durham, NC: Pitchstone, 2020), 119. Their observation—that this may be due to CRT's origins in legal theory—is plausible, to which one might add that its distance with regard to sources from European Hegelian and post-structuralist texts is also likely a contributing factor.

[2] Theodor W. Adorno, *Jargon der Eigentlichkeit: Zur deutschen Ideologie* (Frankfurt: Suhrkamp, 1964). English translation: *The Jargon of Authenticity*, trans. Knut Tarnowski and Frederic Will (London: Routledge, 1973).

We have noted several times that one of the conclusions which the early critical theorists draw from Hegel is that what counts as knowledge is historically conditioned. When we add the further critical twist to this—that society as currently constituted involves alienation, that the way people think and the way people live and relate to the world around them is not harmonious but deeply fractured and contains fundamental contradictions—then it becomes clear that the modes of thinking and writing that society regards as clear are themselves deceptive or, to use the technical jargon, ideological. Apparent clarity and coherence are part of the illusory apparatus that disguises the deep problems that beset our culture. The question for the critical theorist then becomes: How does one raise awareness of this? One cannot simply do it using the standard criteria of clarity and rationality of the surrounding world, for, as just noted, these things are themselves embedded within an alienated and fragmentary social structure. Instead, one does it by reflecting the lack of unity in the very form of discussion.

I have often made this point in class with reference to the writings of Judith Butler on gender. Butler is quite capable of writing clear, elegant prose. Her occasional journalism provides numerous examples.[3] Yet her scholarly writings on gender are dense and something that the typical undergraduate student finds hard, if not impossible, to follow. That, of course, is a large part of her point: the obscure style is an important aspect of her work. She is not just arguing that stable categories such as "man" and "woman" need to be destabilized; through the opacity of her prose and the recondite structure of her argument she is in a sense destabilizing her readers by refusing to provide them with a clear, well-founded place to stand and judge her work.

This point—that form is an important means of communicating the critical, disruptive nature of what is being communicated—is important for

---

[3] See, for example, Judith Butler, "Wise Distinctions," *London Review of Books*, November 20, 2009, https://www.lrb.co.uk/blog/2009/november/wise-distinctions.

understanding the Frankfurt School. Some of their obscurity (at least for Anglo-American readers) lies in the fact that their philosophical background in German idealism is not so familiar to the Anglophone world as it would have been to their European readers. Any reader of Hegel can vouch for this. But some of it also lies in their conscious commitment to exposing the alienation and the contradictions that lie below the surface of what would appear to be a natural, given, and unassailable social order. In a sense they were rather like the modernists of the broader culture such as T. S. Eliot, Igor Stravinsky, and Pablo Picasso, since their work too set out to expose the lack of coherence underpinning a Western civilization that had sloughed off its old Christian faith.

This use of form as a means of communicating the fragmented and alienated nature of the modern world is most evident in two of the early Frankfurt School's central texts: Adorno's *Minima Moralia* (*MM*) and Horkheimer and Adorno's *Dialectic of Enlightenment* (*DE*).[4] The former, composed in three parts between 1944 and 1947, is a collection of aphorisms, somewhat reminiscent in its fragmentary style and structure of Nietzsche's *Gay Science*. The latter was originally privately printed in 1944 as *Philosophical Fragments* and then formally published in 1947 with its new title and the original now moved to the status of a subtitle. It consists of five long essays and one chapter of brief notes and comments. Neither book presents a single, sustained linear argument. Instead, they both offer a series of reflections or, perhaps better, interventions, on a set of related themes that point to the underlying problems of modernity without reducing those problems to a single cause. The effect of reading these works is both disorienting, as the quest for a single, dominant idea or approach proves elusive and challenging as neither is susceptible to a single, obvious interpretation.

---

[4] Theodor W. Adorno, *Minima Moralia: Reflections from Damaged Life*, trans. E. F. N. Jephcott (New York: Verso, 1974); Max Horkheimer and Theodor W. Adorno, *Dialectic of Enlightenment: Philosophical Fragments*, trans. Edmund Jephcott (Stanford: Stanford University Press, 2002).

Nevertheless, there are a number of indisputable themes that these works contain, and given the status of both (especially *DE*) as foundational texts for critical theory, it is worth expounding these since a basic knowledge of them will enable us to understand more deeply the aims of the Frankfurt School in particular and critical theorists in general.

The Domination of Nature

At the heart of *DE* is the notion that human history is the story of humanity's attempts to control nature. Now, as soon as I write that statement, I am aware of a problem: Horkheimer and Adorno never actually offer a precise definition of nature, something that might initially strike you as odd. Do philosophers predicating their view of the world on the idea of control of nature not have a duty to define their terms at the outset? In one sense, of course, yes they do. But Horkheimer and Adorno are Marxists of a strongly Hegelian variety and are thus acutely aware that what is understood by the term "nature" is itself a function of the historical circumstances in which the word is being used. Put simply, what the ancient Athenian, the medieval Franciscan friar, the Renaissance humanist, the Enlightenment philosopher, and the modern capitalist thought of as "nature" will differ. Further, terms are to be understood in relation to their opposites. We noted in chapter 2 that Hegel saw the definition of lord and bondservant to be codependent: each was defined in terms of his relationship with the other, and as the relationship changed over time, so did the definitions. So, in *DE*, the meaning of nature will emerge from the way in which human beings interact with, and think about, the world.

Early in the first essay in *DE*, "The Concept of Enlightenment," Horkheimer and Adorno declare that "what human beings seek to learn from nature is how to use it to dominate wholly both it and human beings."[5] Here we see that which we have already noted as a theme that

---

[5] *DE*, 2.

binds together early and later critical theorists, and which transcends the divide between Hegelian Marxists and the post-structuralists: a concern to see power and domination as central themes in how to understand the dynamics of society and, to put it in somewhat colloquial terms, to understand what is really going on. Power, the struggle for mastery of the world around and of other human beings, is the basic dynamo of human history. Relationships between human beings and their environment can be analyzed using this category.

So what is this nature which humans seek to dominate? We might summarize it by saying, "that which is there for humans to dominate but which is not itself human." That does not seem to take us very far, but an abstract definition that goes further is not really possible. Human beings have always instinctively strived to survive, and that means that they have sought to control the world around them in such a way that will not be annihilated. But the ways in which they seek to do this have changed over time. Thus, what Horkheimer and Adorno do in this first essay is lay out a schematic history of how human beings have related to "what is there" in the natural world, seeing this search for domination as taking a series of forms.

From Magic to Disenchantment

The first chapter of *DE* addresses what contemporary Canadian philosopher Charles Taylor calls the *social imaginary*:

> I want to speak of "social imaginary" here, rather than social theory, because there are important differences between the two. There are, in fact, several differences. I speak of "imaginary" (i) because I'm talking about the way ordinary people "imagine" their social surroundings, and this is often not expressed in theoretical terms, it is carried in images, stories, legends, etc. But it is also the case that (ii) theory is often the possession of a small minority, whereas what

is interesting in the social imaginary is that it is shared by large groups of people, if not the whole society. Which leads to a third difference: (iii) the social imaginary is that common understanding which makes possible common practices, and a widely shared sense of legitimacy.[6]

What Taylor is pointing to is the fact that what human beings believe about the world, themselves, and the relationship between the two, is not the result of self-conscious engagement with arguments and of pressing everything back to first principles. Rather it is the result of intuitions shaped by how they live life in community. To put this in the more politically loaded language of critical theory, it is a matter of an ideologically formed consciousness, the manipulative nature of which is hidden to those subject to it. To them it appears natural and simply the way the world is. And that is what Horkheimer and Adorno are trying to explore. So what is the social imaginary of modern human beings, according to *DE*? It is one where nature has been disenchanted.

This is a clue to one influence behind the overall tendency of the historical scheme in *DE*: Max Weber, the German sociologist. He saw the rise of the modern society as involving a slow but steady process whereby the transcendent, the sacred, and the patterns and values of public life built upon them have retreated in the face of science that seeks to rationalize everything through measurement and calculation. This is disenchantment, and it has led to a situation where public life acknowledges only the empirical and the calculable as important.[7] Horkheimer and Adorno agree with Weber's basic observation, but they wish to move beyond him. Weber's view is quite consistent with what they would call the approach of traditional

---

[6] Charles Taylor, *A Secular Age* (Cambridge: Belknap, 2007), 171–72. Taylor has devoted an entire book to discussing the concept: *Modern Social Imaginaries* (Durham, NC: Duke University Press, 2004).

[7] See "Science as Vocation," in Max Weber, *The Vocation Lectures*, trans. Rodney Livingstone (Indianapolis: Hackett, 2004).

theory: that descriptive, explanatory approach we noted in chapter 4. As critical theorists, Horkheimer and Adorno seek to show the problems and contradictions inherent in this process of disenchantment. The basic pattern they discern in history is one that begins with magic, moves on to religion, shifts into metaphysics, and then culminates in a thoroughly disenchanted positivism, with human beings in each phase seeking to master nature. As always, they are concerned with how such a development facilitates and serves deeper political interests.

The phase of magic involves a close identification of the elements of material reality with supernatural forces. Thus, the volcano is a god, the woods are the places inhabited by spirits and demons, and the village is subject to the whim of a local deity. Imagining the world as such, human beings responded in what *DE* describes as a mimetic way, an attempt to develop rituals that respect the given reality of what we might call somewhat paradoxically supernatural nature. This is *mimesis*, an attempt to control nature by likeness of kinship. To drive out a terrifying demon, for example, the shaman himself dons a terrifying mask to scare the spirit away. Whatever the shaman does to the spear or the doll is thought to be done to the person represented. This is a world of little or no religious or philosophical abstraction. As with later science, magic is concerned with the achievement of certain ends; but unlike science, it does so in a manner that sees nature as a subject, as having a "personality," so to speak, and not merely as raw material.[8]

With this as the historical starting point, *DE* paints a picture of human development that involves an increasing distance between human beings and the world around them. First rise the ancient gods who live on Olympus and are not so much identified with the natural elements as seen to symbolize them and have control over them. Then there emerges monotheism, with one God in charge of all of nature and with human

---

[8] *DE*, 6–7.

beings made in his image. This closeness of God and man, this imaging of the former in the latter, paves the way for the human mind to be seen as an analog of the divine mind and thus as having a similar role in sovereignty and control. Eventually, this leads to the development of metaphysical concepts for categorizing and explaining nature. We might point to Thomas Aquinas as a great exemplar of this approach, with his critical appropriation of the categories of Aristotelian thought and his grounding of reality in the being of God. These metaphysical categories themselves are eventually detached from belief in God but then come under devastating criticism at the Enlightenment from figures such as David Hume. And, finally, as these metaphysical categories collapse, all that is left is nature "stripped of qualities . . . the chaotic stuff of mere classification," and human beings cease to be the image-bearers of God but rather examples of the "all powerful self . . . a mere having, an abstract identity."[9]

The net result of this historical transformation of humanity's understanding of nature is that we cease seeking to influence nature by acting in ways that make us like it in terms of its givenness (an offering of fire, for example, to the volcano as a means of preserving the village in the valley below). Instead, we see nature as something that can be mastered through work. Reality becomes prosaic, and humanity's task becomes one facilitated by what we now think of as science: experiments, measurements, and calculation. And these things in turn facilitate the development of general laws of nature.

This is of great importance for understanding the Frankfurt School's relationship to the nature and use of reason in modern society. Essentially, what *DE* sees happening at the end of this process is the rise to dominance of what is called *instrumental reason*, that reason which is defined by its focus on measurement and calculability and driven by a basic urge to exert mastery. Instrumental reason considers important only those things that can

---

[9] *DE*, 6.

be assessed in empirical, objective terms. Other things—God, love, music, literature—are significant only to the extent that they feed into this picture. Do they inspire people to work harder? Do they allow for relaxation so that the worker can be more productive? What is their cash value in the marketplace of exchangeable goods? We are all no doubt aware of these kind of arguments today whereby the public value of any given human activity is reduced to its measurable significance: Will this degree lead immediately to a higher paying job? Does this academic discipline have a practical payoff? The issue of instrumental reason remains as significant for us as for the early Frankfurt School.[10]

It is important to remember once again at this point that the interest of critical theorists is not the typical one of traditional philosophy. They are interested in why certain modes of thinking emerge and become dominant at certain points in history, and they see the answer to this not as lying in the intrinsic truth or superiority of such modes in comparison with what they replace but rather in how they serve the emerging social order. We noted in chapter 3 how Karl Korsch observed that Hegel's thinking about historical change enjoyed great vogue in early nineteenth-century Prussia as a new bourgeois order was supplanting the old regime of landed nobility, but then fell out of favor as Kant's rather more fixed philosophical categories re-emerged. His argument was that once the bourgeois order had stabilized, a revolutionary philosophy of change was no longer needed. Indeed, it came at that point to pose a threat. So with the rise of disenchantment and scientific positivism, the question for Horkheimer and Adorno is not so much "Is this better than orthodox Christianity?" but "Why does this development take place at this particular point in time?" Or, more pointedly, "Who benefits from scientific positivism?"

---

[10] For instrumental reason as a constant focal point for the Frankfurt School, see J. M. Bernstein, "The Idea of Instrumental Reason," in Gordon, Hammer, and Honneth, *The Routledge Companion to the Frankfurt School*, 3–18 (see chap. 3, n. 24).

Disenchantment as Ideology

Before answering that specific question, it is important to note that *DE* sees the critical movement in the Enlightenment as a dialectical one whereby human beings are first liberated from God but then returned to a form of bondage. The irony is that it is the thing that liberates them—reason—that then places them in this new form of servitude. Specifically, what the rise of instrumental reason does is present a view of reality that parades itself as neutral, as "just the facts." This kind of reason has no place for the metaphysical fancies of old-style religion or philosophy and therefore breaks their hold on the social imaginary. But then this scientific objectivity, focused on scientific laws, measurability, and predictability, tilts society ineluctably toward seeing human beings not as subjects—as free, acting individuals—but as objects. They become just one more kind of thing that can be treated as raw material and defined in terms of the criteria of measurement and calculability. In other words, to give a Marxist twist, they can be defined in terms of how much they produce and how efficiently they do so and under what conditions. This is the reification that Lukács spoke about in his analysis of class struggle. In a memorable phrase, *DE* comments, "Animism had endowed things with souls; industrialism makes souls into things."[11] And as previously noted, one of the great ironies that *DE* observes in this narrative is that that which liberates then comes to dominate. This is the dialectical move, where a thing turns into its opposite. The great thinkers of the Enlightenment—perhaps most notably David Hume and Immanuel Kant—dealt death blows to traditional Christian orthodoxy with their philosophical reflection. But in shattering the metaphysical foundations of religion, they offered only a short-term liberation before the new ideology of instrumental reason replaced the old moral codes and practices of Christianity.

---

[11] *DE*, 21.

The irony of this result is clear when one considers the famous definition of Enlightenment given by Kant in his 1784 lecture, "What Is
Enlightenment?":

> Enlightenment is man's emergence from his self-imposed
> immaturity. Immaturity is the inability to use one's understanding
> without guidance from another. This immaturity is self-imposed
> when its cause lies not in lack of understanding, but in lack of
> resolve and courage to use it without guidance from another. Sapere
> Aude! "Have courage to use your own understanding!"—that is the
> motto of enlightenment.[12]

Here the note of a coming-of-age signified by the assumption of personal
responsibility and realization of individual freedom is obvious. For Kant,
Enlightenment brings human beings out of bondage and into adulthood, an
adulthood characterized by personal independence and liberty. To use the
language of *DE*, the Enlightenment destroys the myths upon which previous
society was built—the mythology of animism, then monotheism, and finally
the metaphysics of those pre-Kantian philosophers for whom knowledge of
what was real was a straightforward process that operated with universal
categories of essences. For Kant and company, breaking free of bondage to
these things is what enlightenment is all about. And yet, according to *DE*, it
has had the opposite effect, ultimately imposing a greater degree of servitude
perhaps than even the old gods demanded. In fact, enlightenment generates
its own mythology which proves just as distorting of reality and imperious
over human beings as that which went before.

The path by which this occurs is, according to *DE*, a straightforward
one: once religious and metaphysical categories cease to be plausible, scientific idiom becomes part of the overall structure of society and thus the
idiom of the all-encompassing ideology of the day. How can a view of reality

---

[12] Immanuel Kant, *Perpetual Peace and Other Essays on Politics, History, and
Morals*, trans. Ted Humphrey (Indianapolis: Hackett, 1983), 41.

that simply presents the facts and laws of material existence in a disinterested fashion be resisted?

The impartiality of scientific language deprived what was powerless of the strength to make itself heard and merely provided the existing order with a neutral sign for itself.[13] Again, to anyone familiar with modern iterations of critical theory, an important note is struck here: the apparent neutrality of scientific discourse is what makes it so powerful; and yet that very concept of neutrality is itself a product of the society in which it occurs and which it serves to justify. As we noted in chapter 4, Horkheimer is clear that the very terms by which a society expresses its values are themselves part of a system that serves to naturalize and thus legitimize its own structures of power and oppression.

The point is one that we can all grasp in terms of personal experience. One of the striking phenomena of recent times has been how science has come to dominate the ways in which societies organize themselves. When the phrase "the experts say" is used on news broadcasts, there is never any doubt who the "experts" are: they are typically what we might call technicians, those whose area of expertise means that they have mastered the techniques necessary to solve a perceived problem. Often they are scientists such as medical doctors. Sometimes they are what we call *social scientists*, but that phrase itself is interesting, granting an aura of objectivity and neutrality to academic fields that stand outside the realm of the real, hard sciences. I have never myself witnessed the phrase being used to refer to a moral philosopher, let alone a religious leader or an artist. And what makes advice couched in the idiom of scientific discourse so powerful is its apparently disinterested nature: it is a report of the facts of the case based upon measurements and calculations that are in principle open to anyone with eyes to see them. What critical theory challenges is precisely this point: the claim to neutrality. It seems to show the political and social conditions that must exist for such

---

[13] *DE*, 17.

notions as "science," "neutrality," "objectivity," and "expertise" to be so culturally powerful.

So why does this neutral, scientific idiom come to dominate and have such cultural authority? Is it because it is simply more true than what has gone before? For the critical theorist, this cannot be the answer as we know that thinkers such as Adorno do not see truth as something which can simply be abstracted from historical conditions. What counts as truth is itself a function of the society in which the claim to truth is made.

Now, there is need for nuance here. In dealing with the rise of scientific positivism, it is not that Horkheimer and Adorno regard, say, modern medical treatments as no better at curing diseases than the king's touch was at curing scrofula in the Middle Ages. That is not what interests them. Rather, they are concerned with how science is understood within a society or, to put it more narrowly, how it is used politically and culturally by the powerful and how it informs the intuitions of the social imaginary.

What instrumental reason, with its generalized laws of nature, does is to reduce individual human beings to individual instantiations of a species, comparable with, and replaceable by, other members of the species. And that fits with the idea that they are just one more exchangeable commodity, where individuality really counts for nothing. The overall effect of this is that human beings become dehumanized. Ironically, therefore, the Enlightenment that sought to place the autonomous self-determining human individual at the center of the universe ends up annihilating individuality. Human mastery of nature, through its focus on what can be measured, analyzed, calculated, and thereby manipulated, ultimately extends to human beings themselves. They too become raw material, and that is presented as an objective, and therefore indisputable, fact. As *DE* expresses it:

> Through the mediation of the total society, which encompasses
> all relationships and impulses, human beings are being turned
> back into precisely what the developmental law of society, the
> principle of the self, had opposed: mere examples of the species,

identical to one another through isolation within the compul-
sively controlled collectivity.[14]

To put this more simply: the very nature of the society in which we now live,
born out of the earlier break that Enlightenment thinking accomplished
with regard to the old religion, with its theological categories and its powerful social institutions, has itself come to tyrannize the individual. Where
once God demanded that individuals surrender their autonomy in obedience to him, now it is science which does so, defining human value only
in the terms that it will accept. And this makes positivist science the new
mythology. It asserts, rather than proves from first principles, that the whole
of reality can be encompassed and exhaustively understood by the scientific
method of measurement and calculation. Such a claim is no more "true"
as a total vision of reality than the old animism that assumed the identity
of material reality with its gods. Rather, it too is ideological. And thus it
informs the social imaginary with a disenchanted picture of the world that
guides behavior but is really no less mythological than the old, enchanted
mythologies of the past.[15]

With this caveat, we can return to the question of why this scientific
positivism, couched in the language of neutral facts, comes to grip the
social imaginary. It should not be a surprise, given the Marxist under-
pinnings of the Frankfurt School, that *DE* sees the answer lying in the
fact that contemporary society is organized around bourgeois capitalism and that this system has a vested interest in the dehumanization to
which instrumental reason leads. The thing which unifies the capitalist
system is exchange value: all things must be comparable with each other
by the unifying factor of exchange: money. The value of each person, like
the value of gold or of gasoline, must be measurable in monetary terms,
and this, of course, means that people can be compared to things and

---

[14] *DE*, 29.
[15] *DE*, 20–21.

exchanged for things. Scientific positivism is the perfect ideology for such a culture because it discounts as unimportant or even as problematic all of those things that are not measurable—desire, love, hate, compassion, and being a father, a wife, a son, or a daughter. These are the things that belong to individual human subjectivity and which cannot be easily priced or exchanged for something of equal value precisely because there is no universal currency into which they can be translated. Indeed, one might perhaps as a Christian comment that it discounts all of those things that actually make us human. And that is *DE*'s point: science/instrumental reason treats people as things, as animated lumps of matter, not as persons. Or, to put it in slightly more philosophical terms, it treats them as objects that are subject to laws beyond their control, not as free subjects. And thus there is an intimate connection between the timing of the scientific revolution and the rise of bourgeois capitalism. The former is an ideological expression of the values needed and encouraged by the latter. Horkheimer and Adorno's colleague, Herbert Marcuse, summarizes this in his essay, "From Ontology to Technology":

> As science was liberating itself, liberating nature from its "external" forces and constituting objectivity as a means in itself, a pure and universal means, an analogous liberation was produced in social relations: man found himself liberated from any individual and "external" dependence. Man entered into the social process as an abstract and universal element, quantifiable in terms of labor power. In the course of this process, the concrete aspect of having different intellectual faculties and needs . . . became reduced to a common denominator, a quantifiable, objective base of exchange, of money, and of means in a universal milieu.[16]

---

[16] Herbert Marcuse, "From Ontology to Technology: Fundamental Tendencies of Industrial Society," in Stephen Eric Bronner and Douglas MacKay Kellner, eds., *Critical Theory and Society: A Reader* (New York: Routledge, 1989), 123.

The net result of both science and capitalism, then, is that the consequent system treats people as simply one more exchangeable commodity. In a chilling comment on fatalities in factories, Horkheimer and Adorno state that "who dies is unimportant; what matters is the ratio of incidences of death to the liabilities of the company." The subject is reduced to being an object, an entry in a ledger book, or a budget, or on an insurance liability policy. The importance of the individual human being has been negated by the reifications upon which the capitalist system depends.[17]

The Problem of Morality

Once human beings are objectified in this way—once they become simply lumps of animated matter, of social value merely because of their productive labor power—numerous problems manifest themselves, not least the question of morality. Lumps of animated matter have no intrinsic moral shape. Yet bourgeois culture depends upon morality. Capitalism thrives on a strong work ethic, strong families, and strong social commitments. Honesty, punctuality, hard work, and a willingness to accept orders from authority figures are all essential to the smooth running of the capitalist system. The problem is that the exaltation of instrumental reason in the Enlightenment raises the issue of how this morality is to be justified and maintained. In a more mimetic culture that sees nature itself as having an objective moral shape of some kind, whether grounded in a form of animism or in the Christian doctrine of creation, the justification of moral principles is relatively straightforward. Why is murder wrong for the medieval Christian? One answer would be that it involves the destruction of the image of God. The moral code is thus theologically grounded.

With the rise to dominance of instrumental reason, two things serve to preclude this answer. First, instrumental reason is not teleological. It posits

---

[17] *DE*, 66.

no intrinsic ends to the nature it seeks to control, seeing it simply as so much raw matter:

> Once the objective order of nature has been dismissed as prejudice and myth, nature is no more than a mass of material.[18]

Because of this, morality cannot therefore be inferred from what merely exists. As the old Enlightenment adage says, one cannot infer an *ought* from an *is*. And yet the bourgeois system requires morality for its functioning. Anarchy would not allow for the flourishing of the capitalist economy. Therefore, various Enlightenment thinkers attempt to give a grounding for morals that provides morality with objective status.

From the perspective of Horkheimer and Adorno, the most important example of this is Kant. Kant formulated morality on the basis that one should always act in a way that respects the humanity/subjectivity of others and in a manner which could be universalized without contradiction. Thus, one should never break a promise because, if one were to allow this, one would be contradicting the very nature of what a promise is and society would also descend into chaos as duplicity was legitimized.

Yet there is a twofold problem here, relating directly to the philosophy that actually underpins this approach. First, it is abstract, dealing in universal principles rather than specific situations; and second, it is dehumanizing. As to the first, in its attempt to give the status of transcendence to a moral rule, it fails to do justice the complexity of real life. One classic objection to the categorical imperative regarding lying is that of the person harboring Jews in their house during the Nazi regime. If the Gestapo come calling and demand to know if there are Jews in the cellar, the homeowner can tell the truth, thus enabling murder. Or he can lie and potentially save the lives of Jews. Which should he do? To speak truth is to have a hand in killing Jews. To lie is to legitimate the lies of others. The abstraction involved in the categorical imperative simply does not reflect the concrete reality—the complex concrete

---

[18] *DE*, 78.

reality—in which human moral subjects have to make decisions. This is one reason why the Greek tragedy *Antigone* has proved perennially fascinating, not least to Kant's successor as the kingpin of German Idealism, Hegel. Faced with the familial obligation of giving her brother an appropriate burial and the king's command that such rites should be withheld from him as a traitor, she is placed at the center of an irresolvable ethical dilemma. Most of us will never face such a situation ourselves, but we certainly know that ethical decision making is always more complicated than straightforward moral regulations would imply. This is because human life involves the interaction of free individuals and is therefore not reducible to a clean set of abstract principles.

This then connects to the second aspect of the problem. The tendency of Enlightenment to trade in generalized abstractions turns human beings themselves into individual examples of an abstraction: human nature, subject to measurement, calculability, and analysis. In short, and to repeat, it turns others into objects, not subjects. Thus, an ethic predicated on treating the others as subjects, as free individuals of unique value, to be treated not as means to an end but as ends in themselves, runs afoul of a view of the world that turns the other into an object of study and analysis. In short, for Horkheimer and Adorno, Enlightenment ethics tries to deliver that which Enlightenment epistemology precludes. That's the dialectical issue at the heart of bourgeois society, the contradiction that can only lead to conflict and disaster.

DE illuminates this by pointing to the Marquis De Sade and Friedrich Nietzsche as two thinkers who spot the sleight of hand upon which the moral order of the emerging bourgeois world represents. Just as Nietzsche attacked the idea of pity as a means of preventing the strong from realizing their strength, so *DE* presents the Sadean protagonist Juliette, from Sade's novel of the same name, as a rationalist who presses rational principles to their ultimate, amoral end.[19] With the assertion of the autonomous

---

[19] "Juliette's *credo* is science. She abominates any veneration which cannot be shown to be rational: belief in God and his dead son, obedience to the Ten Commandments, preference of the good to the wicked, salvation to sin." *DE*, 76.

individual and the correlative dissolution of all natural bonds of obligation and dependence, morality becomes a chimera, a smokescreen maintained only because it protects the interests of a particular group. Juliette realizes this and in her sexual indulgence treats all other human beings as objects for domination or, to put it in Marxist terminology, as commodities to be consumed for the satisfaction of personal desire. *DE* asserts a connection between the way bourgeois society operates and the morality of power and domination that Sade and Nietzsche advocate. Now that rational, industrial production has delivered such control of nature into human hands and thereby removed the need for magic and religious observance, domination becomes a pleasurable end in itself. It is not that Juliette's survival depends upon her sexual indulgence. Rather, her transgression of the remnants of the old order in terms of its morality brings her pleasure. One might say that such transgression is the last avenue for asserting her freedom and autonomy—those values exalted by the Enlightenment—in the face of the rationalized world the Enlightenment has produced. Therein lies an example of the dialectic of Enlightenment.[20]

To the objection that the perversions which Sade, in the voice of Juliette, advocates are wrong, the question "Why so?" is unanswerable on the terms of the society where exchange value has become the only criterion for judging the worth of any given action. In this disenchanted context, love—that which many would regard as central to the human experience— is itself exposed as a sham, a point from which Sade does not hesitate to draw the most extreme conclusion:

> It is not just romantic love which has been condemned as metaphysics by science and industry but love of any kind, for no love can withstand reason: neither that between wife and husband nor between lover and beloved, nor the love between parents and children. . . . Sade, however, applies the same even to exogamy, the

---

[20] *DE*, 81–83.

foundation of civilization. According to him, there are no rational grounds to oppose incest, and the hygienic argument formerly used has now been invalidated by advanced science, which ratifies Sade's cold judgment.[21]

In sum, to ascribe moral significance to the biological connection between parents and children, or to the romantic attachment of husband and wife, is to create a social structure that stands at odds with a society that sees all human beings not as subjects but as objects. Such relationships would, after all, interfere with the strict nature of exchange that bourgeois capitalism requires and that makes all human beings merely units on a balance sheet or strategic business plan rather than free agents. Sade (and Nietzsche) expose this obvious implication of rejection of an inherent moral shape to the universe which scientific positivism demands. Their anti-authoritarianism demonstrates how the reduction of life to the measurable and calculable can be used to shatter some of the bourgeoisie's most cherished institutions and moral imperatives. As *DE* expresses it in the conclusion to the Excursus on Sade and Nietzsche:

> The dark writers of the bourgeoisie, unlike its apologists, did not seek to avert the consequences of the Enlightenment with harmonistic doctrines. They did not pretend that formalistic reason had a closer affinity to morality than immorality. While the light-bringing writers protected the indissoluble alliance of reason and atrocity, bourgeois society and power, by denying that alliance, the bearers of darker messages pitilessly expressed the shocking truth.[22]

In short, DE regards the morality of the Enlightenment as a smokescreen that only the likes of Sade and Nietzsche had the honesty to expose as a sham. There is a basic contradiction in bourgeois culture: it requires

---

[21] *DE*, 91.
[22] *DE*, 92.

morality in order to have a compliant workforce, but its adherence to an anti-theological, anti-metaphysical philosophy where instrumental reason is the dominant ideology is subversive of any attempt to construct a broader moral framework.[23] This is critical theory at its most pungent, arguing that appearance is the opposite of reality, a theme to which we shall return below in "The Whole Is the False."

The Problem of "the Other"

Anyone with even the briefest acquaintance with the idioms of postmodern theory will have come across the term "the Other" at some point, with the capitalization giving it an aura of portentous significance. This significance in fact lies in the idea that one group's identity depends upon it defining itself over against another. In this, it is reminiscent of Hegel's lord-bondservant dialectic, noted in chapter 2, where the meaning of each term at any given point can only be understood in terms of the one subject's relationship with the other.

---

[23] In his work, *Eclipse of Reason* (London: Continuum, 2004), 16–17, Horkheimer sums up this argument with great clarity and rhetorical power: "What are the consequences of the formalization of reason? Justice, equality, happiness, tolerance, all the concepts that . . . were in preceding centuries supposed to be inherent in or sanctioned by reason, have lost their intellectual roots. They are still aims and ends, but there is no rational agency authorized to appraise and link them to an objective reality. Endorsed by venerable historical documents, they may still enjoy a certain prestige, and some are contained in the supreme law of the greatest countries. Nevertheless, they lack any confirmation by reason in its modern sense. Who can say that any one of these ideas is more closely related to truth than its opposite? According to the philosophy of the average modern intellectual, there is only one authority, namely, science, conceived as the classification of facts and the calculation of probabilities. The statement that justice and freedom are better in themselves than injustice and oppression is scientifically unverifiable and useless. It has come to sound as meaningless in itself as would the statement that red is more beautiful than blue, or that an egg is better than milk."

In *DE*, this concept is used to explain the phenomena of Fascism and Nazism. *DE* argues that these are products of rationalism. Three things are of relevance here. First, there is the Sade-Nietzsche exaltation of power over others to which treating others as objects leads. *DE* does not treat anti-Semitism in this context as the crude manifestation of economic interests in the manner in which the older strict materialism of the Marxism of the Second International might have done. But it does connect anti-Semitism to the form of economic life that capitalism represents and the kind of social imaginary that capitalism fosters. If the exchange of commodities is the basic principle upon which society is built, then this comes to penetrate every aspect of life and, as stated previously, shapes how human beings come to be understood. Once another human being ceases to be a subject to me and becomes simply an object of value only because of its exchange value (e.g., what it is worth in terms of its productive labor power), it becomes easy for me to treat that person as just one object among many. Thus, where one worker is easily replaceable with another, then workers are just interchangeable cogs in the machine. And this in turn cultivates a way of thinking that makes it easier to regard other groups as not being human. Economic behavior in capitalist society means that the social imaginary has been shaped in such a way that this becomes very plausible indeed. In the case of the Nazi Party, the target of such is obvious: Jews. Hypothetically, regarding Jews—or any other group that is perceived to be different to the one to which I belong—as subhuman is easy once the general conception of human nature has been degraded as it is under bourgeois capitalism.

The second strand of this "Othering" flows from the point made in the excursus on Sade and Nietzsche, where power and domination are seen as the inevitable result of the disenchantment of the world. Power and domination cannot exist in a vacuum. One cannot dominate in the abstract. One can only dominate some *thing* or some *one*. So when a political philosophy that exalts power and domination emerges—say Fascism or Nazism—there must be an object of domination in order for the masters to be masters. The man who sits in his basement and claims to rule the universe is simply mad.

Unless he actually does rule the universe, the claim is delusional. The point is a Hegelian one but appropriated by Horkheimer and Adorno with regard to Nazi anti-Semitism: ironically, Nazis needed Jews as the "Other" in order to be Nazis.[24] They need to pronounce an inferior race to dominate in order for themselves to be the master race. This is a theme that is a staple of later critical theories. Concepts of masculinity require concepts of effeminacy in order to exist. Concepts of "whiteness" require concepts of "blackness" in order to exist. Heterosexuality requires homosexuality in order to exist. The sense of value and superiority in each of the former needs each of the latter.

The third strand of this "Othering" involves the projection of the fears and insecurities of one group onto another. The idea of projection is not new with the Frankfurt School. As noted in chapter 2, in the nineteenth century, Ludwig Feuerbach argued that the concept of God was really a projection of human aspirations onto a (nonexistent) divine being, a point picked up and developed by Marx in his own critique of religion. In Freud the concept is associated with guilt: that which the Superego considers to be bad or weak in an individual is then projected onto, or ascribed to, another. We are probably all familiar with claims sometimes made in the media or portrayed in soap operas and movies that the most outspoken critics of homosexuality are secretly struggling with the issue themselves. This kind of claim rests upon an appropriation of Freud. And it is this idea which shapes the understanding of Fascism and Nazism put forward in DE.[25]

Indeed, this is elaborated in the chapter in DE entitled "Elements of Anti-Semitism: The Limits of Enlightenment." The important thing to remember, of course, is that Horkheimer and Adorno assume as basic that the capitalist system, precisely because it turns people into objects and reifies them as a category, to use Lukács's terminology, is ineradicably alienating. It simply cannot deliver on its promises of liberation and is therefore doomed

---

[24] DE, 79.

[25] DE uses exactly this example in describing the dynamics of projection in DE, 159.

to disappoint. There will be economic crises, people will find that they are treated as disposable commodities, and life will be hard, difficult and unrewarding—we might say unfair and unjust—to many. How does the system therefore keep going? What mechanisms or cultural phenomena does it generate that help to sustain it?

In this context, *DE* draws explicitly on the concept of projection. Ironically, given how the modern left has made LGBTQ rights a central part of its platform, *DE* presents Fascism and Nazism as the result of the repression of homosexual desire. The guilt that such desire generates in individuals pushes them to direct their violent impulses of self-loathing outwards:

> The psychoanalytic theory of pathic projection has identified the transference of socially tabooed impulses [i.e., homosexuality] from the subject to the object as the substance of that projection. . . . Because it [the individual] cannot acknowledge desire within itself, it assails the other with jealousy or persecution, as the repressed sodomite hounds the animal as hunter or driver.[26]

This theory may today strike us as speculative and simplistic, but its importance lies in the way it seeks to address that question that has perplexed Marxist theorists since Marx himself: Why does the working class support reactionary causes? *DE*'s answer, in part, is that repressed desire needs an outlet, a violent, destructive outlet to assuage its inner guilt.

DE then combines this with another argument: not only does the capitalist system turn subjects into objects, it even convinces the subject that it too is an object. That may sound somewhat obscure, but the basic point is this: not only does capitalism treat people as things, it makes people—individual, conscious people—treat themselves as things. This is critical because it then makes individuals complicit in the overall structure of bourgeois society, with all of its problems and contradictions.

---

[26] *DE*, 158–59. Cf. Adorno's comment in *MM*, 50: "Totalitarianism and homosexuality belong together."

The argument for this runs as follows: Industrialized capitalism makes production, the making of goods for exchange, the central activity of society. As technology advances, the demands of physical labor decrease, but—and here is the key move—the notion of production then colonizes the area of mental work. In other words, thinking is itself required to be productive, that is, to contribute directly to the economic structure of society. All other thinking—what *DE* dubs "armchair thinking"—becomes an unnecessary luxury.[27] In short, all of those thoughts and feelings that we have that make us truly human, such as love or the joy to be found in listening to a beautiful piece of music, are downgraded in importance for the way we think of ourselves. At best they are to be seen as merely private matters, indulgences, or hobbies. What really matters is how we function in the larger economic structure of society.

We see this in our own day with philosophies of education. The humanities and the liberal arts are typically regarded as less important or—and this is significant terminology—"useful" than the sciences or those degrees that lead directly to professional careers in the finance or service sectors of the economy. Horkheimer and Adorno would say that this is entirely predictable in a world where "the economy" has been reified and where individuals need to acknowledge that and tailor their behavior, including their mental lives, accordingly. As *DE* says elsewhere:

> Thought, stripped down to knowledge, is neutralized, harnessed merely to qualifying its practitioner for specific labor markers and heightening the commodity value of the personality.[28]

In short, the individual thinks of himself primarily as an object and behaves accordingly, never challenging the system but adapting his behavior, including his intellectual behavior, to what the system demands of him.

---

[27] *DE*, 166–67.
[28] *DE*, 163.

Where this becomes significant to the rise of Nazism and the appeal of anti-Semitism is this: it cultivates a kind of stupidity among the population that can no longer think for itself. When the system sets the values by which one must live in order to survive and excludes as irrelevant or even dangerous the kind of thinking that might criticize the system and thus damage or even destroy it, the moral agency of the individual is eliminated. As *DE* expresses it:

> The individual no longer has to decide what he or she is supposed to do in a given situation in a painful inner dialogue between conscience, self-preservation, and drives. For the human being as wage earner the decision is taken by a hierarchy extending from trade associations to the national administration; in the private sphere it is taken by the schema of mass culture, which appropriates even the most intimate impulses of its forced consumers.[29]

We will discuss the Frankfurt School's thinking on mass culture in chapter 7, yet here is an important feature to consider: The claim is that capitalism annihilates the individual in such a way that the individual becomes simply a function of the overall system. The self as an individual, reflective, responsible, self-conscious agent vanishes because the individual has been absorbed by the system as a whole. The system makes the decisions. The system therefore defines the individual. And this turns the population into an easily manipulable mass that can be led to project the things that it fears most onto a target that can be presented to it by a strong, political demagogue such as Adolf Hitler. That it happens to be Jews who are the focal point of this projection rests upon the long history of anti-Judaism in European culture. Their long-established outsider status makes them easy and vulnerable targets.

---

[29] *DE*, 168.

The Whole Is the False

Adorno's most famous statement is probably the cryptic comment in Fragment 29 of *MM* that "the whole is the false." Like so much of early critical theory, the meaning of the statement is opaque unless one has some knowledge of the philosophical background against which Adorno is working. Here, it is clearly Hegel of whom he is thinking who states in the Preface to his *Phenomenology of Spirit* that "the true is the whole."[30] To grasp Adorno's point, then, we need to understand what he is reacting against in Hegel.

Hegel's understanding of the historical process was that its subject—what he calls Spirit—ultimately guides and shapes reality. Reality—consisting of institutions, structures, law codes, and the like—is the result of the actions of countless individuals, often working at cross purposes with each other and with no consciously agreed universal vision of what is to be achieved. And yet, according to Hegel, the overall result makes sense. The tendency of society is to make people ethical through personal interaction and cooperation, even if they do not realize that is what is happening. Hegel refers to this as "the cunning of reason"—that which we might say works behind the scenes to guide society in the right direction.[31]

Set against the background of Adorno's thinking, particularly as set forth in *DE*, his enigmatic statement in *MM* likely has a variety of meanings, but among them is surely a criticism of the kind of confident optimism that seems to mark Hegel's understanding of history in particular and much post-Enlightenment thought in general: for Adorno, history is not inevitably moving in a positive, liberating direction. In fact, as Auschwitz indicates, the great technological products of modernity can be deployed for very destructive purposes. Less obviously, but also destructively, the institutions

---

[30] Hegel, *Phenomenology*, 11 (see chap. 2, n. 3).
[31] Stephen Houlgate, *An Introduction to Hegel: Freedom, Truth and History* (Oxford: Blackwell, 2005), 199.

of Western democracy can be deceptive, presenting themselves as manifestations of freedom while really being instruments of subjugation and oppression. In part this is the burden of the first excursus in *DE* where Horkheimer and Adorno discuss the character Odysseus. His significance for them lies in the fact that he can only survive and succeed in his world by suppressing and even denying his own identity.[32] As Marx turned Hegel upside down with regard to replacing his idealism with materialism, Adorno turns him upside down with regard to replacing his confidence in the historical process with a pessimistic view of the same.

Conclusion

We have noted repeatedly that modern iterations of critical theory have moved well beyond the immediate concerns of the early Frankfurt School. Indeed, those in the post-structuralist strand represented most signally by Michel Foucault have very different philosophical roots, rejecting the systematic Hegelian roots of Adorno and company. And yet in *DE* we see once again significant common ground in terms of the critical approach to society. The suspicion of the Enlightenment, the observation that things can tend to turn into their opposite, and the way in which powerful interests cloak themselves in language and concepts that seem neutral, objective, and disinterested are all points of continuity with later non-Hegelian strands of critical theory. As a result, the *Dialectic of Enlightenment* is rightly considered *a*, if not *the*, foundational text of the broader tradition. And, in its excursus on De Sade, it points toward a theme in critical theory that will explode onto the world stage in the 1960s: the role of sex and sexual

---

[32] "From the standpoint of the developed exchange society and its individuals, the adventures of Odysseus are no more than a depiction of the risks which line the path to success. Odysseus lives according to the ancient principle which originally constituted bourgeois society. One had to choose between cheating and going under." *DE*, 48–49.

liberation in modern political discourse and the broader social imaginary with regard to what it means to be human and to be free. That is the subject of our next chapter.

A Postscript on *Dialectic of Enlightenment*

There are huge problems with the historiography of *Dialectic of Enlightenment*. For a treatise attempting to penetrate to the heart of the modern political project, it is remarkable for its failure to engage with any of the great advocates of the Western liberal tradition, such as John Locke and Thomas Paine. And it treats "Enlightenment" as a monolithic whole, reducing it to a single tradition of instrumental reason, ignoring the diversity of thought in the eighteenth century, with no interest in the ways in which others engaged with the emergence of the modern world, such as orthodox Christianity (e.g., Jonathan Edwards, John Wesley, and John Henry Newman), Protestant liberalism (e.g., Friedrich Schleiermacher), and Romanticism (e.g., Friedrich Hölderlin and Samuel Taylor Coleridge). The authors seem to have selected a narrative that suits the points they wish to make. One might, if one were in an impish mood, suggest that their history is merely ideology dressed up as disinterested analysis.

And yet, for all its historiographical shortcomings, a number of the problems with which the text wrestles are of perennial importance. It is often the case that historical movements turn into their opposite. The transgender movement is perhaps the most obvious contemporary example. Resting upon a theoretical foundation that sought to dismiss physical reality as giving gender an essence, it destroyed the authority of the body. Yet as it now manifests itself politically, it demands acknowledgment of the essentialism of what it means to be a man or a woman, albeit grounded in psychological feelings, not physiological reality. Anti-essentialism has become essentialism.

We might also sympathize with *DE*'s repudiation of the idea that life can be reduced to that which is measurable and to that which can be addressed through the categories offered by empirical science. To repeat an earlier comment, a medical doctor can tell us how to save a life but he cannot give us an account of why a life should be saved without stepping outside of his field of expertise. Yet you would be forgiven for not realizing this, given how a medical expert appearing on television, sporting a white coat and a stethoscope, seems to carry the authority of omnicompetence. Further, as Christians, we know that most important things in life are not measurable or calculable. Instrumental reason gives us no insight into love, friendship, loyalty, beauty, self-sacrifice, and all the other things that make us human. It is why the Bible contains narratives, wisdom literature, poetry, and songs. Human life cannot be captured in an algorithm.

And yet even as we might find some affinity with *DE* in its rejection of the despotic demands of instrumental reason, there is a problem in its analysis of life, a problem we have already noted before: the failure to have any normative notion of human nature. This difficulty is intrinsic to the assumptions of the approach. Rooted in the historicism of Hegel and Marx, and driven by the concept of alienation, *DE*'s understanding of what it means to be truly human is ultimately something projected into the future. Only when alienation is brought to an end will the cycle of dialectical negations conclude. Only then will men and women truly realize themselves as truly human. Only then will they know what being truly human means. For all the sophisticated argumentation in *DE*, we are left with nothing more than the pious hope that an unalienated humanity will emerge from the historical process, though we have no way of knowing in advance of that moment what such might look like.

Christians cannot accept this. According to orthodox Christianity, to be human has already been fully manifested in Jesus Christ. What humanity truly is has been revealed. In him, the end of time has already in a sense arrived. And this presses us once again to a consideration of the church. The church is the body of Christ, the place where the Spirit dwells, and where Christians are (paradoxically) both resurrected already in Christ and awaiting the final resurrection at the end of time. In short, the church is here and now the inbreaking of future eternal life into the present. The underlying problem that Marxists such as Horkheimer and Adorno are wrestling with—how do we overcome the alienation of this present age?—is, according to Christian claims, already overcome in Christ. Not perfectly, for sure, for Christian teaching sees Christians as themselves imperfect and the church itself as an admixture of true believers and frauds. But nonetheless, the church is the place where alienation is overcome.

Any Christian response to critical theory cannot therefore concede that human nature does not at some deep level have a content. We can—indeed, we must—acknowledge that human behavior does vary from time to time and from place to place. To fail to do this would be to ignore what is patently obvious to anyone who has studied history or traveled to another country. But we must not fall into the anti-essentialist trap of rejecting any notion of human nature as a mere social construct. Shorn of Marxist eschatology, this is what later critical theorists have done, seeing any attempt to talk about human nature in normative terms as clandestine attempts by one dominant group to control the categories by which everyone is to understand the world. Christianity, with its notion that human beings are made in the image of God, does not have that option. It has to assert that there is some authoritative human nature that transcends our cultural particularities.

And so we return again to how we do this: in the life of the church. It is there, as we worship together, hear the Word, and share in the sacraments, that we answer the problems highlighted by *DE*, but with more adequate resources than *DE* has at its disposal. We demonstrate that life is not reducible to impersonal categories, that every human being is a person and not a thing. And that God's grace, not the economic transformation of society, is that which alone can overcome the problems of the alienated human condition.

CHAPTER 6

Critical Theory and Sexual Revolution: Wilhelm Reich and Herbert Marcuse

Introduction

One of the areas where critical theory is most often cited as important for contemporary political and cultural discourse is that of sex and gender. Indeed, various strands of feminism and, more recently, the variety of approaches to these topics referred to broadly as *queer theory* have proved remarkably potent in our current cultural climate, touching everything from medical ethics and human reproduction to marriage and drag queen story hours. Heated discussions of sexuality and gender are no longer merely the topics of abstruse university seminars; they are the common currency of social media, TV shows, HR policies, and water cooler conversations. You may not be interested in queer theory, but queer theory is interested in you.

In general, the immediate origins of the various theories behind much of contemporary thinking about these issues do not lie directly with the early critical theories of the first generation of the Frankfurt School. Rather the key figure is Michel Foucault, the French post-structuralist, whose influence in the humanities over the decades since his death is hard to exaggerate. His work on the history of sex and sexuality is a landmark study in the field of how these have been understood and used in cultural discourse, shaping much of later discussion.[1] And Foucault was deeply suspicious of the kind of totalizing system that Hegel and his heirs, including Marx and his progeny, represented but which we have noted as providing much of the background to the Frankfurt School. In a sense he represents the real crisis in anthropology: While Hegelian Marxists arguably regarded unalienated humanity as something to emerge in the future, with Foucault and company, there is no such eschatological fulfillment or revelation, only the constant flux of discourses of power.

And yet the single most important figure in the development of queer theory is Judith Butler, an unabashed admirer of Hegel, as her doctoral dissertation indicates.[2] And therein lies an important point: for all of the differences between Foucault and Butler in their respective attitudes to Hegel, there are key affinities that they share with the Marxists of the earlier Frankfurt School. They may reject the teleology of the latter, but they have numerous immediate concerns in common. These include a sensitivity to power as fundamental to the social construction of what constitutes knowledge and personal identity, a deep distrust of anything that presents itself in the culture as normal or natural, and a consequent deep commitment to methodologies that seek to unmask power and destabilize what counts as

---

[1] Michel Foucault, *The History of Sexuality*, trans. Robert Hurley, 3 vols. (New York: Vintage, 1990). All three were published prior to Foucault's death in 1984. A fourth volume was published posthumously (New York: Pantheon, 2021).

[2] Judith Butler, *Subjects of Desire: Hegelian Reflections in Twentieth-Century France* (New York: Columbia University Press, 2012).

stable and assured knowledge, social structures, and thus the whole status quo. They are anti-essentialist and deeply critical of claims to absolute truth.

To this we might also add that they also share a concern for sex and sexual desire. In this sense, Marcuse and Foucault both represent responses to a world profoundly altered by the Freudian revolution in psychoanalysis in the early twentieth century. Both are wrestling with the kind of anthropological question I noted in chapter 1 and which really underlies the presenting problems of our modern age: What does it mean to be human, if anything at all, and how does sexual desire function in any answer we might care to give? Freud infamously placed sexual desire at the center of his answer to this question. In doing so, he made the move that would inevitably make politics explicitly sexual. Whether he did that because he was capturing some perennial aspect of human nature or whether he was part of the development of new categories for discourses of power in the late nineteenth century is somewhat immaterial. He did so and thereby helped to create the world to which figures such as Marcuse, Foucault, and Butler then addressed themselves. That is also our world, and so some understanding of how contemporary political discourse was shaped by the thinking of Freud and his impact upon the Frankfurt School via the likes of Wilhelm Reich and Herbert Marcuse is helpful in understanding the critical imagination of today's politics.

Freud, Civilization, and Sexual Desire

We noted earlier that Marxists such as Korsch, Lukács, and the Frankfurt School moved consciousness to center stage in their discussion of why Marxist revolutions had not occurred in advanced industrial societies and why parties of the far right were making significant gains among the proletariat. In the context of the early twentieth century this also meant that the world of Sigmund Freud would inevitably become a matter of political interest. His role in the rise of psychoanalysis is akin to that of Augustine in discussions of grace: later debates inevitably had to go through Freud because of the immense influence he had on the categories and concepts used in the field. For example, his exploration of the unconscious and his arguments concerning the fundamental irrationality of human behavior were clearly going to be of importance to anyone trading in concepts such as false consciousness and wrestling with questions about the attractiveness of authoritarianism.

On the surface, however, Freud and Marxism were very strange bedfellows. Freud was a pessimistic thinker; Marxists tilted strongly in a utopian direction. Freud saw human nature as being at its foundation fundamentally the same across time and space; Marxists saw human nature as the product of history and as changing over time. Clearly, any appropriation of Freud by the followers of Marx would therefore have to be a critical appropriation that corrected his insights in terms of the larger Marxist framework. But before reflecting on the nature of the Marxist appropriation of Freud, it is first useful to grasp a few relevant elements of his thought that proved to be of particular relevance to early critical theory and that provide the background to modern sexual identity politics.

There is the role that Freud sees sexual prohibitions playing within the constitution of society. Freud regards human beings as motivated by the desire for happiness and the avoidance of suffering. This is what Freud calls the *pleasure principle*.[3] To put it in rather colloquial terms, this is what makes human beings tick, the great engine of human life: we want to be happy. Yet Freud does not operate with a subjective notion of happiness whereby it is defined as whatever any individual happens to enjoy. For him, human happiness is found supremely in genital pleasure, that is, orgasmic sex.[4]

It is important to note here that Freud tends to regard males as normative for what it meant to be human, hence the focus on genital pleasure as

---

[3] Sigmund Freud, *Civilization and Its Discontents*, trans. James Strachey (New York: W. W. Norton and Co., 1989), 25.

[4] Freud, *Civilization and Its Discontents*, 33, 56.

central to happiness. To put it bluntly, Freud posits that men find that sexual intercourse eventuating in orgasm is the archetypal form of happiness. The problem, of course, is that if men simply went about the pursuit of sexual pleasure willy-nilly, then the world would rapidly descend into a chaotic nightmare. Women's lives would be utterly wretched as they would find themselves victims of continual sexual violence. Further, the condition of most men would also be problematic as the world would really be the preserve of a few strong males. And even these strong males would only enjoy life for a short period of time as new, younger, stronger claimants to the title of dominant male would always be rising to challenge them.

Because of this, Freud believes that human beings have traded off the possibility of complete (if rather temporary) freedom and happiness for a handful of males for the possibility of extended life for the many.[5] They have done this through forming what Freud calls civilization or what we might refer to as culture: a society governed by a system of rules and behaviors that restrict the sexual aims of individuals. This leads to a certain level of frustration but also to a society that is much safer. Indeed, it is this that makes society "civilized." Here is how Freud himself expresses it:

> It is impossible to overlook the extent to which civilization is built upon a renunciation of instinct, how much it presupposes precisely the non-satisfaction (by suppression, repression, or some other means?) of powerful instincts. This "cultural frustration" dominates the large field of social relationships between human beings.[6]

It should be clear how this will be of significance to the early critical theorists: with a Freudian anthropology, sexual codes are repressive. They stop people acting on their desires. They therefore stop people from being who they would desire themselves to be. This is not necessarily a bad thing socially, for aforementioned reasons. But it does inhibit the free

---

[5] Freud, 73.
[6] Freud, 51–52.

development of the individual by socializing him into a world where his sexual desires are repressed.

This concept of repression offers suggestive parallels to the Marxist critique of bourgeois society as oppressive. To translate Freud into Marxist terms, sexual codes are a form of ideology, establishing and enforcing a particular understanding of normative human nature and how humans should behave toward each other. This is not a novel development for post-Freud Marxism. Indeed, the theme of sexual codes as being part of economic oppression is present in Marxism from its early expressions, for example Engels's critique of the economic origins of the family, *The Origin of the Family, Private Property, and the State* (1884). Here he connected the rise of the monogamous patriarchal family to changing economic conditions and saw the family emerging as "the cellular form of civilized society," which anticipated in microcosm the larger conflicts that would develop in society at large.[7] This critique of family, specifically in terms of the sexual codes which define and maintain it, will be a staple of critical theorists, such as Reich and Marcuse. What is novel is the sophisticated taxonomy and understanding of human psychology that Freud provides, particularly with its focus on sexual gratification as central to human nature and personal fulfillment.

The suppression of dark sexual instincts raises a further question for Freud: What happens to all of this pent-up sexual energy? Freud's answer is that it is redirected, or "sublimated" to use the technical term, into other activities.[8] Religion, art, politics, science, and sport—cultural pursuits that we might be tempted to take at face value, as being intrinsically meritorious and ends in themselves—become in Freud's world manifestations of the frustration of erotic desire. Religion calms the fear of death. Art gives pleasure—not as intense as sex, for sure, but something that takes the edge

---

[7] See *The Marx-Engels Reader*, ed. Robert C. Tucker, 2nd ed. (London: W. W. Norton, 1978), 739.

[8] Freud, *Civilization and Its Discontents*, 51–52.

off the sexual frustrations that are a necessary concomitant of civilized life. Politics and sport offer avenues for conflict and struggle, for those destructive impulses we all have, and yet they do so in a manner that restricts their aim and channels them toward relatively harmless outcomes. The boxer does not kill his opponent but merely beats him in a carefully regulated and controlled environment. The American does not kill the Russian but achieves real feelings of superiority and satisfaction when Team USA beats Team Russia in a soccer match. Even the pleasure of solving a scientific problem, like that gained from painting a picture or listening to a piece of music, brings momentary happiness. And, at a more sinister level, war allows for the explosion, still within a context controlled by civilization broadly considered, for the satisfaction of our most dark and destructive impulses. Again, this will be important for the development of critical theory. Refracted through a Marxist lens, these compensations start to look like manipulative diversions that distract from the miserable state of human beings laboring under a system of bourgeois sexual morality designed to maintain an oppressive political system. As Marx saw religion as the opium of the people, so Freudianism allows for this opiate-like effect to be seen across the full range of cultural pursuits.

Freud and the Structure of Human Psychology

This overall theory of civilizations rests upon Freud's elaborate psychoanalytic anthropology. For him, human behavior is shaped by three things: the Id, the Ego, and the Superego. The Id is the primitive part of the mind, characterized by instinct in the form of dark and destructive desires that, if unleashed, would lead to the violence that civilization is designed to repress. Occasionally, the Id will emerge—in those dreams in which we do things we would never do in real life or when we explode with uncharacteristic rage or act in a transgressive way that we later look back on with incomprehension—moments when we might describe ourselves as "losing control," which is itself an interesting and suggestive turn of phrase. Those are the instances when the Id asserts itself and the usual controls—Ego and Superego—prove incapable of suppressing it. Such moments are also (disturbingly from a "civilized" perspective) rather pleasurable precisely because they allow the individual to be who he really is, without the controls of civilization forcing him to be false to his desires.[9]

The Ego is the conscious, rational component of being human that acts as a mediator between the desires of the Id and the requirements of life in the real world. We might describe the ego as the "self" that we are conscious of being. Like the Id, the Ego wants to pursue pleasure and avoid pain; but, unlike the Id, the Ego seeks to develop realistic strategies for achieving these that balance immediate pleasure against long-term consequences. Yes, killing that enemy who has insulted and infuriated me might bring immediate and intense satisfaction but then it might lead to life imprisonment or even a death sentence. Thus, I control my rage and suppress the desire of the Id, perhaps by rationalizing to myself the idea that my enemy will be punished in the end anyway, either in this world or the next. Consequently, I do not kill him, postponing my pleasure for the sake of avoiding pain. This is what Freud characterizes as the *reality principle* in which the Ego balances the desire for immediate pleasure over against the long-term consequences. Again, a happily married man away on a business trip may well feel a desire to sleep with the woman he has been flirting with at the hotel bar but he resists the temptation to do so because the moment of intense pleasure such would provide is outweighed by the ongoing and devastating problems and pain it will introduce into his relationship with his wife.

The third concept, the Superego, connects the Id and the Ego. This is one of the most important elements of Freud's thought for understanding

---

[9] "The feeling of happiness derived from the satisfaction of a wild, instinctual impulse untamed by the ego is incomparably more intense than that derived from sating an instinct that has been tamed. The irresistibility of perverse instincts, and perhaps the attraction in general of forbidden things finds an economic explanation here." Freud, *Civilization and Its Discontents*, 29.

his usefulness to critical theorists. The Superego provides the foundation for what we might call the voice of conscience. It represents the behavioral codes that cultivate pleasurable feelings (such as pride or satisfaction) and unpleasant feelings (guilt/shame) relative to thoughts we might have and actions we might perform. As such, it operates as that which regulates what society would deem our moral compass and behavior. The Superego involves the internalization of society's values so that they become intuitive. For Freud, it is formed early in a child's life and is therefore shaped more than anything by the family context.

We can illustrate this with a simple example. Why do most of us not steal? It is not primarily because there are laws that forbid it and punishments prescribed by such laws if we are caught. Most of us do not steal because we simply "know" that it is wrong. If we were tempted to steal, say, a purse someone had just accidentally left on a park bench, our conscience would pinch us, we would start to feel shame even at having had the thought (and we would thus subject ourselves to a kind of mental pain), and we would therefore resist the temptation. We might even pick the purse up and return it to the person, in which case we would feel a little warm glow of pride at having behaved so well. The same applies to that man in the bar we used as the previous example. He resists the temptation presented by the woman he has been flirting with because the subsequent strain of lying to his wife about his infidelity would cause immense feelings of guilt and make his life miserable. This is the Superego in action, psychologically punishing transgression and rewarding obedience in accordance with the moral standards that were internalized in our childhood, through the teaching of our parents, school, and church.

The key significance of Freud's Id-Ego-Superego construction, the point that makes it so very helpful to Marxist critical theory, lies in the way it separates the individual conscious self (the Ego) from the social personality (the

Superego).[10] To put this another way, what Freud's distinctions do is drive a wedge, and thereby create potential tension between how I experience my self and who society demands that I be. This offers an obvious structural parallel with a Marxism that sees alienation—that disconnect between who a person should be and what society demands that he be—at the heart of its political critique. What will emerge in the Frankfurt School's appropriation of Freud is that such alienation must be understood in terms that give a significant place to sex and sexual desire.

It should also be clear from this that the Superego shares an affinity with the notion of false consciousness. Both refer to socially constructed and then internalized ways of thinking that drive the decision making of the individual. Such decision making seems to the individual natural and rational and is backed up by a raft of cultivated instincts of which the individual might be completely unaware. The false consciousness of Lukács and Korsch is a natural bedfellow with the Superego of Freud.

Freud, Infant Sexuality, and the Oedipus Complex

One further aspect of Freud that is important for the Frankfurt School appropriation of his thought is his understanding of how the Superego is formed. Key to this is the Oedipus complex. This is the name he gives to the psychological results of the relationship between children and parents, an idea which itself rests upon the notion that sexual desire is a basic part of human nature from the very start, even in infancy.

Freud sets out his case for infant sexuality in his *Three Essays on the Theory of Sexuality*, a book which brought to an end "that epoch of cultural innocence in which infancy and childhood were regarded as themselves

---

[10] See Philip Rieff, *Freud: The Mind of the Moralist* (New York: Viking, 1959), 59–61.

innocent."[11] Freud here offers a taxonomy of growth from infancy to adulthood which focuses on the nature and direction of sexual desire, with each stage marked by fixation on a particular part of the child's physical anatomy. First comes the oral stage, in which the mouth is central to desire and where breast feeding is thus an activity with sexual significance, as is the act of thumb sucking.[12] This is followed by the anal stage, when the control of bowel movements becomes a preoccupation.[13] Then there is the phallic phase where sexual satisfaction via masturbation is key, to be followed by a stage where sexual activity is minimized, even latent.[14] Finally, there is the genital phase, marked by a turning away from masturbation and toward finding a real-life sexual partner, with engagement in full sexual intercourse as its consummation.[15]

The idea of infant sexuality is not simply important for Freud or even for those in the Frankfurt School who draw on his work. It is arguably central to modern political culture where many of the most heated debates of our own day focus on childhood sexuality and gender identity. What Freud is arguing is that inner desire, specifically inner sexual desire as it relates to our own bodies, is the foundation of who we really are from our earliest moments onwards. That has an obvious implication, though Freud does not care to draw them out: it politicizes sex. In a world where you are your sexual desires, then rules about how you can behave sexually are in reality rules less about behavior and more about who society will allow you to be.

---

[11] Steven Marcus, introduction to *Three Essays on the Theory of Sexuality*, by Sigmund Freud, trans. and ed. James Strachey (New York: Basic Books, 2000), xxxii. Anthony Giddens also credits this work with providing a scientific foundation for the social acceptance of sexual diversity in Western society. Giddens, *The Transformation of Intimacy: Sexuality, Love, and Eroticism in Modern Societies* (Stanford, CA: Stanford University Press, 1992), 32–34.

[12] Freud, *Three Essays*, 45–47.

[13] Freud, 51–53.

[14] Freud, 42–45.

[15] Freud, 73–74.

And it also makes the family a focal point of political conflict as families are the places where infants and children receive their initiation into society's prevailing sexual codes.

This brings us to Freud's notion of the Oedipus complex, named after the mythical king of Thebes who was fated to kill his father and then marry his mother, albeit without him realizing what he was doing. Freud saw this complex as central to the formation of Superego. His argument is as follows: an infant child experiences sexual desire for the parent of the opposite sex and a deep fear of (and desire to exclude) the parent of the same sex. So little male children desire their mothers and are terrified of their fathers because of the latter's obvious strength and the fact that they have an intimate access to the mother denied to the child. The net result is that the child wishes to murder his father and have sex with his mother. Clearly, this is a good example of the kind of sexual impulse that would prove socially disastrous if left unchecked. And so for Freud, normal childhood development involves the overcoming of this condition and ultimately the child's identification with the parent of the same sex. This is part of the healthy formation of the Superego, that which cultivates feelings of guilt and shame. The child learns to feel guilt for desiring to kill the father and wanting to have a sexual relationship with the mother. We might recast this by saying that the Superego comes to play in life the role of moral authority initially taken by the father. It is the internalization of the behaviors necessary to please the father figure.[16]

This theme in Freud will be significant for the early critical theorists in their struggle to understand the appeal of figures such as Hitler and Mussolini to the working classes. The Fuehrer and the Duce, so the argument will go, are strong father figures. Children raised to respect such in their own families, and indeed to love and to depend upon them, will be

---

[16] See Sigmund Freud, *The Ego and the Id*, trans. Joan Riviere (New York: W. W. Norton, 1989), 22–36.

attracted to precisely the same figures in the broader political world of their adulthood.

But there is one significant problem for any Marxist appropriation of Freud. Freud is, at least from a Marxist perspective, an essentialist when it comes to human nature. To put this in simple terms, he believes that human nature at its core does not change significantly over time. The desires of the Id and the structure of Ego and Superego remain as constants throughout the history of the human race. General taboos against incest, cannibalism, and unfettered killing are hardy perennials of human civilization because these are necessary for any civilization anywhere, at least to Freud's modern Western mind. This clearly stands in significant tension with Marxism, given that the latter is acutely attuned to the historical nature of humanity. For Marxists, the meaning and significance of human nature is tied to historical process. To be a human in Pericles's Athens, Charlemagne's court, and Napoleon's France were three different things. And Marxism with a Hegelian twist, as in that of the Frankfurt School, is very aware of the historical nature of the human mind and the way that it thinks, that is, its consciousness. The challenge, then, is how Marxists might appropriate Freud without committing themselves to a very un-Marxist essentialism.

Nevertheless, Freudian themes—sexual desire, the importance of the family, the Oedipus complex—will all inform the program of the critical theorists. As they engage with Freud, they will come to frame the cultural revolution for which they are looking in profoundly sexual terms, something that continues to be the case, perhaps even more intensely so, today with the rise to influence of militant advocates of LGBTQ+ rights. Indeed, it is especially in the critical theorists' iconoclastic attack on sexual morality and on the institution of the family that a clear line of continuity between the early Frankfurt School and our current political iterations of critical theory can be most obviously seen.

Appropriating Freud: Wilhelm Reich

The key to understanding the usefulness of Freud to the critical theorists lies in their ability to take his theories and refract them through an historicist lens. For figures such as Herbert Marcuse, Theodor Adorno, and Wilhelm Reich, Freud's view of culture as repressive, specifically in the sexual realm, was fundamentally sound as an analysis of the present. What Freud fails to do from their perspective is understand that the specific repressions he identifies are themselves not the necessary concomitant of being a civilized human. Rather they are social constructions that are part of the ideological structure of society as it exists. We might put it this way: they are repressions necessary to maintain bourgeois society in particular, not human society in general. This thinking is likely familiar to many readers in the criticism that is often voiced of "bourgeois" or "middle class" morality and values. Such things represent a particular way of life—and a way of life that its critics might well describe using the term "inauthentic" as a means of implying its falsity and manipulative nature. Substitute those adjectives for "white," "male," or "cisgender" and the structural similarities with much modern critical theoretical parlance is obvious.

The criticism of Freud by the Frankfurt School can be summarized as the belief that he fails to be critical enough of his own theories and instead grants them a natural status that hides the ideological function that lies behind them. Freud himself is a bourgeois and, brilliant as he is, fails to see the background of his own thinking that tilts him in an essentialist direction. His theories may well involve a criticism of society, or religion, and of certain sexual attitudes, but they are ultimately put in the service of helping individuals overcome their neuroses, not of transforming the overall nature of human society itself.

Reich makes this point clear in *The Mass Psychology of Fascism* when he notes that it is not cultural activity in itself that requires, for example, repression of children's sexual urges but only certain forms of cultural activity, specifically those of the bourgeois/capitalist epoch that require strong families to produce a compliant and submissive workforce.[17] Nevertheless, once the historicist point was acknowledged, Freud became the basic theoretical lodestar for the critical theory of Reich and company with regard to the rise of Nazism and Fascism.[18]

Reich's *Mass Psychology of Fascism* is itself an excellent example of how Freudian categories can be deployed to explain the false consciousness of the working class. Reflecting on why traditional housewives—those, from Reich's perspective, with most to gain from the kind of social liberation promised by the parties of the left—are so attracted to Nazism, he makes the following argument. Proletarian women who are liberated are part of the industrial workforce. They are therefore economically exploited by the capitalist system in which they are wage slaves. But they are liberated; they have a level of political self-consciousness that pushes them leftward in their thinking. Yet there are also housewives who suffer exactly the same kind of economic hardship, but while the former are more likely to vote left, the latter tend to vote for the conservative parties of the right and even for the Fascists. Why? Reich's answer is that, while economic deprivation promotes rebellion, sexual repression as embodied in the traditional family structure promotes acquiescence to the status quo. And the reason for this is that sexual repression leads to an internalization of repression and a consequent fear of liberation, particularly sexual liberation. Indeed, the stay-at-home mother is tightly bound to her own sense of identity to precisely those institutions that cultivate and impose sexual repression: the nuclear family, with its ties of obligation, and to the church, with its stringent moral codes. She

---

[17] Wilhelm Reich, *The Mass Psychology of Fascism*, trans. Mary Boyd Higgins (New York: Farrar, Straus, and Giroux, 1970), 28–29.

[18] In the monumental study of the personality types drawn to authoritarian movements and leaders, the Frankfurt School acknowledged that it "leant most heavily" on Freud for the theoretical understanding of the structure of personality: see Theodor Adorno, Else Frenkel-Brunswik, Daniel J. Levinson, and Nevitt Sanford, *The Authoritarian Personality* (London: Verso, 2019), 5.

cannot break free, for to do so would lead to destitution and social deprivation. More than that, both institutions—family and church—wield power through the guilt they have cultivated in their members with regard to sexual transgression. The Superego keeps the housewife in check through its feelings of shame with regard to liberation and pride with regard to raising a family, sexual fidelity, and keeping a household. Her conservatism is not enforced by some heteronomous and violent external power. She does not stay at home with the children under fear of arrest or imprisonment if she does otherwise. This behavior is decided by her own Ego in its negotiation with the Superego. In short, her sexual repression is a decisive formative factor in her consciousness, such that she has no interest even in hearing about any economic scheme that might liberate her and improve her condition. Indeed, to challenge the economic structure would be, from her perspective, to go against the Superego and to feel guilt and shame in betraying that upon which she depends like a child upon a parent. For that reason, the housewife votes for the reactionary parties of the right.[19]

What is particularly interesting here is the way Reich weaves together the Freudian concern with sexual codes and the traditional Marxist concern for religion. Family and church work to repress sexual liberation as a means of repressing the desire for political liberation. These are the institutions that play a vital role in the formation of the Superego. We noted in chapter 2 that Marx saw religion as promoting what later theorists would call false consciousness and thus as offering an account of why religion remained attractive even after the Enlightenment had done such damage to it and how it kept its adherents from truly understanding the poverty of their material conditions. Religion is, for the classical Marxist, a reactionary ideology. Here Reich locates its power not so much in its dulling of present pain through promises of eternal bliss in the afterlife. Rather, he sees its significance as lying in its sexually repressive function. This is in line with Freud's own understanding of religion: it exists in part to articulate and

---

[19] Reich, *Mass Psychology*, 30–31.

enforce sexual taboos. It is thus sex, and not religion, that is more basic to human life. Indeed, for Reich, the church is significant in this context because it continues the sexually repressive work that the family has already established as foundational:

> The interlacing of the socio-economic structure with the sexual structure of society and the structural reproduction of society take place in the first four or five years and in the authoritarian family. The church only continues this function later. Thus, the authoritarian state gains an enormous interest in the authoritarian family. It becomes the factory in which the state's structure and ideology are moulded.[20]

Reich thus broadens the lines along which religion must be critiqued: it must not only be exposed as a metaphysical sham that promises mythical rewards in the afterlife that dull the real pain of actual life; it must be understood as playing a role in the sexual economy and therefore primarily be exposed as sexually repressive and as working in tandem with the idea of the strong family unit. It continues the internalization of bourgeois sexual codes that have been set in place by the family in the earliest years of childhood and thus fosters a Superego that leads to acceptance of the status quo. That is why political parties, particularly those led by a strong father figure, can count on the loyalty of housewives: they will change nothing of any significance.

Of course, this is one of the areas where critical theory collides with traditional views. Are families not good things? Is the stable unit of a loving home comprised of a father and a mother to look after their children not a boon to society at large? Are such notions not simple common sense? For Reich and those like him, this is exactly how they would expect the typical member of society to react, with such reactions merely indicating how deeply the mentality of the culture is gripped by false consciousness. Just

---

[20] Reich, 30.

as Marx proclaimed the critique of religion to be a necessary component of revolutionary thinking, so Reich and those influenced by him place sexual morality in the same role. Critical thinking requires scrutiny of the ways society instinctively and intuitively understands itself, especially in those matters which seem particularly obvious and unassailable as truths. Nowhere is this truer, Reich believes, than in the realm of sexual codes. And therefore, critique of sexual codes with a view to their abolition becomes the path to social revolution.

Yet sexual codes are not the only means by which people are manipulated. The sublimation of sexual desire, its redirection toward other things of which Freud speaks, also plays a role in Reich's understanding of the problems that exist in the German society of his day. Eroticism is significant in understanding the appeal of the violent politics of the Nazi Party. We noted in chapter 5 that Horkheimer and Adorno thought Fascism the result of guilt for inner homosexual desires. Reich offers a different understanding: military uniforms, of a kind with which Nazism and Fascism clothed themselves, project an image of sexual allure. Military service is marketed as something that makes men virile and irresistible to women. And the violence that marks war is, of course, something that appeals to the dark and destructive elements of the Id. Natural sexual desire is frustrated and thence perverted through repressive bourgeois culture into something more sadistic: warmongering political nationalism. Hence the attraction of ideologies such as Nazism that sanction street violence. This functions as a substitute gratification for that which a normal, healthy sex life would provide in a properly ordered socialist world.[21]

While this may seem at first glance to be nothing more than the speculative musings of a cultural commentator overly preoccupied with reducing everything to sex, Reich is pointing to something important: human behavior, especially evil and destructive human behavior, cannot be explained in terms of pure rationality. Anyone who has observed video footage of people

---

[21] Reich, 31–32.

looting storefronts during what started as peaceful political protests will likely have been struck by the looks often not so much of rage but of exhilaration on their faces. Violence is not a rational thing, yet it exerts a dark and compelling influence over human beings. How many of us enjoy crime dramas or find the evil characters in movies to be the most fascinating, even attractive, in a strange, albeit unwholesome, way? Reich's analysis in terms of sexual repression of the appeal of Nazism and its concomitant cult of violence and power may ultimately be reductive, but it is hard not to acknowledge that he is at least taking seriously the fact that a simple explanation of Hitler and his gang in terms of economics or class conflict is not adequate. Nazism did not answer a rational need; it satisfied more sinister desires.[22]

In all of this, Reich is drawing out an obvious—and highly significant— implication of Freud's thought, one we previously noted and which has come to shape our own contemporary political and cultural landscape: once human beings are understood as being defined by sexual desire, the regulation of sexual desire must be understood not so much as restricting behavior as policing identity. In short, Freud gives Reich a conceptual apparatus that means that the cultivation of revolutionary consciousness requires the dismantling of bourgeois sexual morality and its central institution, that of the family, and then its redirection in ways that are, at least from a bourgeois perspective, morally shapeless. For to argue that sex has a moral shape is to impose upon human beings a definition of what they should be, to assume

---

[22] In a 1940 review of Hitler's *Mein Kampf,* George Orwell (a man of the left, but no Marxist or critical theorist) commented that it was precisely the irrational violence of Nazism that made Hitler so appealing, offering the following sardonic comment by way of illustration: "The Socialist who finds his children playing with soldiers is usually upset, but he is never able to think of a substitute for the tin soldiers; tin pacifists somehow won't do." Hitler, he observes, understands that human beings do not just want comfort; they want "struggle, self-sacrifice, not to mention drums, flags, and loyalty parades. However they may be as economic theories, Fascism and Nazism are psychologically far sounder than any hedonistic conception of life. The same is probably true of Stalin's militarized version of socialism." George Orwell, *Essays* (New York: Alfred A. Knopf, 2002), 251.

a certain moral essence that defines human nature. Such codes are inevitably alienating in that they will serve the bourgeois economic order that is by definition unjust. In other words, revolution requires a culture fully committed to making the sexual nature of human beings obvious and destroying any notion that sex in itself possesses an intrinsic moral shape to which human beings must conform in order to be truly human. Again, to impose a moral shape on sexual desire is to impose a normative notion of what it means to be a human being.

Reich is clear about the political implications of such a move. Indeed, at the heart of his major work of social criticism, *The Sexual Revolution*, is a sustained and detailed polemic against the notions of monogamous marriage and the stable family unit. As noted earlier, Reich sees these as the breeding grounds for conservative and reactionary citizens, and they are therefore to be dismantled via the revolutionary government taking control of society's sexual education.

And the concepts of the family and sexual fidelity in the context of monogamous marriage are to serve a threefold social function: economically they connect to private ownership, providing a means by which the bourgeoisie can protect its property via blood ties and family lineage; politically they embody in microcosm the submission to authority that bourgeois society at large requires; and socially they keep women and children dependent upon the male breadwinner.[23]

---

[23] Wilhelm Reich, *The Sexual Revolution*, trans. Therese Pol (New York: Farrar, Straus and Giroux, 1974), 135–36. Our era may be very different, given the normalization of women in the workplace and of childcare, but that would likely not impress Reich, as the basic dynamic shaping the raising and education of children is still that of capitalism, though now the relationship of family loyalty has been attenuated by that of the demands of the market upon the individual. Yet it is quite clear that the liberalizing of sexual codes has proved entirely compatible with the economies of advanced capitalism and that sexual liberation has not proved to be the force for Marxist revolution that he assumed it would.

The importance of this is that it provides us with a great example of what critical theory does. It is radical in the truest sense of the word. We noted in the work of Lukács and then of Horkheimer that the critical approach being proposed by this stream of Marxist thought is not reformist. Reich is not looking at monogamy or the family and seeing that there are some problematic areas which need to be addressed in order to make them function better as institutions. He is not, for example, proposing that paternity leave or changes to the tax code might be used to improve marriage and the family by eliminating certain pressures that create problems. Nor is he suggesting that what is needed is a sounder educational system that would help parents school their offspring in matters of sexual behavior in a more balanced way. Not at all. For Reich, the very institutions of marriage and the family, both their social reality and the ideological rationale which they embody, cultivate, and perpetuate, need to be dismantled wholesale. As with later iterations of critical theory—whether of gender or of race—the goal is not the reform of the system but the replacement of the system with something wholly different, for the current system only really exists for the purpose of maintaining specific forms of injustice.[24]

This is why Reich offers a critique of marriage which, in classic critical theory style, focuses upon the contradiction which it represents. There is, Reich asserts, a basic contradiction between the economic and sexual interests that marriage represents. Traditional monogamous marriage meets the economic demands of bourgeois capitalism: a stable unit for the production of children and for the domestic work of the woman which thus enables the man to give more of his time and effort to his employer. It also reinforces the idea that well-being depends upon the stability of the system via the stability of the institutions by which it is constituted.

---

[24] See, for example, the recent work of Sophie Lewis, *Abolish the Family: A Manifesto for Care and Liberation* (London: Verso, 2022). The connection of the abolition of the family to "care" and "liberation" is entirely consonant with the earlier arguments of Reich.

Furthermore, it provides a context for sexual activity that is controlled and where the natural consequences of sex (pregnancy and children) do not create chaos for society as a whole by posing serious challenges to the social structure. Sexually, however, marriage also arouses the desire of those involved (particularly the woman).[25] This means that the demand for monogamy that lies at the heart of marriage is itself a deeply repressive and problematic thing. Marriage promises sexual satisfaction and releases sexual desire from its repressions but then ends up frustrating it by demanding the impossible: that human sexual desire and satisfaction be found in sexual relations with only one person and that for life. In a sense, therefore, it is simply an extension of the sexual repression that applied before marriage. So it attempts to provide the economic system with a stabilizing institution but that institution is itself profoundly unstable. Nor will laws on divorce solve the problem because in a patriarchal economy divorce simply places the woman in a very vulnerable social and economic position. In short, marriage dooms the parties to unhappiness, an alienation both sexual and economic, but that unhappiness cannot be solved unless there is a wholesale restructuring of society that abolishes the family unit in favor of something utterly different.[26]

To use the terminology of more recent critical theorists, Reich is arguing that marriage is systemically unjust. In its very essence it serves to perpetuate the problem of sexual repression and thereby props up the broader bourgeois culture. It is thus antithetical to human flourishing, and it therefore does the exact opposite of what it claims to do. It cannot be reformed; it must be abolished. The parallel with arguments, for example, about American democracy as systemically racist—as pretending to give everybody an equal voice in elections while yet marginalizing significant sections

---

[25] Reich notes that virginity is prized, but that male sexual activity before marriage is generally not regarded by the society of his day with the same censoriousness as that of women: *Sexual Revolution*, 147.

[26] Reich, 147–53.

of the population—should be obvious. Systemic criticism is not a new thing for critical theory. It is there in Reich's commentary on marriage. Indeed, it is a key component of the principles of critical theory as adumbrated in the work of Lukács and expounded by Horkheimer.

It is also worth noting a further implication of Reich's thinking that stands in clear continuity with many of the debates surrounding the progressive politics of our own day: the rejection of the authority of biological relationships in constituting a good and just society. In Reich's thought, parents have no intrinsic authority of a kind that might be used to hinder a child's sexual development. For example:

> The free society will provide ample room and security for the gratification of natural needs. Thus, it will not only not prohibit a love relationship between two adolescents of the opposite sex but will give it all manner of social support. Such a society will not only not prohibit the child's masturbation but, on the contrary, will probably conclude that any adult who hinders the development of the child's sexuality should be severely dealt with.[27]

The point is clear: parents who try to teach their children sexual codes that hinder the free sexual development that Reich considers necessary for true human freedom will find themselves subject to state intervention. In short, "parental rights" are social constructs that serve a particular form of society; given this, the very notion of parenthood must shift toward a functional definition that places actions, rather than intrinsic biological relationship, at the heart of the concept.

Again, this is consistent with developments in our own day. The whole transgender issue has brought this to the fore in an unprecedented manner, with schools claiming exclusive rights to know a child's chosen gender identity and feeling no obligation to share that information with

---

[27] Reich, 23.

parents. It is surely an interesting situation where an educational institution considers itself to have the authority to definitively know who a child is (according to its own gender philosophy) and to deny that information to the child's actual parents. This trend is represented by the broader functional definition of parenthood that is emerging both in our culture at large and in legal thinking: to be a parent is increasingly to fulfill certain defined tasks, not to have a biological relationship to a child which brings with it certain obligations. On what basis could such a thing become imaginable? On the basis of a view of the world and of human identity and relationships of the kind articulated by Reich, where the biological family is viewed as a socially constructed and repressive tool of the broader political interests of bourgeois society, specifically as they require the cultivation and internalization of specific sexual codes in children.

Marcuse, Sex, and '68

While Reich's work is foundational for understanding the appropriation of Freud by Marxist critical theory, it is Herbert Marcuse who proved the most influential sexual revolutionary in terms of inspiring the political revolutionaries of 1968, the year of student protests across Europe and the United States, and the various social changes that flowed thereafter.[28]

Marcuse, like Reich, accepts the broad framework of Freud's thought while also subjecting it to historicist criticism, though in a somewhat more elaborate fashion. He sees human civilization as being driven historically by *Ananke* or scarcity—basically the lack of those things by which human beings sustain their existence. This forced people to work together to produce sufficient food and goods to survive.[29] With the advent of capitalism, however, it is clear that old concerns about survival are mitigated. We can

---

[28] The central text for this is Herbert Marcuse, *Eros and Civilization: A Philosophical Inquiry into Freud* (Boston: Beacon, 1966).

[29] Marcuse, *Eros and Civilization*, 138.

all understand why this is the case: Various factors, such as the tremendous power of industrial production and increasing scientific control over
productive processes, mean that the constant threat of *Ananke* disappears.
Thus, where once a family farmed the land with manually operated ploughs
and scythes in total dependence upon the seasons and with little knowledge
of or access to fertilizers and pesticides, now their use of tractors, combine
harvesters, and an array of chemical agents has massively increased the yield
per capita of the agricultural workforce. The same applies to factories: for
example, where once a single garment of cloth took many days to make,
now a machine operated by one man can produce hundreds, maybe thou-
sands in a day.

This then raises the obvious question for Marcuse: If sexual codes
existed to repress sexual activity and drive it into the domestic sphere in
order to harness people's communal energy so as to stave off *Ananke*, why
do these same codes persist now that scarcity of essential goods is no longer
an existential threat? Here Marcuse distinguishes repression into two kinds:
basic and surplus. Basic repression will always be necessary because some
curbing of individual human instincts is required for human society to operate at any level. Surplus repression, however, refers to repressive codes and
practices that go beyond what a free society requires to stave off *Ananke*. In
his own words:

> *Surplus-repression:* the restrictions necessitated by social domination.
> This is distinguished from (basic) *repression:* the "modifications" of
> the instincts necessary for the perpetuation of the human race in
> civilization.[30]

The question as to why surplus repression exists, therefore, has for Marcuse
a political answer: it exists in order to maintain the unjust power structures
and forms of life in capitalist society. It is not that capitalism keeps people
on the verge of physical starvation. Rather it is connected to the way in

[30] Marcuse, 35.

which bourgeois society maintains scarcity even when there are, in theory, enough goods to go around. *Ananke* plays a role as the basic motivator for both kinds of repression, basic and surplus, but it does so for the latter—and here is the Marxist twist—because capitalism as a system depends upon an unequal distribution of goods and upon cultivating the fear that any individual who breaks with the system will find themselves destitute.

It also depends upon the invention of unnecessary needs—luxury goods that fulfill no real purpose, built in obsolescence that makes useful goods redundant or useless within a short period of time. In short, the characteristics of what we would call the consumer society are predicated on the creation of desires, on the capitalist system's ability to fulfill them, and on the system always threatening to generate shortages whereby the desires will not be met.[31] We can all likely understand this point: the desire for smartphones has been created by the smartphone industry; that each generation of smartphones quickly becomes obsolete (whether because of a short battery life or the constant transformation of what count as cool aesthetics that indicate the owner's status) is not a bug in the system but rather a central feature. The smartphone industry is designed to create its own needs, desires, and shortages.

This kind of society also resonates with the notion of reification we noted in Lukács: the initial free association of individuals to stave off Ananke has taken on a life of its own; no longer is it dependent upon people but people are now dependent upon it. It creates the needs that it then satisfies, establishing the absolute dependence of the individual upon the system. The persistence of surplus repression is thus also a function of reification.

Marcuse also speaks of what he calls the *performance principle*. This is his historicist appropriation of Freud's reality principle.[32] For Marcuse, the

---

[31] Marcuse's major elaboration of this is his *One-Dimensional Man: Studies in the Ideology of Advanced Industrial Society* (London: Routledge, 2002).

[32] "*Performance principle:* the prevailing historical form of the *reality principle*." Marcuse, *Eros and Civilization*, 35.

performance principle is the product of history and of social conditions. Thus the criteria by which it makes its judgments about delayed gratification and about how and where to repress the instinctive drive for pleasure are those of the society in which the individual finds himself. So, for example, in capitalist society individuals are taught to save money and to work hard in order that they will have a good and well-funded retirement. The values of thrift are thus an integral part of the performance principle. The same is true with sexual discipline: the young unmarried man does not sleep with the young woman with whom he is in love even though he desperately wants to do so. He knows that such behavior could lead to a pregnancy that will impose social protocols upon him (marriage, lifelong responsibilities, financial obligations) that outweigh the brief moment of sexual pleasure he might enjoy. The key for Marcuse is that the performance principle can be changed—by technology or by a revolutionary transformation of the economic system, for example.

We might illustrate this by thinking of how the advent of the pill and easy access to abortion have changed the performance principle with regard to sexual behavior since the 1960s. Prior to this, sexual codes restricting sexual relations to monogamous married couples made sense. If previous generations of men and women had simply engaged in promiscuous sex, then the result would have been socially chaotic: lots of babies born to women who were already economically vulnerable in a patriarchal society. *Ananke* was thus a real threat, and monogamy made perfect sense. Once you have the pill and access to abortion, however, then monogamy ceases to have an economic rationale. Sex can become something enjoyed for pleasure without any need for long-term commitment because pregnancy can be easily avoided or terminated when necessary. So why does monogamous marriage remain an ideal, and why are those (particularly women) who flout its principles regarded as morally deviant? Marcuse's answer is simple: the old sexual codes now articulate the power of family, the church, and the middle class who wish to maintain their position of dominance via an economic system that keeps *Ananke* a reality for those who lack power. Think, for example, of the rates of single-parent families in inner-city America and the social problems that has generated. Marcuse would argue that such problems do not derive from single parenthood but rather from the capitalist system that assumes affluent stable families while yet unequally distributing wealth so as to ensure that those who do not fit into such a mold are weak, vulnerable, and dysfunctional. It is not the promiscuity of the populace that is the problem. It is the system within which this promiscuity occurs.

Marcuse differs from both Freud and Reich, however, in his understanding of the role of genital satisfaction in thinking about sex. For Freud, as mentioned previously, the growth into adulthood is marked by the moving of the focal point of sexual gratification, focusing ultimately upon the genitals. Genital orgasm thus becomes the center of pleasure. Reich is similar: it is orgasm that plays the critical role. Marcuse, however, sees this shifting focus as involving a steady restriction of sex toward the reproductive function and the limitation of the body's sexualization to the genitals. As such, sexual, erotic desire is focused on the private, domestic sphere and kept out of the workplace and labor practices of society.[33]

This creation of a private sphere, separate from the public, economic realm, is something of wide interest to the early Frankfurt School, as we shall see when we note the criticisms they make of the culture industry and consumerism. From a Marcuse framework, what is important here is that this is also part of his revision/criticism of Freud and his fixation of adult sexuality on the genitals. He regards Freud as reinforcing bourgeois culture because this restriction of sexualization to the genitals has two unfortunate consequences. First, it desexualizes the rest of the body and its activities. Second, it tilts the purpose of sex strongly toward reproduction and hence toward the importance of the monogamous family. Both of these are functions of the capitalist reality principle.

---

[33] Marcuse, 200.

The first connects to the dehumanized nature of labor in the capitalist economy where people are not free individuals but fungible commodities that can be thought of in terms of their labor value rather than their intrinsic humanity. Once work becomes drudgery, once laborers are alienated from the fruits of their labor, they are dehumanized. There is no coming together of the pleasure principle and the reality principle. Alienation is thus profound and tending always under capitalism to become worse. What Marcuse calls for is the abolition of the sexual repression that has led to this narrow focus on the private sphere as the place for pleasure. Work itself is to be a pleasurable exercise, and this can be achieved by returning to the polymorphous sexuality of childhood:

> Reactivation of polymorphous and narcissistic sexuality ceases to be a threat to culture-building if the organism exists not as an instrument of alienated labor but as a subject of self-realization—in other words, if socially useful work is at the same time the transparent satisfaction of an individual need.[34]

Exactly what this kind of talk means is unclear and likely only plausible to one like Marcuse whose work no doubt gave him intrinsic pleasure. Indeed, like so much of the utopian dimension in Marcuse's thought, he is more confident in asserting that utopia can be achieved than in describing exactly what form it will take in any detail. How the reactivation of polymorphous sexuality involving the whole body can in practice bring together the pleasure principle and the reality principle in a factory or a coal mine is not obvious, nor does Marcuse care to speculate in detail how such an interesting confluence of Hegel, Marx, and Freud might occur. But Marcusan fantasies aside, what is important for our study is simply this: sexual codes and theories are for Marcuse deeply political and embedded in the history of oppression and intimately connected to the way the values of society, with all of its unjust, oppressive structures, are internalized. Thus, to shatter the

---

[34] Marcuse, 210.

unjust system of capitalism and overcome human alienation, one must therefore not simply reorganize the economic structure of society but also reorganize the manner in which sexual desire and pleasure is understood. When that is done, the very nature of what is desired and how such desires are to be enjoyed will be transformed.

The second—the tilt in capitalist society towards seeing sex as primarily reproductive—points toward the need for the revolutionary program to shatter sexual codes built around the normative end of reproduction. So, for example, homosexual sex—by definition sterile and for the sole purpose of pleasure, not reproduction—becomes in itself a revolutionary activity. Its very existence defies the reality principle of capitalism, and its legitimation within a society is not simply an expansion of the canon of socially acceptable sexual behaviors. Instead it involves a revolution in how sex is understood and thus presents itself as a serious challenge to the bourgeois society that has made the monogamous family central to human relations and social organization. And although Marcuse did not live to see gay marriage normalized in the West, it is easy to see how he would have understood it: as a fundamental and revolutionary subversion of a central, oppressive institution of bourgeois society. By removing reproduction from the normative relationship that marriage represents, the whole bourgeois system of production is challenged.

This connects to one more point of significance in Marcuse's thinking: the performance principle, the internalized way of thinking and acting within society, is not the same as false consciousness. It is not that reality is one thing but the way the individual is taught to intuitively think and act is another. Far from it. The performance principle, of which sexual mores are one crucial part, really does reflect reality as it is constituted because it addresses the problem of *Ananke* as it is formulated in bourgeois society. Revolution can only be achieved by a fundamental refusal to play by the rules of the reality principle. Talk of a return to polymorphous sexuality might on the surface appear to be little more than Freudian jargon pressed into the service of a Hegelian-inflected Marxism. Yet the chaotic, shapeless sexuality it represents is profoundly affected by the revolutionary politics of 1968 and beyond. Today, the basic point—political revolution requires sexual revolution—is deeply embedded in the radical politics of our own day.

This also brings to a head a tendency we can still see in modern iterations of critical theory and political movements born out of the same: a fundamentally antithetical posture to whatever actually exists in order to bring about some revolutionary new form of society, without critical theorists feeling the need to give any real positive substance to the latter. Marcuse's dream, like that of many radicals after him, seems to be that, if one can only tear down the current system of sexual codes, a new, better system—a system undefinable beyond vague, aspirational jargon—will arise to replace it. As Goethe's Mephistopheles declared to Faust, "I am the spirit that negates."[35]

Conclusion

Nowhere in contemporary Western society is the impact of revolutionary changes in attitudes and behavior being felt more profoundly than in that of sex and sexuality. And this revolution, while being technologically enabled (How could sex come to be seen as primarily cost free and recreational, without such things as contraceptives, antibiotics, and abortion?), finds two of its most influential theorists in Reich and Marcuse. And, at root, what

---

[35] See, for example, the aspirational statements of Black Lives Matter. "About," Black Lives Matter, accessed July 11, 2023, https://blacklivesmatter.com/about/. They clearly know what they are against and their statement describing their aspirations contains plenty of positive-sounding rhetoric but offers almost nothing in terms of positive substance. Ironically, the website also offers official BLM merchandise. It is hard not to imagine Herbert Marcuse seeing this as a fine example of how easily the revolution itself conforms to the performance principle, or Georg Lukács noting how powerful and omnipresent commodification is.

we witness in the sexual revolution is nothing less than a transformation in what it means to be human. Walter Benjamin, close friend of Theodor Adorno, noted this as early as 1920:

> This age is participating in one of the greatest revolutions ever to take place in the relations between the sexes. Only someone who is aware of this development is entitled to speak about sexuality and the erotic in our day. An essential precondition is the realization that centuries-old forms, and along with them an equally ancient knowledge about relations between the sexes, are ceasing to be valid. Nothing forms a greater obstacle to realizing this than the conviction that those relationships are immutable at their deeper levels—the mistaken belief that only the more ephemeral forms of erotic fashion are subject to change and to history, because the deeper and supposedly unalterable ground beneath is the domain of the eternal laws of nature. But how can anyone sense the scope of these questions and not know that what history shows most powerfully are the revolutions in nature?[36]

What Benjamin sees so clearly here is that the very idea of humanity is tied at the deepest level to matters of sexual desire and sexual behavior. The sexual revolution is an anthropological revolution, and both Reich and Marcuse saw that with clarity. Our world, where sex is constantly a matter of political debate, is a world where human nature is in effect up for grabs.

---

[36] "On Love and Related Matters," in Walter Benjamin, *Selected Writings*, ed. Howard Eiland and Michael W. Jennings, 4 vols. (Cambridge: Belknap, 1996–2003), 1:229.

A Postscript on the Sexual Revolution

Anyone who reads Reich's *Sexual Revolution* today will be amazed at just how much of his prescriptive analysis has come true. Indeed, it is one of those books whose author could not possibly have known at the time he wrote it just how prophetic his work would prove for future generations. From its argument that traditional sexual codes were oppressive to its polemics against parental authority and its demand that the government should work to dismantle family sexual taboos, it might have been composed as an intervention in the sexual and educational politics of the twenty-first century. We live in Reich's world now, where a close identity between the ideas of political and sexual liberation is assumed. That some of the most ferocious political battles of our day surround the role of sex in children's education also witnesses to the advance into the mainstream of what might once have been considered his more far-fetched ideas.

Yet there is also an obvious and tragic irony to the work of Reich and Marcuse on sex and revolution. The burden of the early critical theorists was to dismantle bourgeois society because it treated human beings as objects not subjects, as things not persons. Six decades past the 1960s and the sexual revolution they represented—not least as inspired by Reich, Marcuse, and their various epigoni—it is clear that sexual freedom has, perhaps more than anything in today's world, turned people into things. And this should not have come as a surprise. Once personal sexual satisfaction becomes the immediate end of sex, the other person becomes nothing more than a means to that end. And once consent becomes the only moral criterion for judging any given sex act, sex itself loses any intrinsic meaning it might once have possessed. We might say that both represent a vacuous anthropology—though, ironically, Reich and Marcuse saw their projects as attempts to realize true humanity.

Thus, contemporary hookup culture represents both the demolition of older traditional codes for which Reich and Marcuse hoped and also the objectification of human beings about which critical theorists fretted. Much the same can be said for the pornification of society via the ubiquity and mass consumption of internet pornography: the actors on the screen are not people but consumer items and the acts performed not for their benefit but for the benefit of the third parties staring at the computer. Sex is commodified and human beings are objectified. Nor is this restricted to the impact of pornography. Feminists such as Christine Emba, Louise Perry, and Mary Harrington have all pointed to various elements of the sexual revolution, not least the ease of accessibility to the pill and to abortion, as having degraded women and furthered their objectification by men—who, strange to tell (at least to those too blind to think ahead), are the major beneficiaries of uncommitted, cost-free recreational sex.[37]

In retrospect, the belief that liberation for society would require liberation from sexual codes and would be achieved by the demolition of such seems ridiculous. This is based upon the claim that society creates sexual dysfunction. There may well be truth to this, but perhaps Freud was correct: maybe a level of sexual frustration is necessary for society to function. To assume that Freud's anthropology is itself myopic because of the capitalist context in which it occurs is just that—a speculative assumption that expresses a hope, not an argument. Indeed, it is another example of the Achilles heel of so much critical theory, past and present: Its historicism and deep suspicion of essentialism prohibits it from articulating a clear anthropology that then prevents it from offering a cogent view of the future in

---

[37] See Christine Emba, *Rethinking Sex: A Provocation* (New York: Sentinel, 2022); Louise Perry, *The Case Against the Sexual Revolution* (Cambridge: Polity, 2022); Mary Harrington, *Feminism Against Progress* (New York: Regnery, 2023). Wendell Berry makes a similar point about the deleterious effects on both community, individuals, and the meaning of sex itself in his essay, "Sex, Economy, Freedom, and Community," in his *Sex, Economy, Freedom, and Community* (New York: Pantheon, 1993), 117–73.

anything more than hopeful pieties. It is a later iteration of the tradition of Marx's comment in *The German Ideology* that, with the end of the division of labor in a communist society it is "possible for me to do one thing today and another tomorrow, to hunt in the morning, fish in the afternoon, rear cattle in the evening, criticize after dinner, just as I have a mind, without ever becoming hunter, fisherman, herdsman or critic." An attractive vision for sure but asserted on the basis of Marx's faith in communism, not any kind of argument or evidence. Indeed, what kind of evidence or argument could there be, given that this utopia lies in the future and all we can do at this point in time is negate that which is? All Marx can really do therefore is speculate that the collapse of capitalism brings this vision to fruition.

The same applies to the sexualized revolution of Reich and Marcuse: at root, it is wishful thinking, a set of assertions built upon a highly tendentious understanding of human sexuality. They can hope that the demolition of sexual codes brings about utopia but they cannot know with any degree of certainty that it will do so. And the evidence thus far indicates that Freud, for all his faults, had a more realistic anthropology. Indeed, he actually had an anthropology. Reich and Marcuse had a dream, an anthropology deferred for a utopian future—and such dreams can be highly dangerous when others attempt to make them a reality.

In closing, it is here tempting to play the critical theory card back at the critical theorists. The sexual revolution required a technological mastery of nature of a kind that they themselves were decidedly ambivalent toward. One can only detach sex from procreation via the use of technology, and in our world that detachment has been so successful that pregnancy and the commitments such natural relations brought have come to be intuitively regarded as matters of personal choice and control. The result is that the very things that have traditionally made human beings human—relationships of obligation towards and dependency upon other persons—have become contractual, not natural. And as technologies such as IVF, surrogacy, and now the very real possibility of producing babies from stem cells have emerged, a vision of children as manufactured rather than begotten has become more plausible. In short, the revolution of Reich and Marcuse is only possible because of technology, technology that further objectifies human beings as things rather than enriching their subjectivity as persons.

In opening the way to making sex a sterile recreation without commitment, Reich and Marcuse ironically facilitated the very dialectical move that early critical theory pinpointed in bourgeois culture whereby that which liberates turns into its opposite, a means of tyranny and oppression. Horkheimer and Adorno saw it with the Enlightenment's alleged exaltation of scientific reason; Reich and Marcuse did it with their push to shatter sexual codes. But perhaps those codes were there for a reason. Perhaps human beings do have a nature, an essence, and perhaps the careful regulation of sexual behavior in a manner that reflects and reinforces natural dependencies and obligations is essential to human freedom. That is a point their approach precluded at the outset. And the results, one is inclined to say, speak for themselves.

This points us to a further conclusion: The answer to the sexual revolution is not an argument. It is a community where properly ordered, functional sexual relationships take place within a broader context that acknowledges the responsibilities that sex involves, particularly toward the children who are begotten thereby. That is where the responsibility falls upon the church to model marriages where husbands and wives demonstrate in their relationship the way in which they treat each other not as objects or things but as subjects and as persons—where sex is not so much the taking of pleasure from another so much as the giving of the self to another in a life of full commitment, in sickness and in health, for richer, for poorer, and till death do them part.

CHAPTER 7

The Culture Industry

Introduction

Today, we are all familiar with terms such as "social media influencer," referring often to those who have been able to use their presence on such platforms as X, Instagram, and YouTube to shape the attitudes of their audiences toward things as varied as brands of cosmetics to attitudes to sexuality and gender. Our world is one where the presence and the importance of various forms of communication are taken for granted. It is why the commercial industry invests billions each year in advertising on television and increasingly online. The significance of the moving image, the slick presentation, and the compelling sound bite are things we all take for granted. And yet this is all a comparatively new development. The radio, the moving image, and then the talkie were developments that took place in the twentieth century and only then did popular culture start to emerge as what it is today: something that could be distributed across vast geographical areas in a consistent form, and something that could also be harnessed to significant commercial interests. And, of course, the members of the early Frankfurt School were witnesses to this new phenomenon.

Indeed, the rise of these new forms of communication and entertainment were of more interest than mere cultural curiosities to these early critical theorists. The central preoccupation of the School in the thirties and forties—that of the rise of Nazism and the failure of significant sections of the working class to support the Marxist left—could not be separated from cultural analysis of the rise of these new media. Of all the contemporary political movements, the German Nazis had leaders who understood the political power of the radio and especially the movies. Indeed, central to Hitler's rise to power was the man who became his Minister of Propaganda, Joseph Goebbels. And it is worth noting that the term *propaganda* was at that time not the pejorative it has since become (which semantic development took place in no small measure because of its association with the likes of Goebbels). Propaganda meant simply that which we now refer to as advertising or public relations.

To connect all this to an earlier theme, the School was exploring the means by which the powerful cultivated ideology and false consciousness within a society. They knew that there was an ideological structure to bourgeois society, and they knew that the proletariat did not see this clearly but were happy to accept their voluntary servitude. And the School identified what they dubbed "the culture industry" as responsible. This term referred to the network of institutions, embedded within the capitalist system of the day, that blinded people to their real condition and their true political interests.

Specifically, this term is used to refer to the ways in which culture is manufactured, and this in a manner that shapes the popular consciousness so as to normalize the bourgeois status quo. "Culture industry" covers such things as movies, theater productions, radio broadcasts, and commercials. All of these serve to cultivate and reinforce the governing bourgeois capitalist ideology and the false consciousness of the proletariat. In short, the purpose of the culture industry is to produce the kind of citizen who will not seek to press for the revolutionary transformation of the basic economic (and thus political) structures of society. This takes different forms and also involves the communication of different messages. But the overall purpose is the same: the creation of a public acquiescence to the bourgeois system. The various cultural analysts associated with the school do not all agree with each other in every detail regarding the significance of this culture industry—most notably Adorno and his friend Walter Benjamin—but they share a common interest in studying the role of the new media in shaping public consciousness.

As with other aspects of early critical theory, the underlying motivation is Marxist, but (again as with other aspects of early critical theory) that does not mean that much of the general analysis cannot be transposed into a non-Marxist framework. The very term "social media influencer" indicates that we all intuitively know that media is not simply reflective of reality but works, often intentionally, to shape reality. To that extent, the fascinating work of the early Frankfurt School remains of interest and relevance today. Indeed, the approach to culture of Horkheimer, Adorno, and their colleagues was multifaceted and sophisticated and offers a very interesting set of perspectives on how modern society thinks and acts the way it does. And cultural criticism of this kind is scarcely a monopoly of the Marxist left: a good case can be made for the nineteenth-century aristocratic Frenchman Alexis De Tocqueville as one of the earlier critics of "the culture industry," given his astute observations on how American democracy reshaped literature and the arts, both in form and content, to serve democratic impulses. What the Frankfurt School does is continue this same tradition by substituting Tocqueville's distinction between elite art forms and those favored by democracy with that between art that liberates and art that serves in the manufacture of social conformity and political passivity.[1]

---

[1] See Alexis De Tocqueville, *Democracy in America*, trans. Arthur Goldhammer (New York: Library of America, 2004), 530–44, 554–68.

A Foundational Distinction

Underlying the criticisms of the culture industry is something that Marxism sees as being an important part of bourgeois culture: the distinction between the public and private spheres. One of the ironies of alienation for Marx is that industrialization means that human beings can only feel themselves to be human in the private sphere. Humans are dehumanized when working in a factory because they own neither the means of production nor what is produced. Instead, they are simply paid money for what they do. Strange to tell, at least for Marx, that which should make human beings human—work—becomes that which prevents them from being free. And this work is done in order to allow for a modicum of so-called free time, in which the concept of "freedom" can be realized in the private pursuit of such things as hobbies and interests that do not directly connect to industrial production. The '80s pop song "Working for the Weekend" captures this: in bourgeois society, the five days of labor are the necessary evil that make a little bit of downtime on Saturday and Sunday possible. It is then that we can go fishing or watch a ball game or simply sit around the dinner table and enjoy fine wine and good conversation. Then at least we can persuade ourselves that we are persons and not just cogs in the machine. As we noted earlier, Marx and his critical theory successors see human beings as alienated, specifically as alienated by a capitalist system that treats them as things or commodities, valued solely in terms of the monetary market value of their labor.

Within a Marxist anthropology, this is deeply paradoxical: the very thing that should constitute our humanness (productive labor) becomes merely an alienating but necessary precondition for feeling a little bit like a real person in our private worlds. Indeed, it is only in the private world outside of work that we can experience some weak semblance of what it means to be free. It is here that we can realize an inner life—the last location of potential freedom. This, of course, makes the private sphere also the place where we can sense some kind of folk memory of freedom and imagine some kind of resistance to the commodification of the human person. And it is for this reason that the capitalist system must ultimately colonize this sphere too if it is to produce fully compliant subjects. Yes, even the private sphere must be brought under the sway of the system. And the means for doing this will be the culture industry.

In the background to this is the idea that modern popular culture represents a distinctive development of the commercial world and that this changes its sociological significance in a fundamental way. Where once music, dance, and literature were communal phenomena and were integrated into the public life of the community, the rise of commerce in the seventeenth and eighteenth centuries both gave birth to private space and transformed such communal folk culture into private entertainments. These transformations were part of the commercial world—publishers, for example, had a vested interest in promoting popular novels in order to turn a profit—but they also gave content to those times and places where the individual was not involved in production or commercial activity.[2] We are all familiar with the phrase, "escape into a good book." That captures beautifully what a novel (and now a film or a piece of privately consumed music) does: it fills that private time with an illusory sense of liberation. It also turns what were once communal productions—dances and musical gatherings—into matters for personal (and in our era of recorded music) private consumption. But the tools for this are bound to the system of production, and so the private sphere of hobbies and entertainment is still dependent upon the capitalist system. And the capitalist system has a vested interest in the content of this private sphere.

Horkheimer explores this in an early essay, "Art and Mass Culture." In an important passage, worth quoting at length, he anticipates much of the later critique of the culture industry:

[2] Theodor Adorno, "How to Look at Television," in David Ingram and Julia Simon, eds., *Critical Theory: The Essential Readings* (St. Paul: Paragon House, 1992), 69–83.

The gradual dissolution of the family, the transformation of personal life into leisure and of leisure into routine supervised to the last detail, into the pleasures of the ballpark and the movie, the best seller and the radio, has brought about the disappearance of the inner life. Long before culture was replaced by these manipulated pleasures, it had already assumed an escapist character. Men had fled into a private conceptual world and rearranged their thoughts when the time was ripe for rearranging reality. The inner life and the ideal had become conservative factors. But with the loss of his ability to take this kind of refuge—an ability that thrives neither in slums nor in modern settlements—man has lost his power to conceive a world different from that in which he lives.[3]

Here Horkheimer points to the creation of a private sphere, a sphere he will go on to characterize as that of art, where human beings were able to dream of a world different to that in which they found themselves. Art once fulfilled an important function, that of pointing beyond current society to something else. As such, it relativized the status quo. But as the bourgeois world tightened its grip, so it is that true art for Horkheimer now only existed in those works that present the horror of the reality of bourgeois life: the isolated, impotent individual pitted against a hostile, impersonal world. He cites both the prose of James Joyce and Pablo Picasso's *Guernica* as good examples. These works are functions of the alienation of modern society and present it in all of its grotesque horror to the audience. They expose the irrationality that lies beneath the veneer of reason with which the bourgeois world covers itself. But such artworks are not the stuff of the culture industry, for the culture industry does not trade in gestures that expose the human condition but rather in masking that condition or distracting the audience from noticing it.[4]

---

[3] Max Horkheimer, "Art and Mass Culture," Zeitschrift für Sozialforschung 9, no. 2 (1941): 278–79, https://www.pdcnet.org/zfs/content/zfs_1941_0009_0002 0290_0304.

[4] Horkheimer, *Critical Theory*, 277–78 (see chap. 4, n. 3).

The world of the culture industry is typically filled not with the aspirational dreams of those who can see beyond the status quo but with the manufactured products of the status quo, tailored towards normalizing the system that produces them. Popular culture thus takes on a deeply political significance. Horkheimer's reference to the ballpark and to movies is very important here. To the critical theorist these are not to be seen as innocent pleasures but rather as part of the social totality—that comprehensive picture of society where everything plays its role in emphasizing and reinforcing the power of the bourgeois system. And even the old "high art" that pointed beyond or posed challenges to the status quo can be co-opted by the commercial culture and turned into a commodity.[5] Again, as we observed in the discussion of Lukács, the tendency of the capitalist world (at least according to Lukács) is the complete commodification of existence. Everything becomes a commodity. And this applies to art too. How, for example, are the paintings of Van Gogh today typically valued? For their message or merely because they were painted by Van Gogh and, bearing his name, can be exchanged for vast sums of money?

We are all aware of other obvious examples of this. A Renaissance painting can be reproduced on a fridge magnet. Museums typically place the gift shop at the exit so that the last exposure the visitor has to its artifacts is one where reproductions of the same are for sale. More recent artwork (—say, Picasso's *Guernica* or Munch's *Scream*)—may have exposed the deep problems of modernity but, when mass produced, they become just another thing to buy—a cool picture to hang on a wall or emblazon on a T-shirt. Of course, the same applies to the cultural artifacts of revolutionary history and thinking. Coffee mugs bearing the image of Karl Marx are easily available on the internet, Black Lives Matter merchandise is a significant income

---

[5] Adorno observes that, when faced with such art, modern culture either assimilates it to the demands of commerce or, if it cannot do that, decries it as elitist and "high culture," thereby sending the message to the population at large that it represents irrelevant snobbery. "How to Look at Television," 70.

stream for the organization, and who has not seen the middle-class pseudo-radical twentysomething wearing the iconic Che Guevara T-shirt? The culture industry is no respecter of the political origins of cultural products. However revolutionary their provenance, the culture industry can turn them into commodities, fold them into the system, and thereby neutralize them.

To return to Horkheimer's statement, the first thing to note, therefore, about this colonization of the private sphere is that the instruments of this colonization are themselves the products of the capitalist system. That then creates a situation where the private sphere becomes dependent upon the very system that is annihilating its significance. And that, of course, is the whole point because it makes it impossible to imagine any alternative to bourgeois culture. Rather like the drug dealer who becomes a vital part of the addict's world because of the addiction that the dealer has himself created and fostered, so the members of bourgeois society are utterly dependent upon the products to which the system has itself habituated them, even in the private sphere that speciously presents itself as a respite from the system.

Marx and Engels noted in the *Communist Manifesto* that capitalist production created new needs and wants, and we saw in chapter 6 that Herbert Marcuse elaborated this into a theory of society and control: capitalism creates needs and then presents itself as the only means by which these needs can be met. We might say it creates problems that it then offers to solve, in return for a general acceptance of its existence. It is all about control. This can be recast in anthropological terms: capitalism creates a certain vision of a normative human being, that of a consumer, not a producer; and having created this reality, then services it. Again, we can all understand this: the next time you are frustrated by your music streaming service crashing and have to turn to that service itself, in order to have the problem solved, remember the frustration you feel is the result of a need that the streaming company has first created. Nobody in the eighteenth century, let alone the fifteenth, experienced the annoyance of a software failure.

Of interest today, of course, is the fact that Horkheimer wrote the statement about movies in 1937. The movie industry was still in its relative infancy at this point—the magical year of 1939, when *Stagecoach*, *The Wizard of Oz*, and *Gone with the Wind* signaled the arrival of the modern movie proper was still in the future. Television, with its reach into the very living rooms of the working population, and the massive commercialization of sport, were some way off. And the world of the personal computer and the internet was inconceivable to any but the most imaginative science fiction aficionados. So if Horkheimer's claim about the power and significance of pop cultural products in 1937 had any merit, then surely today that ring of truth sounds even louder. Once society's concept of how to fill the private sphere becomes dependent upon the consumption of commercially produced entertainment, then the social imaginary comes to think of the entertainment industry as vital to the well-being of society. Any comparison between the salaries earned, say, by professional athletes and movie stars with those earned by nurses and police officers surely reveals something about the respective position these different professions occupy in the social hierarchy of our day. For some reason—and Horkheimer would argue that the reason is ideological, the need of the bourgeois system to colonize and thereby control the private sphere— we consider entertainers to be among the most important people in our world. And they reinforce the anthropology of man as passive consumer rather than active producer.

Passive Conformity

We noted in chapter 5 that the goal of a bourgeois society governed by instrumental reason was to turn people into things and subjects into objects. And the supreme accomplishment of such transformation occurs when people come to think of themselves intuitively as things and as objects. At that point, all subjectivity—and thus all possibility of resisting the system—is eliminated. The culture industry plays a key role in this, both in the media it uses and in the message it sends. It is a primary means of manufacturing conformity.

As to the former, Horkheimer and Adorno make an interesting observation about technology and its impact in *DE* by drawing a distinction between the telephone and the radio:

> The [telephone] liberally permitted the participant to play the role of subject. The latter democratically makes everyone equally into listeners, in order to expose them in authoritarian fashion to the same program put out by different stations. No mechanism of reply has been developed and private transmissions are condemned to unfreedom.[6]

The essential passivity of the medium of radio applies similarly to movies and television. Each provides entertainment that is passively consumed, that requires no active or intentional engagement from the consumer beyond the choice to listen or to watch. Reading a book or a newspaper still involves a form of active engagement with the medium, even if the message in every copy of the newspaper sold is inevitably the same. What these new forms of media do is place little to no demand upon the audience in terms of subjective agency. The listener or the viewer is (at least in the account given in *DE*) merely a passive receptacle. In other words, the very medium presses toward turning the human subject into an object.

We can all sense the truth in this to some degree. There is a difference between watching a live play at the theatre and watching the same production on television. That difference may be hard to articulate, but typically the mediation of the play via a screen makes it somehow less immediate and less engaging. In a live production—as in a live lecture—the actors feed off the energy and atmosphere created in part by the audience. There is a subliminal dialogue of sorts that happens. No such thing occurs with a radio broadcast, a TV show, or a movie.

This is where the contrast with the telephone is important. To speak on the telephone is to engage in a conversation, albeit a technologically

---

[6] *DE*, 95–96.

mediated one, where two parties actively interact with each other. Neither is exclusively passive in the engagement. Each individual remains a subject, an agent engaging with the other in intentional, free ways. This is not the case with radio. There even the very technology itself shapes the consciousness of the one listening. It serves to turn the active agent into a passive object, a producer into a consumer. Bourgeois ideology becomes much more powerful when combined with a passive population. False consciousness sees the capitalist system as absolute and also the individual as completely impotent. And the key connection between the explicit message of the culture industry (e.g., "We can meet all your needs"), the method of the culture industry (the creation and then satisfaction of those needs), and the passivity that the very means of delivery cultivates, makes this a powerful and potent ideological force. If the early Marx worried that religious practices and institutions anesthetized poor people to the painful reality of their actual lives, that role is played for the Frankfurt School by the entertainers, movie makers, and advertisers of the culture industry.

Stereotyping Reality

This loss of the subject is also reinforced by a second aspect of what we might call mass media or mass entertainment: the uniformity of the programs. While the earlier media revolution of the printing press made it easy to communicate the same message to large numbers of people, the advent of radio and the movies expanded this in dramatic ways. Now media that promoted passivity of reception also presented to vast numbers of people the same vision of life, often (as with radio and later television) at the same time. Passivity of reception, consistency of content, and uniformity of time all combined to press toward a political homogenization of society.

This uniformity is important for a number of reasons. First, and most obviously, it serves a clear ideological purpose in the way that it naturalizes the system within which the culture industry operates. In fact, conformity reflects the underlying nature of commercial society. Just as the difference between a Ford automobile and one produced by Chrysler is so negligible as to be basically "illusory," so the products of MGM and Warner Brothers are really no different. The characters, the plotlines, and the lavish displays of conspicuous consumption are common to both. What television adds to this is the fusion of the radio's ability to deliver its product to the private domestic space of the home along with the aesthetics of the visual moving image.[7]

Second, uniformity serves the production of stereotypes, both in terms of characters and plots. Now, it is important to make a distinction here between stereotypes in general and stereotypes as they are used in the culture industry. Adorno, for example, is clear that stereotypes fulfill an important function with regard to navigating life in this world:

> Since stereotypes are an indispensable element of the organization and anticipation of experience, preventing us from falling into mental disorganization and chaos, no art can entirely dispense with them.[8]

What Adorno is pointing to here is the fact that making sense of the world requires us to have generalized concepts of things within that world, and that artistic productions are no exception to this. For example, if my water heater breaks down, I need to call a plumber. I may not know the specific plumber whose number I find on the local website for local businesses, but I have a concept of what a plumber does that guides me as to the kind of person I am looking to hire. The same applies in artistic productions. If I watch a performance of *Macbeth*, I will not understand the plot unless I have some general prior concept of monarchy, of what loyal and disloyal retainers are, and of what a wife is supposed to be. At a more popular level, no soap opera or sitcom will make much sense unless the audience has some generalized categories for understanding the characters on the screen. Stereotypes as such are thus important.

---

[7] *DE*, 97.

[8] Adorno, "How to Look at Television," 78–79.

It is therefore not the existence of stereotypes that is the problem. It is the function that they come to fulfill. The danger is that stereotypes become reified and then start to control how the individual thinks about the world. And the more often the stereotypes, whether of character or of plot, are reproduced in the artifacts of the culture industry and passively consumed by the audience, the more unquestionable they become. To quote Adorno:

> The more stereotypes become reified and rigid in the present setup of the culture industry, the less people are likely to change their preconceived ideas with the progress of their experience. The more opaque and complicated modern life becomes, the more people are tempted to cling desperately to clichés which seem to bring some order into the otherwise un-understandable [incomprehensible]. Thus, people may not only lose true insight into reality, but ultimately their very capacity for life experience may be dulled by the constant wearing of blue and pink spectacles.[9]

In short, the culture industry makes products that come to grip the imagination with a vision of reality such that the actual experienced realities of life end up being understood in terms of these confected categories. This is so powerful that not even experience can change the way individuals think about the world around them. What is interesting here is the pessimism that clearly underlies Adorno's thinking. The audience is passive; the medium and its message are in complete control. This will be a point of difference with the approach of Walter Benjamin, which we will discuss later in this chapter.

The moving picture is critical to this political project because it offers something that appears to be a closer replication of reality than a painting or a photograph. The flux, the movement, and the interactions of the actors all seem "real." The advent of talkies (and then color film) further closes this gap. This, according to *DE*, is increasingly the goal of production:

---

[9] Adorno, 79.

The whole world is passed through the filter of the culture industry. The familiar experience of the moviegoer, who perceives the street outside as a continuation of the film he has just left, because the film seeks strictly to reproduce the world of everyday perception, has become the guideline of production. The more densely and completely its techniques duplicate empirical objects, the more easily it creates the illusion that the world outside is a seamless extension of the one which has been revealed in the cinema. . . . [L]ife is to be made indistinguishable from the sound film.[10]

In short, for the audience, real life does not provide the framework for interpreting movies; movies provide the framework for interpreting real life.

Given the context of the Frankfurt School, the obvious examples of such movies would be those produced by Nazi propaganda. In 1940, Fritz Hippler, president of the Reich Film Chamber, directed one of the most notorious examples, *Der ewige Jude* ("The Eternal Jew"), which traded in crass racial stereotyping with regard to Jews and to which we can easily apply the insights of the Frankfurt School. Scenes show Jews seducing women. Excerpts taken from an earlier movie, *The House of Rothschild*, are included to imply that the world is controlled by a conspiratorial cabal of Jewish bankers. Connections between Judaism and Bolshevism are asserted both in the commentary and in the accompanying images consisting of photographs of Jewish Marxist leaders and newsreels of communist agitators in action. Jewish artists, such as the innovative director Max Reinhardt, are named and shamed as representative of degenerate art. There are allusions to cross dressing, homosexuality, and sexual license. One scene depicts a sexual assault by a Jewish man on a non-Jewish woman. There is footage of worship in a synagogue, where the men apparently nod their heads in manic fashion while reading the Scriptures, making the congregants look like mindless automata. Toward the end, a live cow is

---

[10] *DE*, 99.

slaughtered in accordance with kosher regulations and bleeds to death on the screen. Repeated use of maps presents the spread of Jews across the world as akin to a plague or contagion. Indeed, throughout the film the commentator uses biological language of disease and parasite with reference to Jews. Their houses are shown as fly infested and filthy. Given that these particular sequences were filmed in the Warsaw Ghetto, the squalid conditions were actually the result of Nazi action, a point conveniently omitted. The purpose is to naturalize—to reify—the notion of Jews as dirty and unhygienic. Most notoriously, in one particularly vile montage sequence, footage of a swarm of rats dissolves into footage of a crowd of Jews. And throughout the movie, which culminates in a speech by Hitler to a crowd of fresh-faced young Nazis, a contrast is drawn between the hardworking, clean, and handsome productive Germans and the devious, filthy and ugly parasitical Jews. The message presented is clear: Jews are not human but are more akin to vermin, carrying a deadly, contagious disease. They should therefore be liquidated just as one might liquidate a colony of rats.[11]

Taken in isolation, the movie might appear repellent but ridiculous. Set within the context of Nazi Germany, where all aspects of German society are being integrated around an ideological anti-Semitism, the movie is a potent instrument for informing and reinforcing the Nazi Party's social imaginary. In particular, the moving images create a deeper affinity between the screen and real life than, say, a photograph would. The result is a negative stereotype of Jews in general that overrides any positive experience a German might have of individual Jews or Jewish communities. The stereotype is reified. Jews become things—verminous, disease-ridden things. And so the Holocaust becomes possible in the German imagination.

---

[11] For an archive of the movie, see *Der ewige Jude*, directed by Fritz Hippler (Berlin: Terra Film, 1940), accessed June 13, 2023, https://archive.org/details /DerEwigeJude1940.

"You Are Not Special!"

We might of course respond by saying that Nazism and *Der ewige Jude* are particularly extreme examples and that such things are not the everyday fare of pop culture. What of Lady Gaga, *Family Feud*, and the typical American lunchtime soap opera? Are they not simply harmless fluff for making free time a bit more enjoyable? Horkheimer and Adorno, however, would reply that such a response is emblematic of a failure to be conscious of how all cultural products are ideological. They all present normative visions of what "real" life should be and how the world operates. This is one reason why today so much is made of the way in which minorities—ethnic, religious, or racial—are portrayed in movies and on television. The fear is that stereotypes end up reifying normative understanding of particular groups or categories and thus turning those to whom the stereotypes are applied into things that no longer need to be treated as subjects. That is the original concern of such figures as Horkheimer and Adorno, and one that permeates later iterations of critical theory.

Further, it is not just categories of people that become reified. The nature and dynamics of life become reified too through the use of standardized plots. Now, one might press back and say that every movie and every soap opera has its own uniqueness, but in fact they all trade in the same character stereotypes. As such, the plots may vary in the details, but the details are themselves interchangeable. The patriarch, the tyrannical boss, the adulterer, and the rebellious child are all stock characters, and the varied plots they are involved in are ultimately all functions of such. And as the dynamics on screen are always the same, so the audience imbibes the message that life itself consists of invariable patterns and outcomes—the patterns and outcomes, of course, that suit the requirements for maintaining capitalism. For example, the detective solves the case, showing that the system works and justice will be done in the end. Or maybe the detective does not solve the case, indicating that the system does not always work but that there is nothing that one can do about it. Either way, the message is that the system wins.

In his discussion of television, Adorno discusses an unnamed play concerning a moment of crisis in the life of a fictional dictator ("a kind of hybrid between Mussolini and Peron"), involving his public and personal collapse. A brutal sadist, he mistreats both his wife and his secretary, causing the former to flee. During her flight, she meets a general, a former lover, who now wishes to protect her. His soldiers surround the palace, and when they learn that the dictator's wife has escaped to safety, they disperse and the dictator, his ego shattered by his wife's desertion, gives up.[12]

Adorno's analysis of this gives important insights into his understanding of how the culture industry develops plots:

> The impression is created that totalitarianism grows out of character disorders of ambitious politicians, and is overthrown by the honesty, courage, and warmth of those figures with whom the audience is supposed to identify.[13]

In short, what the plot does not do is point to any notion that Fascism and dictatorships may be the result of the social system that exists. Fascism is a bug in the system, not an integral part of it. The underlying message is that the evils that Fascism represents can be overcome within the current system by the application of honesty, honor, goodwill, and love. Love, if you like, will conquer all. The plot also depends upon a clear line between good and evil, such that it is clear who the good guys and who the bad guys are. Again, this rests upon that deeper refusal to see the system as at all responsible for producing and enabling a sadistic dictator. The existence of a military, and of a military that clearly possesses immense political power, is never questioned and certainly not seen as being part of the problem. On the contrary, it is presented as key to the solution. In short, the status quo is being affirmed, even as imperfections are acknowledged. The message is that these

---

[12] Adorno, "How to Look at Television," 79.

[13] Adorno, 79.

imperfections—Fascism, a brutal dictator—are deviant malfunctions that can be overcome, not necessary parts of the system.

Adorno does not use the term *systemic*, but that is clearly the concept underlying his critique. What he is pressing for is a more thoroughgoing criticism of the assumptions that underlie the play's plot and which are being quietly preached to the audience both by positive plot developments and by a refusal even to acknowledge the validity of the kind of critical questions that Adorno wants to ask. The audience is being taught a way of looking at the world without even being aware that that is what is happening. In sum, as Adorno puts it,

> What matters in mass media is not what happens in real life, but rather the positive and negative "messages," prescriptions, and taboos that the spectator absorbs by means of identification with the materials he is looking at.[14]

But there is also a dialectical move in the standardized plots of movies. In *DE*, Horkheimer and Adorno reflect upon audience perception of young female actresses, starlets, as they appear in the movies. The message, they claim, points in two opposite but paradoxically complementary directions. First, the existence of the starlet, plucked from obscurity by some powerful movie mogul who just happened to notice her in the secretary pool, indicates that there is a path from the prosaic, mundane life of workplace drudgery to the glamor of Hollywood, to wealth, and to fame. Yet two other messages are also being communicated. The first is that the chances of this happening, while real, are infinitesimally small. And the second, flowing from the first, is that it is really a matter of luck, and so there is nothing the individual can do to bring it about. The net result is that the girl in the audience is given hope but also pressed into a position of passivity.[15]

---

[14] Adorno, 80.
[15] *DE*, 116.

But this does not simply apply to the young girl gazing with envy at Greta Garbo (then) or Margot Robbie (now) on the screen. The dialectical genius of the culture industry is that the closeness of identification it achieves between members of the audience and the stars on screen eventually becomes its opposite, a total distancing of the two. In the words of *DE*, "The perfected similarity is the absolute difference."[16] This is a typically obscure Frankfurt School statement, but its meaning is not particularly complicated. What *DE* is claiming is that the fact that movies invite members of the audience to identify with those on the screen also pushes them toward seeing each and every human being as replaceable by another. If I can imagine myself as George Clooney, then so can the man sitting next to me and so on. There is therefore nothing unique about any of us. And that, of course, is key to the capitalist enterprise, where the worker is treated—and comes to think of himself—as a thing, a tool, that can easily be replaced and has in himself no intrinsic value as a particular individual. In the words of *DE*:

> The culture industry has sardonically realized man's species being. Everyone amounts only to those qualities by which he or she can replace everyone else: all are fungible, mere specimens. As individuals they are absolutely replaceable, pure nothingness, and are made aware of this as soon as time deprives them of their sameness.[17]

Elsewhere in *DE*, Horkheimer and Adorno make the comment that "the culture industry endlessly cheats its consumers out of what it endlessly promises,"[18] and this would seem a good example. That which presents itself as offering hope actually induces a state of political passivity at the same time as providing an analgesic to obviate the pain that the system causes. Entertainment cultivates passivity and hopelessness while distracting the audience from the latter through keeping it entertained. And that

---

[16] *DE*, 116.
[17] *DE*, 116–17.
[18] *DE*, 111.

applies both to the stereotypical characters and the stereotypical plots that the culture industry produces. The culture industry is key to ideological conformity and false consciousness in the modern world.

A Conspiracy Theory?

One standard objection to this critical approach to cultural products might be that it is not the intention of, say, the screenwriter or the director of the typical soap opera or movie to produce reifications in a manner that consolidates the cultural power of those in control. This, of course, was not the case with *Der ewige Jude*. The writer and director were clearly very intentional in the way they wished to essentialize Jews as a subhuman, unhygienic, bacillus-like species that required extermination like rats. But what of the more mundane, less obviously political products of the culture industry such as we might today categorize as light entertainment or prime-time viewing? Does the theory of the "culture industry" not imply that the makers of such fare are engaged in a conscious, even conspiratorial, project to gull audiences into unconsciously adopting certain ideological intuitions?

Adorno addresses this issue directly in his essay on television. His argument is that production is always a team exercise and is also deeply informed by the cultural framework within which such productions take shape. Examples of the latter might well be the kind of product that currently enjoys popularity in the marketplace. For example, detective dramas with strong female leads are very much in vogue today in a way that was unknown in the 1970s. Therefore, to sell an idea for a movie or TV series, the author needs to take account of the nature of contemporary public tastes. But then there are budget constraints that will affect where and how the movie is filmed. The producer and director will both have their own opinions on the production, and that will play into its final form in a significant way. And beneath the level of leadership, there are no doubt countless other factors that come into play. Today, the term "production values" is often used with reference to movies and shows. This points toward what

Adorno is trying to express: The author is only one part of the final product. The overall result is that movies, like TV shows, cannot be reduced to the psychology or intentions of the author.[19] They are far more complicated entities than that. The overall production is therefore the result of a complex set of factors.[20]

This is reminiscent of Hegel's concept of the "cunning of reason," his notion that the historical process produced the right result, despite the mass of contradictory motivations and actions that marked the individual human agents who brought it about. But this, of course, is Adorno, for whom (unlike Hegel) the whole is not the truth but the false. Thus, the result of the interaction of the various elements of bourgeois culture is not the overcoming or transcending of the bourgeois system but rather its reaffirmation and reinforcement.

In fact, one might say that the movie and television industries, precisely because they are commercial enterprises, can never destroy that upon which their very existence depends. Indeed, in *DE*, Horkheimer and Adorno make the point that there is an increasing coalescence of entertainment and advertisements, reflecting and strengthening the commercial foundations of the culture industry.[21] We see this in our own day with commercial sponsorship of sports matches, something that in the case of American football has even altered the dynamics of the game, as time needs to be made for commercial breaks. And even where programs are "commercial free," the audience is often reminded that this is because of a commercial sponsor. *DE* gives the example of an uninterrupted Toscanini concert on the radio, but we

---

[19] "To study television shows in terms of the psychology of the authors would almost be tantamount to studying Ford cars in terms of the psychoanalysis of the late Mr. Ford." Adorno, "How to Look at Television," 77.

[20] Adorno, 76–77.

[21] *DE*, 131. In another essay, "Culture Industry Reconsidered," Adorno comments that "cultural entities typical of the culture industry are no longer *also* commodities, they are commodities through and through. . . . Brought to bear is a general uncritical consensus, advertisements produced for the world. So that each product of the culture industry becomes its own advertisement." Theodor Adorno, *The Culture Industry* (London: Routledge, 2001), 100.

might think perhaps of *Masterpiece Theater* or a Ken Burns documentary on PBS.[22] And, broadening out from traditional media, the free services provided by such things as YouTube and Gmail are also explicitly connected to commercial interests, even if payment is not given in terms of money but personal information to the advertising algorithms of corporations. Culture is a commodity and therefore it is advertising, as Horkheimer and Adorno would say.

All of this, according to Horkheimer and Adorno, serves to enervate the revolutionary potential of modern media. We have a half century more of perspective on the entertainment world than Adorno had, and one thing is very clear: even movies that purport to be politically radical and to offer biting critiques of the West and of the economic system it represents, are themselves dependent upon that very system for their existence. Thus, if movies by Michael Moore did not make money, they would never be shown in cinemas—more than that, they would never be made at all. And were he alive today, Adorno may well be of the opinion that Moore's films reassure the bourgeois audience that, by watching them, they are advancing the cause of social justice while they are in fact simply furthering the injustices of that system by purchasing its products. Much the same might be said of the person who buys a BLM T-shirt or an Extinction Rebellion coffee mug. In each case, revolutionary politics has been turned into a marketable commodity, and true transformative protest is enervated and replaced by designer protest as consumer product. Indeed, Hollywood radicalism is always faux because it is so wedded to the mechanisms of the world of commerce. That would be Adorno's verdict.

Walter Benjamin: A Dissenting Voice?

The argument of Horkheimer and Adorno—that modern media such as radio and movies essentially turn the audience into passive consumers and

---

[22] *DE*, 128–29.

thus reinforce the status quo—was not shared by all of those associated with the early Frankfurt School. Walter Benjamin, a close friend of Adorno, took a somewhat different approach to the arrival of modern mass media. Indeed, from 1927 to 1933 he himself wrote and presented a large number of radio broadcasts, indicative of the fact that he saw not only potential risks but also potential gains from using such a medium.[23]

Benjamin's key theoretical work in this regard is his famous essay, "The Work of Art in the Age of Its Technological Reproducibility."[24] Central to his argument in this essay is the way in which mechanization has facilitated the mass reproduction of artworks, something that has a fundamentally transformative effect upon the meaning, significance, and experience of art. Benjamin is, of course, aware that artworks have always, in principle, been reproducible but he argues that technology has changed this in a qualitative way.[25] We can certainly grasp what he means here: it has always been possible, for example, for somebody to copy a sculpture by Michelangelo or a painting by Leonardo Da Vinci. But that process would in the past have been long and laborious and have involved great technical skill on the part of the one making the copy. Nowadays, many of us have prints of original artwork hanging on the walls of our homes and our offices, prints that were produced en masse, at very little cost and in a very short period of time.

---

[23] The surviving transcripts are available in English translation as *Radio Benjamin*, ed. Lecia Rosenthal, trans. Jonathan Lutes, Lisa Harries Schumann, and Diana K. Reese (New York: Verso, 2021). Benjamin's thought is notoriously difficult to parse, partly because of his obscurity of expression and partly because of its unique and eclectic fusion of Marxism and Jewish mysticism and messianism. Two accessible introductions are: David Ferris, *The Cambridge Introduction to Walter Benjamin* (Cambridge: Cambridge University Press, 2008) and Uwe Steiner, *Walter Benjamin: An Introduction to His Work and Thought* (Chicago: University of Chicago Press, 2010).

[24] The essay occurs in three versions. I am using the text of the second version as found in Walter Benjamin, *Selected Writings*, ed. Howard Eiland and Michael W. Jennings, 4 vols. (Cambridge: Belknap, 1996–2003), 3:101–33.

[25] Benjamin, "The Work of Art," 102.

And, of course, they were produced by machines and not by the applied skills of a particularly talented human being.

Benjamin argues that this changes what he calls the *aura* that surrounds traditional artwork. Originally, a work of art was produced at a specific time and tied to a particular place. It also involved the application of the unique talents—perhaps even genius—of the artist. It was thus embedded in a particular culture and derived its power—its aura—from that. Benjamin defines aura as "a strange tissue of space and time: the unique apparition of a distance, however near it may be."[26] What he is pointing to here is the power that art originally possessed over its audience. We can perhaps taste a little of this in comparing the experience of seeing a photograph of a great work of art—say, the roof of the Sistine Chapel—in the pages of a coffee table book with that of actually being in the Sistine Chapel itself. Standing in the very place where Michelangelo worked, where the Renaissance popes strolled, and where the cardinals gather periodically to elect a new Bishop of Rome, we marvel at the mind and technical genius of the artist, the uniqueness of the place, and feel the power of the frescoes. It is hard to articulate why that should be so, but it is nonetheless undeniable. The same can be applied to music: to hear a live performance of a piece of sacred music by Palestrina in a medieval cathedral is different to hearing it performed in a concert hall or, even more so, on our iPhones. Something is lost when the work is removed from its original context, some element of magic or, to use Benjamin's term, aura. No such experience is felt when we look at the photographs or listen to a recording.

For Benjamin, the advent of the camera and of the moving picture served to shatter this aura by detaching art from the ritual practices and social structures in which it originally developed and flourished. Once any work of art is in theory reproducible on a mass scale, the function of art changes dramatically. In Benjamin's words, "instead of being founded

---

[26] Benjamin, 104–5.

on ritual, it is based on a different practice: politics."[27] As so often in Benjamin's writings, his clipped prose makes such portentous statements less than transparent on first reading, but his claim amounts to this: traditional artworks, grounded in human skill and deriving their meaning from a specific time and place, meant that they were surrounded with a mystical power that reinforced the cultures of which they were a product. Once artworks can be mass produced, they lose this power but, given their continuation in this new form, their function must therefore be understood in a new way. Benjamin argues that art then becomes something susceptible to political use by the powerful.

Benjamin is somewhat ambiguous about this loss of aura. He thinks it can tilt the audience in one of two directions. First, the loss of aura might alienate the onlooker. The sense of mystery, transcendence, and religious power that the Sistine Chapel generated to those who first saw it, rooted as it is in uniqueness of place, time, and artist, is replaced by a sense of deep loss. We regret that we no longer live in a world where such aura is possible and where a sense of the greatness and glory of God combined with the technical genius of a specific artist to produce something unique and to give us a sense of touching the transcendent. And as a result, we seek to recapture the sense of meaning and belonging that such a world had. This then makes us vulnerable to the use of aesthetics deployed by politicians to reproduce such feelings.

We might think here of Leni Riefenstahl's infamous film of the 1934 Nuremberg rally, *Triumph des Willens* ("The Triumph of the Will"). This is a superb example of the kind of thing he is suggesting. The film presents all kinds of images and sounds—the medieval skyline of Nuremberg, locals dressed in traditional costume, Nazis in uniform marching in unison, music, drumbeats, flags, fires, speeches, etc.—in order to generate a kind of aura around Hitler and the Nazi movement. The film is powerful, not because it offers an argument for National Socialism but because it projects a particular

---

[27] Benjamin, 106.

image of Nazism, and one which can replace something which the Germans have lost and long to recover: a sense of belonging to a glorious nation, to something transcendent which gives them a feeling of significance. There is a kind of aura here—but it is the aura attached to the Fuehrer. It is easy today to think of parallels in our own political world where the politicians and parties may be much less sinister than Hitler and the Nazi Party but where a similar play on images of past glories is made in order to attract voters. We too live in an age of political aesthetics.

In pointing to the way in which modern mass production can fuel Fascism and Nazism, Benjamin's approach can be seen to supplement the account given by Horkheimer and Adorno. But Benjamin (as one might expect from someone happy to give radio addresses) does not see this as unavoidable or inevitable. This is where the ambiguity in his reaction to the loss of aura is significant. In fact, he thinks that the demolition of aura and the tradition upon which it rested might also be a moment for liberation, enabling individuals to break free of the power structures of the past. The sheer disposability of artworks in the modern era speaks to this. For example, Benjamin notes that the difficulty of producing art in ancient Greece made it virtually inevitable that the Greeks would invest the works with eternal value. By way of contrast, Charlie Chaplin shot 125,000 meters of film for *A Woman of Paris* and threw 122,000 of those away.[28] The production of art is comparatively cheap and easy. And while Adorno sees movies as cultivating passivity and impotence in the audience, Benjamin sees them as potentially offering a vision of resistance:

> The majority of city dwellers, throughout the workday in offices and factories, have to relinquish their humanity in the face of an apparatus. In the evening these same masses fill the cinemas, to witness the film actor taking revenge on their behalf not only by asserting *his* humanity (or what appears to them as such) against

---

[28] Benjamin, 108–9.

the apparatus, but by placing that apparatus in the service of his triumph.[29]

Benjamin is ultimately ambivalent, perhaps even ambiguous, on how modern media will impact the political situation, but that ambivalence is itself important because it allows for an option effectively denied by Horkheimer and Adorno: modern media might also be used as a means of resisting the system. It also leads to Benjamin's famous conclusion to the essay, where he declares that, as Fascists have aestheticized politics, so communism must respond by politicizing art.[30]

Again, his clipped prose has an enigmatic quality but what he is pointing toward is the way that fascism and Nazism use art to create mass movements by offering images and symbols that seem to offer a sense of belonging and a sense of power and importance that the mundane reality of bourgeois life denies them. The underlying system of exploitation remains the same, but Fascism offers aesthetic experiences that hide this reality and thus disempower the masses. The response from the communists, therefore, should be to expose this political use of aesthetics and the system of exploitation by stripping away the mythology such promote and to present as an alternative a politicized aesthetics where art is consciously used by social revolutionaries to press the radical political message of Marxism. Art then becomes not merely a product of the political context but a force within the political context.

We might think here of the plays of Bertolt Brecht, a friend of Benjamin. Brecht not only pressed politically radical messages through the plots of his plays, he also presented the dramatic action on stage in ways that were deliberately jarring: actors speaking directly to the audience, staging techniques such as uncomfortably bright lighting, the use of explanatory placards, and interruptions of dramatic action with songs. His intention was,

---

[29] Benjamin, 111.
[30] Benjamin, 122.

among other things, to prevent the audience from being merely passive consumers of his plays. He wanted to force them to think about the kind of social issues that his plays were addressing. Politics as aesthetics rather than aesthetics as politics.[31]

Adorno, Benjamin, and the Political Significance of Art and Entertainment

Of all the areas covered by the early Frankfurt School, the material on the culture industry is perhaps the most useful to Christians. In our highly technologized and entertainment-saturated world, it alerts us to the many ways in which our imaginations are formed. It is not simply—or even primarily—arguments that shape our thinking. The aesthetics and the forms of cultural discourse are also significant. Years ago, Fox used to broadcast *The Simpsons* at the very time in the evening when families would typically sit down around the dining table and eat a meal together. It is interesting that a program that satirizes the family would be timed to undermine one of the actions that brought a family together. Reading the likes of Adorno is one way to alert us to such things.

Benjamin's contribution to early critical theory's approach to art and media represents an interesting alternative to the work of Adorno. Certainly, his rejection of the necessary and inevitable passivity of the audience in the world of modern entertainment is important. Indeed, it is hard not to see Adorno's understanding of modern media as connected to his overall pessimism about the real possibility for political change and to his barely disguised cultural elitism. The former is clear from the way in which he

---

[31] The basic texts in the debates among Western Marxists about aesthetics and politics can be found in Theodor Adorno, Walter Benjamin, Ernst Bloch, Bertolt Brecht, and Georg Lukács, *Aesthetics and Politics: The Key Texts of the Classic Debate within German Marxism, with an Afterword by Fredric Jameson*, translation editor Ronald Taylor (London: Verso, 1980).

seems to grant no room for the possibility of active resistance to the culture industry: both in its technological form of production and in the messages it preaches, television (or radio or cinema) objectifies human beings and convinces them that this objectification is natural. The latter, his elitism, is most apparent in his treatment of jazz, a musical form for which he has withering contempt.

Adorno's criticisms are rooted in his technical understanding of music. In essence, he sees the improvisations of jazz as being of nothing but ornamental significance while the underlying rhythmic form (4 times 8 beats) as being unvarying. Thus, an appearance of freedom was given by improvisation but, in reality, the fundamentals were fixed and invariable in comparison to other music. The theory may seem far-fetched today. It also fails to address jazz as performance (it is perhaps significant that Adorno's earliest writing on jazz in 1936 was based purely on recordings and transcriptions). Jazz is a live dialogue. It is also an ever-changing genre. It has often resisted the status quo and overturned it. Almost as soon as one style becomes commercialized, another emerges. Thus, traditional jazz gives way to swing which gives way to bebop, which gives way to modern jazz, and so on. Had Adorno been able to see jazz more through Benjamin's lens, he might not have missed such obvious counterevidence to his "jazz as the oppressed identifying with the oppressor" thesis.

The details of Adorno's critique of jazz are interesting because they suggest that his disdain for popular culture distorts his analysis of its political significance. On this score, Benjamin's belief that the new media could in fact be part of the dismantling and repudiation of bourgeois culture through the raising of human consciousness seems a far more fruitful approach.

Yet Benjamin's own approach is not unproblematic. The most obvious area of difficulty lies in his foundational argument that mass production destroys the aura of works of art. In a sense, this is true: now one does not need to see Caravaggio's *Crucifixion of St. Peter* and *Conversion of St. Paul* in Santa Maria del Popolo in Rome, where they hang opposite each other in the context of a Christian house of worship. I can find them reproduced in a book or printed as posters. I can even download them onto my cell phone. Yet mass production has had an odd effect on art: as copies have become (in the case of a download) virtually free, so originals have increased massively in value. Think, for example, of the work of Van Gogh. As posters of his *Sunflowers* have proliferated and become so cheap as to be virtually worthless, so the original painting has become priceless. Bourgeois culture itself has generated a new kind of aura, it would seem, whereby the original now has an escalated value. And so Benjamin's analysis needs both supplementation and modification.

Having said this, there is possibly no area in early critical theory that is more relevant to our own day than the critique of the culture industry. This is not to advocate for the approach either of Adorno or Benjamin (the latter of whose work we have barely touched in this chapter). But is to say that in an era where image has become vital to political success, where Hollywood stars carry significant public influence and where social media is clearly disrupting traditional forms of power and authority, the kind of questions raised by the early Frankfurt School are more pressing now than at any time since the 1930s. The problem continues to be the solution that critical theory offers (or refrains from offering).

One of the key developments, of course, is the rise of the internet and social media, a form of entertainment that is itself not merely passive. Anyone with internet access can have an X or an Instagram account or a Facebook page. These are not passive media in the sense that Adorno identified the radio as being but perhaps more akin to the telephone. Dialogues and interaction do take place. The same applies to online gaming, again something that carries a message (think of the values embodied in *Grand Theft Auto* or *Call of Duty*) but which also involves active participation. And then there is the vast amount of information available online, such that it is impossible for one group to have complete control of the messages that are being disseminated to the people. What might the early Frankfurt School make of such?

I suspect Adorno's elitism would lead him to despise the products of the internet as so much distraction from real problems. He would likely see the interactive nature of social media as a deception, conning consumers into thinking they have power and influence. True, some social media campaigns have had real impact, #MeToo being perhaps the most obvious. But Adorno would no doubt counter that these victories have occurred within the system. They have thus not led to the overthrow of the system but rather to an increased dependence upon it. The capitalist system allows social media to be powerful only to the extent that it can accommodate it, and those in power can use it to enhance their own control over what really matters: money.

As to the democratization of news and information, that can itself be disempowering because one can end up not simply having no idea who is speaking the truth but also becoming cynical about the very notion of truth itself, that the world is just a mass of incommensurable opinions. Now, we noted at numerous points that the notion of "truth" as an objective standard is repudiated by the early critical theorists. But even so, they do accept the notion that some claims move society in the right direction while others are intrinsically reactionary or retrogressive. And that requires the ability to see the contradictions in any cultural system. When that system involves a chaotic mass of information, then a deep and cynical relativism takes hold. And that is in itself utterly disempowering. As such, it helps to fulfill that underlying pessimism that characterizes Adorno's work: the individual is impotent in the face of the world. When everything is relativized, when no narrative is superior or more coherent than any other, resistance is futile.[32]

Benjamin would likely see the technology as offering both a challenge and an opportunity. The challenge would derive from the way in which the politicization of aesthetics is potentially enhanced by the internet and

---

[32] This point is made with force by Marxist literary critic Terry Eagleton, *The Illusions of Postmodernism* (Oxford: Wiley Blackwell, 1996).

social media. Fascism and forces of reaction have more scope for displaying their aesthetics to more people. We might think, for example, of the various young people who, to use the media phrase, "pledged allegiance to ISIS online." What were they doing? They were committing themselves to a movement of which they had no real-world experience, only the images and slogans that they encountered online.

And yet it is also arguable that the distinction between politicized aesthetics and aestheticized politics lies in the ideological eye of the beholder. When ISIS recruits the disillusioned young man in London via its online campaign of images, we recoil at the politicization of aesthetics because of the violent and reactionary nature of the cause promoted. But when Disney promotes progressive sexual and gender themes in movies aimed at children, is this really any different? The early critical theorists might point to the latter as increasing human liberty rather than impeding or reversing it, but that simply begs the question of how one makes such a judgment and on what criteria. I am inclined to say that it really depends on what position you hold on sex, sexuality, and gender. That will determine your reply. And so perhaps the Frankfurt School's critique of the culture industry is most compelling when it is used to make us aware of the ways in which aesthetics shape our thinking rather than in prescribing the ways in which our thinking should be shaped.

A Postscript on Aesthetics

The importance of the criticism of aesthetics for Christians should by now be obvious. We do not hold to the Marxist premises of Adorno and Benjamin, but we all know how powerfully images and music can shape the way we think about the world. The battle over gay marriage, for example, was not lost in the public square because the traditional arguments for marriage were exposed as incoherent. It was lost because the social imaginary came to be populated with the images and narratives of happy gay couples in sitcoms, soap operas, and beyond.

While this has obvious implications for understanding the political culture, we should also see it as connecting to the life of the church itself. If the battle for the minds in the world is to a significant degree waged via aesthetics, then we need to take aesthetics in the church seriously too. What do we fill our minds with in terms of the products of the wider culture industry? How does the content and form of what we consume shape the way we think? And, perhaps above all, how does the culture industry infiltrate the church herself? Years ago, Jeanne Halgren Kilde demonstrated that evangelical church architecture in the nineteenth century came to be shaped by that of the theater.[33] Today many churches look like conference halls, with pastors mimicking TED talkers and praise bands looking and sounding suspiciously like Coldplay. This is not necessarily wrong, but it is at least worth a moment's critical reflection. It is surely interesting that sacred space has come to look no different than commercial space. The church has its own culture industry, nestled in the wider culture industry of the world around us. We too therefore need our Adornos and Benjamins, rooted in a very different understanding of the world, to make us think about the significance of such.

This may well be one reason why many thoughtful Christians have in recent years been turning away from their broad evangelical roots to more formally liturgical Christian traditions such as Anglicanism, Orthodoxy, and Roman Catholicism. What these traditions have in common is a deep connection between their understandings of theology and the form and structure of worship. The structuring principle is their understanding of God's grace rather than the need to meet the immediate tastes or expectations of their congregants. The result is typically something that is profoundly different to the aesthetics and expectations of the culture around them. This is not to express an opinion on the theological soundness of any

---

[33] Jeanne Halgren Kilde, *When Church Became Theater: The Transformation of Evangelical Architecture and Worship in Nineteenth-Century America* (Oxford: Oxford University Press, 2002).

of these traditions, but it is to alert us of the fact that there is a connection in Christianity—or at least there should be—between belief and practice, doctrine and liturgy. Historic liturgies from East and West assume this, and it is something that we today should wrestle with more than many of us typically do. Aesthetics, as Adorno and Benjamin knew, are not neutral but serve an ideological purpose. We need to make sure that our churchly aesthetics serve the correct theological purpose.

CHAPTER 8

Negating the Spirit That Negates

In chapter 1, I ended by noting the affinity between critical theory and Goethe's Mephistopheles, the self-described spirit that negates. Revolutionary theory is, by definition, destructive. The status quo is one of alienation, a situation normalized by all departments of the culture. To overcome alienation, then, everything must be destabilized and overturned. Even the very categories used by the culture need to be challenged and overthrown. Justice that imposes a ban on theft of private property for the rich man and the destitute woman is not justice. Equality of opportunity in a world where the cultural system means some opportunities will never be available to many because of their skin color, sexuality, or ethnicity, is not equality. And color-blind racial policies are not color-blind if the overall framework of society tilts always in favor of the white man. These are the kind of critiques that critical theory makes of Western society. And as we have seen, the basic elements of such are already evident in the work of the early Frankfurt School.

All of this raises a number of questions. First, why bother with critical theory when so few have actually read the central texts or reflected in any depth upon their contents? Second, is there anything in critical theory that might prove useful to Christians? Third, if we decide to interact as Christians with critical theory, what might be a pastorally and pedagogically responsible way of doing so? And fourth, if the approach of critical theory is always to probe behind the constructions of any system of truth to allegedly manipulative cultural structures that naturalize or legitimate such, how can the church respond in a manner that is compelling to those tempted by the spirit that negates? Is critical theory in principle unfalsifiable, given that any objection or argument against it can be dismissed or dismantled as ideological? Or, to put this final question another way, if all theory serves power, how can Christianity offer an alternative that can outmaneuver such criticism?

Why Bother with Critical Theory?

The answer to this question should by now be obvious: the categories and claims of critical theory are to a large extent the intuitions of our age. For sure, few have read Adorno and Horkheimer, still less the work of Lukács or Korsch. But the concepts that they developed at a theoretical level are the instincts of the political and cultural discourse of our age. Social relationships are reduced to matters of power and manipulation. Traditional morality is seen as a smoke screen for one group subordinating another. Stereotypes are understood as turning others into objects. And claims to truth are treated with suspicion. We instinctively ask not what is true, but who is making the truth claim and what ulterior motive they have for so doing. The list could go on but what is clear even from these is that the critique of ideology that drove the early critical theorists is, shorn of its self-conscious theoretical foundations, the intuitive spirit of the day.

This is why having some grasp of those theoretical foundations is important. To echo Hegel, if you want to know about a given culture or society, you need to understand the philosophy that it embodies. When you do that, you can also come to see the broader significance and deeper implications of patterns of thought and behavior that might otherwise be hidden from view. It is my hope that this book has gone some small way to helping us become more self-conscious about the ideology of our own age and indeed of the ideology with which we ourselves often unconsciously operate.

Is Critical Theory at All Useful to Christians?

In his major analysis of the emergence of secular Western society, Charles Taylor observes that the conflict between belief and unbelief cannot be reduced (as it often is in the popular Christian and indeed atheist imagination) to a straight fight between theists and atheists. To do so is to fail to see that atheism is far from uniform in its understanding of the world. In fact, Taylor claims, the fight is at least a three-way conflict between Christians, exclusive humanists, and Nietzschean anti-humanists. What makes this conflict fascinating is that the sides line up differently depending on the issue at hand.[1]

First, it is useful to clarify the terminology. "Christians" (or theists) is straightforward: those committed to some kind of transcendent sacred order beyond our immanent social order, grounded in a belief in God. They believe that the latter, the social order, must be understood in light of the former, the sacred order. At the level of cultural analysis and commentary, Augustine would be an obvious ancient example, Benedict XVI is a fine modern one.

"Exclusive humanists" are the heirs of the mainstream Enlightenment, with their confidence in the scientific method and in the fundamental rationality of the universe and of human beings. While they may demur from ascribing transcendent value to human morality, they would argue that reason can deliver a stable, moral world where such things as altruism can be shown to make sense. In this category, we might include a contemporary advocate for reason such as Stephen Pinker.

---

[1] See Charles Taylor, *A Secular Age* (Cambridge: Belknap, 2007), 636–39.

As the name suggests, "Nietzschean anti-humanists" stand in the tradition of thinking represented by the German philosopher, Friedrich Nietzsche. They see humanity as marked at a deep level by irrationality and by struggles for power and domination. Reason simply cannot by itself make sense of human existence, behavior, and history. In such a category, we should place thinkers who draw not only on Nietzsche but also on Freud. Michel Foucault, the French post-structuralist, would be a good example, as would the American art critic, Camille Paglia.

What is interesting is how these three groups align relative to different questions that arise in our culture. If the question is about whether God exists, then the conflict sets Christians against both the exclusive humanists and the Nietzschean anti-humanists. Benedict XVI would find no common ground with either Pinker or Foucault on this point. If the question is about whether there is a basic rational and/or moral structure to the universe (or, we might say, about whether there are such things as truth and goodness), then the conflict sets Christians and exclusive humanists against Nietzschean anti-humanists. Benedict XVI and Pinker would at least agree that truth claims can be made and assessed for their veracity. They would also likely agree that moral judgments about right and wrong are possible, even if their criteria for assessing such would be very different. Foucault is not interested in truth so much as how claims to truth—and also to moral value—arise, who decides what is true or good, and how such claims function within the wider culture. Finally, if the question is about whether human beings, as currently constituted, are innately good, then the conflict sets Christians and Nietzschean anti-humanists against exclusive humanists. Benedict XVI and Foucault would both acknowledge an ineradicable darkness and irrationality in human beings (though for different reasons and with different purposes) while Pinker would assert that irrationality can be combated through reason and education.

Given this, we can see how a Christian historian or cultural critic might well find points of contact with authors whose overall approach and philosophy are antithetical to Christianity. Yet Taylor goes further than simply pointing to the complexity of the struggle that marks modernity. He also points to potential gains that the unbelieving perspectives have brought in their wake, a position he characterizes as that of a fourth party. Thus, for Taylor, the practical primacy of life here and now, which both exclusive humanism and the Nietzschean reaction asserted, represents a helpful development. Christianity can, at times, exhibit an otherworldliness that downplays or discounts the significance of life in this world, and the other two approaches can thus raise questions that make this absence clear. Indeed, erroneous systems can yet highlight blind spots and lacunae in approaches to the world that Christians may have missed or neglected. It seems, for example, that the Enlightenment focus on universal human dignity and the Nietzschean/existentialist focus on the need and urgency of individual choice and responsibility, can both be used to highlight the practical lack of these emphases and their implications (which are both clearly biblical) in, say, the theology of the Middle Ages.

In light of this, we can see overlapping concerns between Christianity and critical theory. The reduction of people to things is clearly something that a Christian should repudiate. When we look into the eyes of another, we want to see them looking at us as individual subjects, not objects. When we interact with other people, we should not treat them merely as instruments, as tools, for our own personal use. We should also have a concern for not reducing value to the terms of instrumental reason and also acknowledge that life here and now is not as it should be, that alienation is a real thing. Of course, we would reject the Marxist assumptions behind the Frankfurt School's approach to these things, just as we might reject Stephen Pinker's arguments for morality. But that does not eclipse the areas of common concern.

Given this framework, we might add a further element of complexity by comparing Christian interaction with critical theory to the function of heretical beliefs within the doctrinal history of Christianity. The words of John Henry Newman are helpful here. While still a Protestant, Newman preached a sermon before the University of Oxford, entitled "The Theory of

Developments in Religious Doctrine," during which he made the following observation about heresy:

> And here we see the ordinary mistake of doctrinal innovators, viz. to go away with this or that proposition of the Creed, instead of embracing the one idea which all of them together are meant to convey; it being almost a definition of heresy, that it fastens on some one statement as if the whole truth, to the denial of all others, and as the basis of a new faith; erring rather in what it rejects, than in what it maintains: though, in truth, if the mind deliberately rejects any portion of the doctrine, this is a proof that it does not really hold even that very statement for the sake of which it rejects the others.[2]

While Newman is here speaking specifically of doctrinal error, the principles he articulates are helpful for the question of Christian use of secular approaches to history and cultural criticism. First, there is the notion that most, if not all, heresies actually embody some singular aspect of the truth. Second, and paradoxically, taken as a whole, the heresy ends up undermining even the truth which it embodied.

An example will help to clarify Newman's point. Arianism is a broad term used to embrace a variety of perspectives in the fourth century that were definitively repudiated as heresy at the Council of Constantinople in 381. Yet even though deemed heretical, these various perspectives grasped an important element of biblical teaching: the need for a clear distinction between the Father and the Son. In emphasizing that, and in rejecting the various forms of modalism that served to elide or deny any such distinction, the Arians were correct. Of course, they also denied any essential unity in God, a serious error and one which rendered them guilty on Newman's

---

[2] John Henry Newman, *Sermons, Chiefly on the Theory of Religious Belief, Preached Before the University of Oxford* (London: Francis and John Rivington, 1844), 338–39.

second point: they ultimately did not give a true account of the one point where they had grasped something of the truth, that is, that God the Father is not God the Son.

The usefulness of Newman's definition of heresy for historians and cultural critics is this: erroneous explanatory schemes can still grasp or, perhaps better, gesture toward elements of the truth even as they fail to articulate them in a manner that is ultimately true or helpful. For example, classical Marxism points to the economic factors that shape human relationships and even human thought. Freudianism highlights the irrationality that often characterizes human behavior. Post-structuralism alerts us to the manipulative nature of discourse. All three of these examples might be said to correlate with some element of biblical teaching: the riot in Ephesus in Acts has an economic motivation (Acts 19:23–27). Human action cannot be reduced to rational decision-making and often involves self-contradictions (the Bible has many examples of such, but the idolator in Isa 44:9–17 is perhaps the most amusing example). And Romans 1 presents as dark a vision of human thought and behavior as anything a post-structuralist might offer. Critical theory, grappling as it does with the questions of what, if anything, it means to be human, raises many questions and highlights many issues that Christians too must address. To that extent, it is important for Christians to engage with critical theory.

Pedagogical Responsibility

If engagement with critical theory is useful, the question of how we might articulate this becomes pressing. Here the analogy with a heresy such as Arianism is apposite. Certainly during the course of 2020 and its aftermath, the lines among Christians seemed to be drawn between those who argued that critical theory was a useful tool and those who argued that it was an irredeemable enemy. Such rhetoric, of course, assumes that the only reasons for engaging with critical theory are to appropriate it or refute it. If my aforementioned argument is sound, however, and we can therefore see critical theory as a response to the challenges of modernity without endorsing its assumptions or conclusions, then "Are you for it or against it?" is not the only question—and certainly not the first question—to be asked. Arianism was a fourth-century attempt to grapple with the theological legacy of the third century. That it was heretical does not mean that a study of Arianism—the questions it asked, the problems it highlighted, the answers it proposed—is useless. Far from it. Such study dramatically deepens our understanding not only of the time in which Arianism developed but also of the orthodoxy which ultimately defeated it.

But here is the rub: no Christian—at least, no responsible Christian—would ever articulate this view by claiming that "Arianism is a useful tool for expressing important elements of the Christian gospel." Still less would they suggest that "eating the meat of Arianism while leaving the bones" is the way to move forward. Concern for the truth precludes such rhetoric. It may be in our current moment that Christians want to appear sensitive to the political or intellectual ethos of the culture, but we need to beware of using language that confuses. Ask me if I think critical theory is important and worth engaging for reasons beyond mere refutation, if it reveals something of the human condition—I am going to respond in the affirmative. Ask me if it could be a useful and constructive tool for cultural analysis—I am going to demur. That language claims too much, even as a merely adversarial approach that simply dismisses reading and wrestling with its key texts and ideas claims too little.

Perhaps this distinction seems a little contrived. If it reveals something about the human condition, does that not necessarily make it useful? The key lies in the term "useful" and its equivalents. Given that critical theory, at least for the early Frankfurt School tradition, claims not simply to be an analytical or descriptive tool but also to be part of a larger revolutionary political program, we need to be careful that the language we use to describe it does not lead us to accept, or even appear to accept, those larger revolutionary goals. The language of "usefulness" would seem vulnerable to that kind of inference.

At this point, it is worth introducing a further important caveat. Some Christians might be tempted to see critical theory as a useful means of exposing, for example, the power structures that underlie our society. As Christians we should understand that the human ability to distort the world, to naturalize and normalize the sinful, and to call evil good and good evil lies at the heart of fallen human condition. We also know that the *critical* dimension of critical theory can be detached from the original Marxist framework from which it emerged. Further, recent years have seen the deployment of critical theory of the more post-structuralist variety appropriated in the cause of undermining the very progressive pieties which critical theory itself helped to establish. For example, Giorgio Agamben has used Foucauldian tools for critiquing discourses of power to address the actions of governments during the Covid crisis. This is a move that in terms of the political spectrum of opinion on lockdowns, vaccines, and the like, would place him on the political right. Strange times—but a critical theory detached from eschatology has no stable political loyalties.[3]

Critical theory that sees any notion of human nature as merely an ideological or social construct, a function of discourses of power, is really no more compatible overall with Christianity than the work of an Adorno. In the hands of Foucault and his epigoni it embodies a set of endlessly destabilizing approaches that can be used to expose and dismantle structures of power. As such, it also ceases to be an exclusive tool of the left and becomes useful to the right too, for it is not a particular political group but rather the powerful, whether right, left, or center, that are the enemy. The spirit that negates, negates all claims to power regardless of who is making them. Thus we now live in a world where the political correctness that shattered the Western canon has itself become an ideology that demands obedience. The cult of the microaggression has become a means for silencing those voices of which powerful progressive establishment disapproves. And in perhaps a

---

[3] See Giorgio Agamben, *Where Are We Now? The Epidemic as Politics*, trans. Valeria Dani (Lanham, MD: Rowman & Littlefield, 2021).

most remarkable irony, the approval of the practical fruits of queer and gender theory are imposed by the wealthiest private corporations in the world today. Indeed, the very rhetoric and concepts of critical theory—the Other, intersectionality, and their like—have become influential tools for wielding power rather than dismantling it. And so, as Horkheimer and Adorno themselves would no doubt point out, things have become their opposite, the liberator has become the tyrant, the tools of freedom have become the weapons of oppression.

Yet we must beware of how far we go in utilizing the tools of critical theory in exposing this. The Christian's critique of power must arise from a normative understanding of human nature. We cannot simply be engaged in the game of showing the immanent contradictions of any given social arrangement, still less engage merely in negation, in some kind of great refusal. We must offer something better, a vision of what it means to be human and a taste of the transcendent. Isaiah's criticism of idolatry and Paul's of human depravity are not rooted in some speculative notion of human nature that will emerge in the future, nor in a commitment to the endless contingency of all social arrangements based upon relationships of power and oppression. They ground their critiques in an understanding of creation, of a normative notion of human nature as possessing an end, a purpose (that of worshipping God in whose image human beings are made) and, most significantly for this conclusion, the inbreak of the future into the present.

A Christian Response

This last comment needs expansion but provides the key to how Christians should respond to the various forms of critical theory. It also reminds us that critical theory cannot be refuted on exclusively theoretical grounds. As we noted, critical theory is remarkably immune to such theoretical refutation. In general, it denies the terms of engagement set by anything that exists within contemporary culture—for example, the culture's definitions of justice, equality, racism, and so on—and so any attempt to show that it fails using these is itself doomed to failure in the eyes of the critical theorist. When the current system delivers good things—the end of segregation, the prosecution of a ruthless landlord—to the critical theorist these are just sops to make it seem that the system works. Remember the point made by Marx: the important thing is to change the world, not merely describe it. And critical theory, as a consciousness-raising activity, is but the more cerebral part of overall revolutionary action.

The way for Christians to acknowledge the importance of critical theory but also to refute it is therefore not simply by producing a more cogent theory. If the fundamental claim of critical theorists is that human beings live in an alienated state that leads them to think of others, and even themselves as individuals, as objects, as things enslaved by systems of power from which they cannot escape and over which they have no power, then Christianity must refute that claim by demonstrating its falsity in practice, or at least by showing that such alienation is not inevitable and insoluble. And the way to do that is in the church.

For Marx, Lukács, Marcuse, and their ilk, humanity was something to be realized in the future. For Foucault and those who follow in his footsteps, human nature is just a construct, the result of discourses of power that produce notions of truth. In both cases, relationships here and now are marked by power and manipulation. Indeed, one searches in vain in their works for discussion of things such as forgiveness and gratitude—at least discussions not marked with cynicism.

This is where the church can refute critical theory. If we take the Marxist notion, that humanity is something to be realized in the future, where the terms of being a free individual and belonging to a community will be overcome, then the church makes the claim that that is already realized in the here and now in the church itself. It is the inbreak of eschatological humanity into the present age. As Paul tells the Colossians, Christians have already died and been raised in Christ (Col 2:12–13). In critical theory terms, alienation has already in one sense been brought to an end. As to reified categories, Paul declares that in Christ there is no Jew or Gentile, no slave or free. In the life of the church, human beings are subjects, not objects. And belonging to Christ and being free in Christ are one and the same thing. All of the central challenges to human existence identified by the critical theorists are resolved in Christ.

And yet this is not merely an argument made by Paul. It is a reality to which he points that is exhibited in the life of the church. It is there that the end of alienation and reification is to be enacted, as Christians forgive each other, give themselves in service and love to each other, and realize here on earth what a nonalienated human community should look like. Is the result perfect? By no means (though, one might note, it is generally far closer to perfection than the Hungarian communist regime within which Lukács played such a craven and sinister role). But it is the place where God addresses human beings as persons and where all humanly constructed barriers are to be demolished. In the proclamation of the Word, in the administration of the sacraments, and in the communal liturgy of the worship service, a new vision of humanity is both realized and displayed before the world. Human relationships in this fallen world may well be typically characterized by power and manipulation; the church, empowered by the Spirit, is to be the place where an alternative reality is manifest, one characterized by love, service, and humility. When I ask God for forgiveness, when I forgive others, I drop my own claims to power. When I love and serve others as fellow Christians, regardless of the cultural categories of the world around us—in Paul's terms, Jew or Greek, today perhaps skin color or ethnicity—I treat them as persons, as subjects, even as I act as a free subject myself. My actions defy the reifications that the world demands. Thus, in the life of the church, both in the liturgical action of the worship service where the gospel is enacted week by week, and in my daily interactions with others, where the gospel is practically demonstrated to the world around, I respond to the claims of critical theory in ways that far surpass in plausibility and power any book I might care to write in their refutation.

Of course, this requires a degree of self-examination on the part of the church. We are all too aware of the many scandals that have damaged the church's plausibility over the years, from support for slavery to the sex abuse crises that have engulfed not just the Roman Catholic Church but Protestant denominations and congregations in recent years. While Christians know that the church is an imperfect institution and that failure is inevitable, it is still important to take seriously the ways in which these things damage the church's plausibility even if they do not disprove the gospel. Critical theorists will jump on such things as providing ammunition for their own arguments against Christianity. We cannot ignore this but must rather acknowledge the problem and seek to address it as best we can. In this perhaps we can be grateful to critical theory in forcing us to answer questions we might be tempted otherwise to ignore or minimize. With the awareness that hostile critical theorists are always waiting for a chance to point out the church's hypocrisy, we are more likely to be vigilant and to do that most important task of continual reformation.

And so, this introduction to early critical theory comes to an end. Yes, the critical theorists of the early Frankfurt School saw something important, that humanity was not what it should be. They recognized how the forces of modernity, with its industrialization, its bureaucracies, its exaltation of efficiency, productivity, and profit margins, and its addiction to the cheap products of the culture industry ultimately prevented human beings from being truly free. And Christians surely have no quarrel with the central claims of such analysis. But they see these things as the result not of bourgeois culture created by capitalism but of human fallenness. Thus, they paradoxically see real hope, not in making earth into heaven, as the Marxists wished, nor in an endless dethroning of the powerful, but in embodying a little bit of heaven on earth in the church, the in-breaking of the end of time into time. The challenge to which critical theory therefore summons the church is to show, not merely to argue, that she has the answers. Critical theory does not so much provide Christians with a useful tool to think about the world as clarify a set of questions to which we have the answers already, if only we open our eyes to see them.

NAME INDEX

A

Adorno, Theodor
  and Frankfurt School, 81
  domination of nature and, 117–18
  fleeing by, 8
  history viewpoint of, 140–41
  Minima Moralia (MM), 116
  plot discussion by, 197–98
  political significance of art and enter-
    tainment and, 208–12
  questions of, 2
  science viewpoint of, 126–27
  stereotypes and, 192–93
  television discussion by, 200–201
  The Jargon of Authenticity, 114
Agamben, Giorgio, 223
Aquinas, Thomas, 121
Augustine, 147, 217

B

Beauvoir, Simone De, 101–2
Benedict XVI, 217–18
Benjamin, Walter, 8, 81, 176, 183, 193,
  202–12, 214
Brecht, Bertolt, 207–8
Butler, Judith, 9, 80, 115, 146–47
  influence of, 80
  introduction to, 146–47

C

Caravaggio, 209–10
Chaplin, Charlie, 206
Clooney, George, 199
Coleridge, Samuel Taylor, 142
Copernicus, 87–88

D

Davis, Angela Y., 8
Destutt de Tracy, Antoine, 29

E

Edwards, Jonathan, 142
Eliot, T. S., 116
Emba, Christine, 178

F

Fanon, Franz, 8
Feenberg, Andrew, 27
Feser, Edward, 7
Feuerbach, Ludwig, 26, 35–38, 40, 54,
  69, 73, 83, 89, 103, 136
Fichte, Johann, 10
Foucault, Michel, 6, 9, 12, 16, 80, 106,
  141, 146–47, 218, 223, 225
Freud, Sigmund
  appropriating, with Wilhelm Reich,
    158–69

civilization and, 147–51
guilt and, 136
infant sexuality and, 154–57
Oedipus complex and, 154–57
sexual desire and, 147–51
structure of human psychology and,
    151–54
Fromm, Erich, 81

G

Garbo, Greta, 199
Goebbels, Joseph, 182
Grünberg, Carl, 81

H

Halgren Kilde, Jeanne, 213
Harrington, Mary, 178
Hegel, G. W. F.
    as revolutionary, 49
    critique of, 10
    cunning of reason concept of, 201
    dominance of, 10–11
    freedom viewpoint of, 31–32
    German idealism and, 25–26
    historical process and, 140
    importance of, 16–24
    influence of, 9
    introduction to, 15
    Korsch's viewpoint regarding, 48–49
    Lectures on the Philosophy of
        History, 19
    lord-bondservant concept of, 21
    philosophy viewpoint of, 88
    The Phenomenology of the Spirit,
        20–21, 140
    the true is the whole and, 140
    thought viewpoint of, 48
Heidegger, Martin, 114
Hippler, Fritz, 194
Hitler, Adolf, 7, 47, 82, 106, 109, 111,
    139, 156, 163, 182, 195, 205–6
Hölderlin, Friedrich, 142
Horkheimer, Max
    alienation and, 94–96
    "Art and Mass Culture", 185–86
    critical theory and, 90–94

domination of nature and, 117–18
false consciousness and, 100–103
focus on, 7
science viewpoint of, 126–27
traditional theory and, 83–89
Hume, David, 121, 123
Husserl, Edmund, 83

J

Joyce, James, 186

K

Kafka, Franz, 71
Kant, Immanuel, 10, 17–18, 25, 27, 49,
    54, 92, 111, 122–24, 130–31
Kautsky, Karl, 44–48, 58
Kellner, Douglas, 50–51
Kojève, Alexander, 21
Korsch, Karl
    contributions of, 13
    Marxism and, 47–57
    Marxism and Philosophy, 48
    philosophy and, 47–57
    philosophy viewpoint of, 88
    truth notion and, 102
Kracauer, Siegfried, 81

L

Lacan, Jacques, 21
Lenin, V. I., 46, 51, 58
Lewis, C. S., 2
Locke, John, 142
Lukács, Georg, 8, 13, 39, 47, 57–67,
    69–76, 80, 82, 84, 90, 102, 123,
    136, 147, 154, 165, 167, 170, 175,
    187, 216, 225–26
Luxemburg, Rosa, 58

M

Marcuse, Herbert
    fleeing by, 8
    "From Ontology to Technology", 128
    knowledge viewpoint of, 94
    personal background of, 106
    quote of, 93
    repressive tolerance and, 104–8

SUBJECT INDEX